Edwin Reed

Bacon versus Shakspere

Edwin Reed

Bacon versus Shakspere

ISBN/EAN: 9783337417529

Printed in Europe, USA, Canada, Australia, Japan

Cover: Foto ©Thomas Meinert / pixelio.de

More available books at **www.hansebooks.com**

BACON *vs.* SHAKSPERE

Brief for Plaintiff

BY

EDWIN REED

Member of the Shakespeare Society of New York

Seventh Edition

REVISED AND ENLARGED

BOSTON
JOSEPH KNIGHT COMPANY
1897.

University Press:
JOHN WILSON AND SON, CAMBRIDGE, U. S. A.

TO

The Honorable Richard Cutts Shannon

ENVOY EXTRAORDINARY AND MINISTER PLENIPOTENTIARY

OF THE

UNITED STATES OF AMERICA

TO THE REPUBLICS OF

NICARAGUA, SALVADOR, AND COSTA RICA

THIS BOOK IS INSCRIBED

BY THE AUTHOR

INTRODUCTORY.

In the following Brief for the Plaintiff, Bacon *vs.* Shakspere, in an action of ejectment, now on trial, it is intended to cite such facts only as are generally agreed upon by both parties, or which can be easily verified, and, in the main, to let those facts, trumpet-tongued, speak for themselves. Like the lines that mark the sea-coast on our maps, each separate proof shades off in a thousand fine corroborating circumstances, which are often very interesting as well as important for a full knowledge of the subject. The question of ciphers is, for the present purpose at least, clearly beyond soundings.

For further information, the reader is respectfully referred, in behalf of Bacon, to 'The Authorship of Shakespeare,' by Nathaniel Holmes, 2 vols. Boston, Houghton, Mifflin & Co., 1887; and to 'The Great Cryptogram' (first part), by Ignatius Donnelly, Chicago, R. S. Peale & Co., 1888; and, on the side of Shakspere, to 'The Bacon-Shakespeare Question Answered,' by Charlotte C. Stopes, London, Trubner & Co., 1889; to 'Studies in Shakespeare,' by Richard Grant White, Chap. VI., Boston, Houghton,

Mifflin & Co., 1886; and to 'Wit, Humor, and Shakespeare' by John Weiss, Chap. VIII., Boston, Roberts
Bros., 1876; not to mention numerous others, on
either side, which it is to be feared the world will
soon be too small to contain.

PREFACE TO SECOND EDITION.

We may say of improbabilities, as we do of evils, "Choose the least." It is antecedently improbable that the "Shake-speare" plays, for which the whole domain of human knowledge was laid under contribution, were written by William Shakspere of Stratford, for he was uneducated. It is also antecedently improbable that Francis Bacon, whose name for nearly three hundred years has been a synonym for all that is philosophical and profound, who was so great in another and widely different field of labor that he gave a new direction for all future time to the course of human thought, was the author of them. And yet, to one or the other of these two men must we give our suffrage for the crowning honors of humanity.

In the claim for Shakspere, the improbability is so overwhelming that it involves very nearly a violation of the laws of nature. No man ever did, and, it is safe to say, no man ever can acquire knowledge intuitively. One may be a genius, like Burns, and the world be hushed to silence while he sings; but the injunction, "In the sweat of thy face shalt thou eat

thy bread," is everywhere as true of intellectual as it
is of physical life. The fruit of the tree of knowledge
can be reached only by hard climbing, the sole instance on record in which it was plucked and handed
down to the waiting recipient having proved a
failure.

In the case of Bacon, also, the assumption may be
said to lie on the very boundary line of credibility.
It implies the possession of faculties seemingly inconsistent, if not mutually exclusive; and yet to a certain degree it is not without precedent. Fortune has
more than once emptied a whole cornucopia of gifts
at a single birth. What diversity, what beauty, what
grandeur in the personality of Leonardo da Vinci!
He was author, painter, sculptor, architect, musician,
naturalist, civil engineer, inventor, and in each capacity, almost without exception, eminent above
his contemporaries. His great painting, the 'Last
Supper,' ranks the third among the products in this
branch of modern art, Raphael's 'Madonna di San
Sisto,' and Michael Angelo's 'Last Judgment' being
respectively, perhaps, first and second. At the same
time, he was the pioneer in the study of the anatomy
and structural classification of plants; he founded
the science of hydraulics; he invented the camera
obscura; he proclaimed the undulatory theory of
light and heat; he investigated the properties of
steam, and anticipated by four centuries its use in
the propulsion of boats; and he barely missed the
great discovery which immortalized Newton. In-

deed, we see in Leonardo da Vinci not a mountain only, but a whole range of sky-piercing peaks.

Another illustrious example is Goethe, scarcely inferior to Bacon, whatever the claims made for the latter, in the brilliancy and scope of his powers. As a poet, Goethe was a star of the first magnitude, a blaze of light in the literary heavens. His 'Faust' is one of the six great poems of the world. As a writer of prose fiction he stands in the front rank, his 'Wilhelm Meister' being a classic, side by side with 'The Heart of Mid Lothian,' 'Middlemarch,' and 'The Scarlet Letter.' By a singular coincidence, also, as compared with Bacon, he was one of the master spirits of his age in the sphere of the sciences. An evolutionist before Darwin, he beheld, as in a vision, the application of law to all the phenomena of nature and life. In botany, he made notable additions to the then existing stock of knowledge; and throughout the vast realm of biology he not only developed new methods of inquiry, but spread over it the glow of imagination, without which the path of discovery is always doubly difficult to tread.

In the light of precedents, therefore, the claim made to the authorship of the plays in behalf of Bacon cannot be discredited.

E. R.

Andover, Mass., September 1, 1890.

PREFACE TO FOURTH EDITION.

NOTHING is more tenacious of life than an old popular belief. It has the force of habit, which the pressure of enlightened opinion, through successive generations, alone can overcome. "O Lord, thou hast taught us," once prayed a good deacon, "that as a twig is bent, the tree's inclined," — a truth drawn from the Book of Nature, and as indubitable as though the writings of Pope were a part of the sacred canon. Trees that have unnatural and uncomely twists in their branches, even if growing on Mt. Zion, must be permitted to die of old age; the science of arboriculture is powerless to affect them. Intelligent and conscientious scholars among us are still defending the historical verity of the first chapter of Genesis. A personal devil is as potent in the minds of some men to-day as he was formerly in the minds of all. How often one hears in Germany the polite ejaculation *Gesundheit* uttered when a person sneezes! Even now, many people turn, almost instinctively, to see in which part of the heavens the moon quarters for a forecast of the weather, though it has long been demonstrated that that luminary has no more influence in this branch of our local affairs than has the most distant star which the Lick telescope reveals to us.

Unfortunately, these old beliefs and habitudes linger in some of the noblest minds to the last. The shadow of a solar eclipse, sweeping over the earth, permits the just and the unjust, the wise and the foolish, to emerge into the light behind it indiscriminately. Evil spirits do not always beg the privilege, when they find themselves about to be exorcised, of taking refuge in a herd of swine and leaping over a precipice into the sea. The butcheries of the Salem witchcraft, marking the close of that delusion, were perpetrated by those to whom the love of God was the chief end of man. One of the last judges in England to send a witch to the gallows was Time's noblest offspring, Sir Matthew Hale. The last in that country to manumit their slaves were the clergy. The Garrison mob in Boston wore broadcloth on their backs, and all the current virtues in their hearts. It is, therefore, no criterion of a good cause that men of acknowledged abilities and culture support it, nor of a bad cause that such men denounce it.

Indeed, Truth has a modest way of entering the world like a mendicant, at the back door. Such a guest is seldom admitted, on his first arrival, at the other end of the house. Copernicus stood there, shivering in the cold, thirteen years before he dared even to lift the knocker. Every great religion has sprung up among the poor. Every great reform owes its origin to the oppressed. Every great invention has had, like the founders of Rome, a wolf for a nurse. It is not to be expected that rebellion against a king of poets will find favor among the nobility that surround his throne. The high priests who, with unsandalled feet, minister in a sacred temple, will not be the first to despoil the idol they worship. No captain in that "fleet of traffickers and assiduous pearl-fishers," to which Carlyle refers, in the most eloquent sentence he ever wrote, will strike his colors or change his outfit so long as the products of his industry under the old régime are bringing him wealth. And what to him are winds and waves or any storm of criticism, whose barque is anchored to the theory of miraculous Inspiration! Showers of verbal aerolites on the mimic stage, only a product of untaught Nature!

Amid the turmoil of our daily life, if we listen reverently, we may hear voices crying in the wilderness, perhaps the voice of a woman, alone and forsaken, in a strange city.

> "No accent of the Holy Ghost
> The heedless world hath ever lost."

From the banks of the Missouri, from the wheat-fields of Minnesota, from far-off Melbourne at the antipodes, out of the heart of humanity somewhere, a response in due time is sure to come.

E. R.

ANDOVER, MASS., January 1, 1891.

CONTENTS.

LIST OF ILLUSTRATIONS.

LIST OF AUTHORS CONSULTED.

[Those marked with a * favor the Baconian theory of the origin of the " Shake-speare " plays.]

ABBOTT, E. A., Introduction to Mrs. Pott's Edition of Bacon's Promus (1882) ; Life of Bacon (1885).

ACADEMY, THE, April 21, 1894.

ADDISON, JOSEPH, The Tatler, No. 267 (1710).

AIKIN, LUCY, Court of James I. (1822).

ALLIBONE, S. A., Dictionary of Authors (1871).

ATHENÆUM, THE (1856, 1871, 1874).

AUBREY, JOHN, Biographical MSS. (1697).

*BACON, DELIA, The Philosophy of Shakespeare's Plays Unfolded (1857).

*BACON SOCIETY, Journals of, London (1886–90).

BARTAS, DU, The Second Week of Creation (1584).

BAYNES, T. S., Fraser's Magazine (1879–80) ; Encyclopædia Britannica, 9th ed. (Art. Shakespeare).

BEAUMONT, FRANCIS, The Mask (1612).

BLACKWOOD'S Edinburgh Magazine, March, 1889.

BLADES, WILLIAM, Shakespeare and Typography (1872).

BRADLEY, HENRY, The (London) Academy, April 21, 1894.

BROWNE, C. ELLIOT, Fraser's Magazine (1874).

BUCKNILL, JOHN C., The Psychology of Shakespeare (1859).

BURNEY, CHARLES, History of Music (1789).

CAMPBELL, CHIEF JUSTICE, Shakespeare's Legal Acquirements (1859).

CHETTLE, HENRY, Kind Heart's Dream (1592).

CHURCH, RICHARD W., Life of Bacon (1884).

CLARK, N. G., Elements of the English Language (1866).

CLARKE, CHARLES and MARY COWDEN, Preface to Works of Shakespeare (1866).

COLERIDGE, SAMUEL TAYLOR, Lectures on Shakespeare (1830).

COLLIER, J. P., Notes and Emendations (1853) ; Shakespeare's Works (1858).

COOKE, JAMES, Preface to English Bodies by John Hall (1657).

CRAIK, G. L., English Literature and Language (1866).

CREIGHTON, CHARLES, Blackwood, No. 145.

DAVIS, CUSHING K., Law in Shakespeare (1884).

DICKENS, CHARLES, Dictionary of Oxford and Cambridge (1879).

DIGGES, LEONARD, Verses to Shakespeare (1623, 1640).

DIXON, WM. HEPWORTH, Personal History of Lord Bacon (1861).

*DONNELLY, IGNATIUS, The Great Cryptogram (1888).

DOYLE, JOHN T. — Shakespeariana (1893) ; Overland Monthly (1886).

DOWDEN, EDWARD, Shakespeare : His Mind and Art (1879).

DYER, T. F. T. Folk-Lore in Shakespeare (1884).

ELZE, KARL, William Shakespeare (1874).

EMERSON, RALPH WALDO, Representative Men (1876).

EVELYN, JOHN, Diary (1641 to 1706).

*FEARON, FRANCIS, Journal of Bacon Society (1886).

FIELD, B. RUSH, Medical Thoughts of Shakespeare, Second Edition (1885).

FLEAY, FREDERIC GARD, Life and Work of Shakespeare (1886).

FLORIO, JOHN, World of Words (1597).

FOWLER, THOMAS, Life of Bacon (1881).

FRISWELL, JAMES H., Life Portraits of William Shakespeare (1864).

FULLER, THOMAS, Worthies of England (1662).

GERVINUS, GEORGE G., Shakespeare Commentaries (1863).

GIFFORD, WILLIAM, Life and Works of Ben Jonson (1816).

GREEN, HENRY, Shakespeare and the Emblem Writers (1870).

GREENE, ROBERT, Groatsworth of Wit (1592).

GUIZOT, F. P. G., Shakespeare and his Times (1852).

HALLAM, HENRY, Introduction to the Literature of Europe (1854).

HALLIWELL.-PHILLIPPS, J. O., Outlines of the Life of Shakespeare (1882).

HARVEY, GABRIEL, Letters and Sonnets (1592).

HAWKINS, JOHN, History of Music (1776).

HAZLITT, WILLIAM, Lectures on the Dramatic Literature of the Age of Elizabeth (1821).

HEARD, FRANKLIN FISKE, Shakespeare as a Lawyer (1883).

HIPPOCRATES, Presages of Death (about 350 B. C.)

*HOLMES, NATHANIEL, The Authorship of Shakespeare (1887).

HUDSON, HENRY N., Shakespeare : His Life, Art and Characters (1872).

HUME, DAVID, History of England.

HUNTER, JOSEPH, Life and Studies of Shakespeare (1845).

INGLEBY, CLEMENT M., Shakespeare : The Man and the Book (1877) ; Essays on Shakespeare (1888).

IRELAND, SAMUEL, Picturesque Views on the Warwickshire Avon (1795).

JOHNSON, SAMUEL, Preface to Works of Shakespeare (1765).

JONSON, BEN, Epilogue to Every Man in his Humour; The Poetaster ; Conversations with Drummond (1619) ; Preface to First Folio Edition of Shakespeare (1623) ; Discoveries (1637).

KNIGHT, CHARLES, William Shakespeare (1851).

LANGLIN, J. N., Shakespeariana (1884).

LOWELL, JAMES RUSSELL, Among my Books, 1st Series (1870).

LYTTON, E. BULWER, Edinburgh Review (1836).

MACAULAY, THOMAS B., Essay on Lord Bacon (1837).

MALLET, DAVID, Life of Lord Bacon (1740).

MALONE, EDMUND, Life of Shakespeare (1821).

MASSEY, GERALD, Shakespeare's Sonnets (1866).

MATTHEW, SIR TOBY, Collection of English Letters (1660).

MINTO, WILLIAM, English Prose Composition (1886).

MONTAGU, BASIL, Life of Bacon (1825).

MORGAN, APPLETON, The Shakespearean Myth (1881); Shakespeare in Fact and in Criticism (1886).

MORLEY, HENRY, English Writers, Vol. X. (1893).

NASH, THOMAS, Epistle to University Students (1589).

NEWMAN, FRANCIS W., The Echo (1887).

NICHOL, JOHN, Francis Bacon: His Life and Philosophy, Parts I. and II. (1888).

NORRIS, PARKER, Shakespeare Portraits (1885).

*O'CONNOR, WILLIAM, Hamlet's Note-Book (1886).

OLDYS, WILLIAM, O. M. (1761).

OSBORNE, FRANCIS, Advice to his Son (1656).

PARMENIDES, Poetic Remains of (450 B. C.).

PEARSON, CHARLES H., National Life and Character (1893).

PEPYS, SAMUEL, Diary (1659-1669).

*POTT, CONSTANCE M., Edition of Bacon's Promus (1882).

QUARTERLY REVIEW, April, 1894.

RAWLEY, WILLIAM, Resuscitatio (1657).

RÉMUSAT, M. de, Bacon: sa vie, son temps, sa philosophie, et son influence (1857).

RYMER, THOMAS, The Tragedies of the Last Age (1678).

SCHLEGEL, A. W. von, Lectures on Dramatic Art (1846).

SHAKESPEARIANA (1883-1893).

SHAW, THOMAS B., English Literature (1852).

SIMPSON, RICHARD, School of Shakspere, 2 Vols. (1878).

*SMITH, WILLIAM H., Bacon and Shakespeare (1857).

SPALDING, THOMAS A., Elizabethan Demonology (1880).

SPEDDING, JAMES, Philosophical, Literary, and Professional Works of Francis Bacon (1858) ; Letters and Life, do. (1870) ; Evenings with a Reviewer (1881).

STAPFER, PAUL, Shakespeare and Classical Antiquity (1880).

STEELE, RICHARD, The Tatler, No. 131.

STOPES, CHARLOTTE C., The Bacon-Shakespeare Question Answered (1889).

*STRONACH, GEORGE, Journal of Bacon Society (1888).

SWINBURNE, ALGERNON C., Study of Shakespeare (1879).

TAINE, H. A., History of English Literature (1871).

*THEOBALD, ROBERT M., Journals of Bacon Society, Vols. I. and II. (1886–91) ; Dethroning Shakspere ; Baconiana (1893–94).

ULRICI, HERMANN, Shakespeare's Dramatic Art (1846).

VERPLANCK, G. C., Works of Shakespeare (1847).

WARD, A. W., English Dramatic Literature (1875).

WEISS, JOHN, Wit, Humor, and Shakespeare (1876).

WELSH, ALFRED H., English Literature and Language (1883).

WHATELY, RICHARD, Bacon's Essays, with Annotations (1864).

WHIPPLE, EDWIN P., The Literature of the Age of Elizabeth (1865).

*WHITE, THOMAS W., Our English Homer (1893).

WISE, JOHN R., Shakespeare : His Birthplace and its Neighborhood (1861).

If we look carefully into the matter, it is not on the prescribed method of Bacon that his fame was built. It was the power of divination in the man which made him great and influential. — Dr. Ingleby.

Bacon was the prophet of things that Newton revealed. — Horace Walpole.

The art which Bacon taught was the art of inventing arts. — Macaulay.

The glance with which he surveyed the intellectual universe resembled that which the archangel from the golden threshold of heaven darted down into the new creation. — Ibid.

His service lay not so much in what he did himself as in the grand impulse he gave to others. — Prof. Minto.

Il se saisit tellement de l'imagination, qu'il force la raison à s'incliner, et il les éblouit autant qu'il les éclaire. — M. Rémusat.

The Novum Organum is a string of aphorisms, a collection as it were of scientific decrees, from an oracle who foresees the future and reveals the truth. It is intuition, not reasoning. — M. Taine.

There is something about him not fully understood or discerned, which, in spite of all curtailments of his claims in regard to one special kind of eminence or another, still leaves the sense of his eminence as strong as ever. — Prof. Craik.

No two critics agree as to the nature or cause of the profound impression he has made on mankind. We are certain only that he is a resplendent orb, in the light of which, across an interval of three centuries, every man still casts a shadow.

BACON *vs.* SHAKSPERE.

————•————

FOR THE PLAINTIFF.

————

I.

THE AUTHOR OF THE "SHAKE-SPEARE" PLAYS.

IT is conceded by all that the author of the "Shake-speare" [1] Plays was the greatest genius of his age, perhaps of any age, and, with nearly equal unanimity, that he was a man of broad and varied scholarship.

I. He was a linguist, many of the Plays being based on Latin, Greek, Spanish, and Italian productions, some of which had not then been translated into English. Latin and French were especially very familiar to him. It is thus apparent that not less than five foreign languages, living and dead, were included in his repertory.

---

[1] Wherever personal reference is made in this work to William Shakspere of Stratford, the name is so spelled, *William Shakspere;* but wherever the reference is to the author of the plays, as such, we treat the name as a pseudonym, spelling it as it was printed on many of the title-pages of the early quartos, WILLIAM SHAKE-SPEARE. In all cases of quotation, however, we follow the originals.

LATIN. — The 'Comedy of Errors' was founded upon the *Menaechmi* of Plautus, a comic poet who wrote about 200 B. C. The first translation of the Latin work into English, so far as known, was made in 1595, subsequently to the appearance of the " Shake-speare " play, and without any resemblance to it " in any peculiarity of language, of names, or of any other matter, however slight." — *Verplanck.*

" His frequent use of Latin derivatives in their radical sense shows a somewhat thoughtful and observant study of that language." — *Richard Grant White's Memoirs of William Shakespeare*, p. xvi.

" He showed his fundamental knowledge of that language, by using its words in their genuine, original meaning, which they have lost with their adoption into English." — *Gervinus' Shakespeare Commentaries,*[1] p. 26.

" After the proofs I have given, it will hardly, I think, be denied that he was quite capable of studying the celebrated story [of 'Venus and Adonis'] in the original sources, and that he certainly did so in relation to Ovid's version of it." — *Prof. T. S. Baynes*[2] *in Fraser's Mag.* 1880.

" He knew Latin, we need not doubt, as well as any other man of his time." — *Stapfer's Shakespeare and Classical Antiquity*, p. 100.

" He makes some of his characters [in 'Love's Labor 's Lost'] use false Latin, that he may show his learning in correcting it." — *T. W. White's ' Our English Homer,'* p. 195.

GREEK. — ' Timon of Athens ' was drawn partly from Plutarch and partly from Lucian, the latter author not having been translated into English earlier than 1638 (White), fifteen years after the publication of the play.

Helena's pathetic lament over a lost friendship in ' A Midsummer Night's Dream ' (III. 2) had its prototype in a Greek poem by St. Gregory of Nazianzus, published at Venice in 1504. — *Gibbon's Decline and Fall*, chap. xxvii.

" The likeness between the Clytemnestra of Aeschylus and the

---

[1] " A German professor, Gervinus, is the author of the greatest book ever written on Shakespeare." — *Stapfer.*

[2] Editor *Encyclopædia Britannica*, ninth edition.

Lady Macbeth is too remarkable to escape notice ; that between the two poets in their choice of epithets is as great, though more difficult of proof. Yet I think an attentive student of Shakespeare cannot fail to be reminded of something familiar to him in such phrases as ' flame-eyed fire,' ' flax-winged ships,' and ' star-neighboring peaks.'

" In the ' Electra ' of Sophocles, which is almost identical in its leading motive with ' Hamlet,' the Chorus consoles Electra for the supposed death of Orestes in the same commonplace way which Hamlet's uncle tries with him. Shakespeare expatiates somewhat more largely, but the sentiment in both cases is almost verbally identical." [1] — *Lowell's Among My Books,* p. 191.

A passage in ' Troilus and Cressida ' is "inexplicable except on the supposition that Shakespeare was acquainted with what Plato wrote." — *Richard Grant White.*

Among the presages of death, given by a Greek writer, 400 B. C., and repeated in ' Henry V.," " Shake-speare " mentions one which is peculiar to the people of Greece, and which no translation of the original work, even into Latin, had brought out.

ITALIAN. — An Italian novel, written by Giraldi Cinthio and first printed in 1565, furnished the incidents for the story of

[1] Gibbon and Lowell were unfortunately restrained by certain supposed exigencies from acknowledging that the author of the plays must have been familiar with the Greek language. Mr. Lowell, however, feels compelled to ask, rather helplessly, not to say absurdly, —

" Is it incredible that he may have laid hold of an edition of the Greek tragedies, Graecè et Latinè, and then, with such poor wits as he was master of, contrived to worry some considerable meaning out of them ? "

This state of mind on the part of so distinguished a critic illustrates very forcibly one of the chief causes of the poverty of Shake-spearean criticism. Mr. Steevens, for instance, suffered himself to be driven to the preposterous conclusion that the play of ' Troilus and Cressida ' is not wholly " Shake-speare "'s, because of certain Grecisms in it, of which, he assumed, " Shake-speare " could have had no knowledge.

'Othello.' The author of the play "read it probably in the original, for no English translation of his time is known." — *Gervinus' Shak. Com.* p. 505.

"He was, without doubt, quite able to read Italian." — *Richard Grant White.*

"When Iago, distilling his poison into Othello's ears, utters the oft quoted lines: —

'Who steals my purse, steals trash ; 't is something, nothing;
'T was mine, 't is his, and has been slave to thousands;
But he that filches from me my good name
Robs me of that which not enriches him,
And makes me poor indeed,' —

he but repeats with little variation a stanza of Berni's 'Orlando Innamorato,' of which poem, to this day, there is no English version." — *Ibid. : Memoirs of William Shakespeare*, XXIII.

"The great majority of the *dramatis personæ* in his comedies, as well as in some of the tragedies, have Italian names, and many of them are as Italian in nature as in name. The moonlight scene in 'The Merchant of Venice' is southern in every detail and incident. 'Romeo and Juliet' is Italian throughout, alike in coloring, incident, and passion. In the person of Hamlet, the author appears even as a critic of Italian style." — *Prof. Baynes in Encyc. Brit.* XXI. 758.

FRENCH. — One entire scene and parts of others in ' Henry V.' are in French.

Plowden's French 'Commentaries,' containing the celebrated case of Hales *vs.* Petit, which was satirized by the grave-diggers in 'Hamlet,' were translated into English for the first time more than half a century after the play was written.

"The author shows his knowledge of even the most delicate peculiarities of the French tongue." — *Richard Grant White's Shakespeare's Works*, II. 206.

"A brilliant proof that the author of the plays was familiar with the French language is the masterly way in which he makes Dr. Caius, in 'The Merry Wives of Windsor,' murder the Queen's English. Those who have ever heard a Frenchman utter this jargon will not hesitate to admit that the poet has grasped and reproduced it with inimitable truth and in the wittiest manner." — *Elze's William Shakespeare*, p. 382.

"The evidence of his knowledge of French is more abundant and decisive, so much so as hardly to need express illustration." — *Prof. Baynes in Encyc. Brit. art. "Shakespeare."*

SPANISH. — The poet drew some of his materials for the 'Two Gentlemen of Verona' from the Spanish romance of Montemayor, entitled the 'Diana,' which was translated into English in 1582, the translation, however, not being printed till 1598. "The resemblances are too minute to be accidental." [Halliwell-Phillipps.]

"Could there be anything more to the point than the description he gives in 'Love's Labor 's Lost' of the Spanish language? Can one who describes the character of a language with such clearness and insight be unacquainted with it?" — *Elze's Shakespeare*, p. 385.

Gervinus calls attention to two of the Comedies in which Latin, French, Spanish, and Italian words and sentences abound, and ventures to suggest a desire, on the part of the author, to exhibit in them *his knowledge of foreign languages.*

II. He had intimate acquaintance with ancient and modern literature, numerous authors, from the age of Homer down to his own, being drawn upon for illustration and imagery in the composition of these works.

"The writer was a classical scholar. Rowe found traces in him of the 'Electra' of Sophocles; Colman, of Ovid; Pope, of Dares Phrygius and other Greek authors; Farmer, of Horace and Virgil; Malone, of Lucretius, Statius, Catullus, Seneca, Sophocles, and Euripides; Steevens, of Plautus; Knight, of the 'Antigone' of Sophocles; White, of the 'Alcestis' of Euripides." — *Nathaniel Holmes' Authorship of Shakespeare*, p. 57.

"The early plays exhibit the poet not far removed from school and its pursuits; in none of his later dramas does he plunge so deeply into the remembrances of antiquity, his head overflowing with its images, legends, and characters. The 'Taming of the Shrew,' especially, may be compared with the 'First Part of Henry VI.' '*in the manifold ostentation of book-learning.*'" — *Gervinus' Shak. Com.* p. 145.

"A mind fresh from academic studies." — *R. G. White's Essay on Shakespeare's Genius,* p. ccxxiv.

"In that play, so marvellously full of thought, 'Troilus and Cressida,' Ulysses rises to the full height of our idea of the wandering Ithacan. Whence came this Ulysses? Not from Homer's brain; for, although Homer *tells* us that the King of Ithaca was 'divine,' and 'spear-renowned,' and 'well skilled in various enterprise and counsel,' the deeds and words of the hero, as represented by the Greek poet, hardly justify these epithets. Here we see that Shakespeare was even wiser than the Homeric ideal of human wisdom. *He made our Ulysses.*'— *Ibid.*

"The early plays mark the productions of a fresh collegian. His familiar acquaintance with college terms and usages makes for the conclusion that he enjoyed the privileges of a university education." — *Charles and Mary Cowden Clarke.*

"The very earliest writings of Shakespeare are imbued with a spirit of classical antiquity." — *Charles Knight.*

"His habits had been scholastic and those of a student. A young author's first work almost always bespeaks his recent pursuits." — *Coleridge's Lectures on Shakespeare,* p. 287.

"The immaturity [of his mind in the early plays] is seen in the extent to which the smell of the lamp mingles with the freshness and vigor of poetic feeling. The wide circle of references to Greek fable and Roman story suggests that the writer had come recently from his books, and was not unwilling to display his acquaintance with them." — *Prof. Baynes in Fraser's Mag.* 1880.

"'Love's Labor 's Lost,' one of the earliest of the plays, is so learned, so academic, so scholastic in expression and allusion, that it is unfit for popular representation." — *O'Connor's Hamlet's Note-Book.*

Stapfer,[1] a distinguished French critic, intimates that in his

---

[1] It may be well to remark that Stapfer, Baynes, and White are unfriendly witnesses, and that Gervinus and Verplanck wrote before

judgment some of the plays are *"over-cumbered with learning, not to say pedantic."*

III. He was a jurist, and his fondness for legal phrases is remarkable.

He had "a deep technical knowledge of the law," and an easy familiarity with "some of the most abstruse proceedings in English jurisprudence." — *Lord Chief Justice Campbell.*

"Whenever he indulges this propensity, he uniformly lays down good law." — *Ibid.*

One of the sonnets [46] is so intensely technical in its phraseology that "without a considerable knowledge of English forensic procedure, it cannot be fully understood." [1] — *Ibid.*

"In an age when it was the common practice for young lawyers to write plays, one playwright left upon his works a stronger, sharper legal stamp than appears upon those of any of his contemporaries; and the characters of this stamp are those of the

this controversy began. Judge Holmes is our senior counsel, but we claim the right at this hearing to put him also on the witness stand. His work on the 'Authorship of Shakespeare' is as temperate in its judgments as it is philosophical and profound in its general treatment of the subject.

[1] "Mine eye and heart are at a mortal war,
How to divide the conquest of thy sight;
Mine eye my heart thy picture's sight would bar,
My heart mine eye the freedom of that right.
My heart doth plead that thou in him dost lie, —
A closet never pierced with crystal eyes, —
But the defendant doth that plea deny,
And says in him thy fair appearance lies.
To 'cide this title is impannelèd
A quest of thoughts, all tenants to the heart;
And by their verdict is determinèd
The clear eye's moiety and the dear heart's part:
    As thus, — mine eye's due is thy outward part,
    And my heart's right thy inward love of heart."

Sonnet XLVI.

complicated law of real property." — *Richard Grant White's Memoirs of William Shakespeare*, p. xlvii.

"His knowledge of legal terms is not merely such as might be acquired by the casual observation of even his all-comprehending mind; it has the appearance of technical skill." — *Edmund Malone.*

"The marvellous intimacy which he displays with legal terms, his frequent adoption of them in illustration, and his curiously technical knowledge of their form and force." — *Charles and Mary Cowden Clarke.*

"In one scene the lover, wishing a kiss, prays for a grant of pasture on his mistress' lips. This suggests the law of pasture; and she replies that her lips are "no common." This again suggests the distinction between tenancy in common and tenancy in severalty, and she adds, "though several they be.'" — *Davis' Law in Shakespeare.*

"Among these [legal terms], there are some which few but a lawyer would, and some even which none but a lawyer could, have written." — *Franklin Fiske Heard's Shakespeare as a Lawyer.*

"In the 'Second Part of Henry IV. [V. 5], Pistol uses the term, *absque hoc*, which is technical in the last degree. This was a species of traverse, used by special pleaders when the record was in Latin, known by the denomination of a special traverse. The subtlety of its texture, and the total dearth of explanation in all the reports and treatises extant in the time of Shakespeare with respect to its principle, seem to justify the conclusion that he must have obtained a knowledge of it *from actual practice.*[1] — *Ibid.*

IV. He was a philosopher.

"In the constructing of Shakespeare's Dramas there is an understanding manifested, equal to that in Bacon's *Novum Organum*." — *Carlyle.*

"He is inconceivably wise; the others, conceivably." — *Emerson.*

---

[1] Italics our own.

" From his works may be collected a system of civil and economical prudence." — *Dr. Johnson.*

" He was not only a great poet, but a great philosopher." — *Coleridge.*

" In some of his [Falstaff's] reflections we have a clear, though brief, view of the profound philosopher underlying the profligate humorist and makesport: for he there discovers a breadth and sharpness of observation and a depth of practical sagacity such as might have placed him in the front rank of statesmen and sages." — *Hudson's Shakespeare. His Art and Life*, II. 94.

Thus was the author's mind not only a fountain of inspiration from its own illimitable depths, but enriched in large measure with the stores of knowledge which the world had then accumulated.

" There is the clearest evidence that his mind was richly stored with knowledge of all kinds." — *Prof. Baynes in Fraser's Mag.*, 1880.

" The range and accuracy of his knowledge were beyond precedent or later parallel." — *Lowell's Among My Books*, p. 167.

" An amazing genius, which could pervade all nature at a glance, and to whom nothing within the limits of the universe appeared to be unknown." — *Whalley.*

" Shakespeare had in his time few equals in the range of his manifold knowledge." — *Gervinus' Commentaries*, p. 25.

" It is childish to discuss the amount of learning possessed by an author who has taught the whole world." — *Stapfer's Shakespeare and Classical Antiquity*, p. 106.

" The great master who knew everything." — *Charles Dickens.*

" Let it be accepted as a truth past all debate, that among the great ones of the earth Shakespeare stands alone, in unapproachable majesty. What was the secret of his power: from whence derived this marvellous insight into human nature under all circumstances, ages, and climes, this accurate knowledge of sciences, arts, governments, morals, manners, philosophies, and codes, this exquisite command of language, never wielded with such skill before or since, by which each character, event, or thought is drawn in lines of living light? This, the greatest of all human mysteries which we have received from our fathers, we must transmit, deepened and heightened rather than lessened by our labors, to our children." — *Allibone's Dictionary of Authors*, II. 2050.

NOTE. — The authorities cited in this chapter give us the best and ripest results of modern scholarship. Nearly all of them are of the latter half of the current century.

II.

WILLIAM SHAKSPERE.

I. THE family of William Shakspere, the actor, was grossly illiterate. His father and mother made their signatures with a cross. Of his two children, Judith, at the age of twenty-seven, was also unable to write her name; Susanna could not read her husband's manuscript, nor even identify it by sight among others. The little we know of his own youth and early manhood affords presumptive proof of the strongest kind that he was uneducated.

" Nature only helped him." — *Leonard Digges*, 1640.

" His learning was very little." — *Thomas Fuller's Worthies*, 1662.

"Old Mother-wit and Nature gave
Shakespeare and Fletcher all they have."
Sir John Denham, 1668.

"Shakespeare said all that Nature could impart." — *Chetwood*, 1684.

" Never any scholar, as our Shakespeare, if alive, would confess himself." — *Winstanley*, 1684.

" He was as much a stranger to French as Latin." — *Gerard Langbaine*, 1691.

" The clerk that showed me this church is above eighty years old. He says that this Shakespeare was formerly bound in this town to a butcher, but that he ran away from his master to London." — *Letter from Dowdall*, visiting Stratford, 1693.

" In him we find all arts and sciences, all moral and natural philosophy, without knowing that he ever studied them." — *Dryden.*

" Without any instruction either from the world or from books." — *Hume's History of England*, III. 110.

" The constant criticism which his contemporaries, from Greene to Ben Jonson, passed on him was that he was ignorant of language and no scholar." — *Richard Simpson's School of Shakspere*, II. 398.

" Where this wonderful creator gained the knowledge of human nature and experience of human motives which have presented him to posterity rather as something divine than a mere mortal artist, it is impossible to learn." — *Prof. Shaw's English Literature*, p. 121.

> " And thou, who did'st the stars and sunbeams know,
> Self-school'd, self-scann'd, self-honor'd, self-secure,
> Didst stand on earth unguess'd at."
>
> > *Matthew Arnold's Sonnet to Shakespeare.*

" The only author that gives ground for a very new opinion, that the philosopher and even the man of the world may be born, as well as the poet." — *Alexander Pope.*

" The untaught son of a Stratford yeoman." [1] — *Richard Grant White.*

II. The Shakspere family, like many others of that period, had no settled or uniform method of spelling their name.[2] More than thirty different forms have been found among their papers, on their

---

[1] No reference to Shakspere personally, made in his lifetime or within a hundred years after his death, in contradiction of the above, can be produced. The only possible exception is Jonson's well-known jest relating to his " small Latin and less Greek," for which see p. 102.

[2] English orthography was then in a plastic state, as orthography always is before the formation of a national literature. Bacon once wrote his own name *Bakon*, with the evident intention, entirely characteristic of him, to simplify our alphabet by substituting for the hard sound of *c* the letter *k*, after the manner of the Greek and primitive Roman languages.

tombstones, and in contemporaneous public records. How William wrote it, it is impossible to say; according to Dr. Johnson, each time differently in the three signatures to his will.[1]

In the registry of his baptism and of his burial, it is *Shakspere;* in his marriage bond, *Shagspere;* under the bust at Stratford, *Shakspeare.* Among other forms discovered in the records of the family are the following: *Shaxpur, Chacksper, Schakespeire, Chacsper, Shexpere, Shackspire, Shakispere, Shaxberd, Shakaspeare, Shaykspere,* and *Schakespayr.*[2] Patronymics often varied at that time, as they do now, in different families and in different sections of the country; but here the variations in the same household were unusually numerous, and to all appearances at hap-hazard.

It is a singular circumstance, nevertheless, that in all the forms tabulated by Wise, nineteen hundred and six in number, the one printed on the title-pages of the plays and poems, SHAKESPEARE, does not appear. It is unique. So far as we know, no person in Stratford or in any other part of the kingdom, previously to the publication of the 'Venus and Adonis,' wrote it in that way. Literature had an absolute monopoly of it.[3]

[1] " Whether it be a privilege of genius never to write one's name alike twice, even on the same day, such was certainly the fact with Shakspeare."—*Mellen Chamberlain, Librarian Boston Pub. Lib.,* 1889.

[2] In Stratford the name was undoubtedly pronounced, as it was often written, *Shaxpere.* It occurs in this form one hundred and four times in the town records. The last syllable, also often written *pur,* was uttered like the first, with a short vowel sound.

[3] It is significant that in many of the quartos a hyphen is inserted between the syllables (Shake-speare), perhaps (as it has been suggested) to give the name a fanciful turn, and distinguish it in another

III. Shakspere's handwriting, of which we have five specimens in his signatures to legal documents, was not only almost illegible, but singularly uncultivated and grotesque, wholly at variance with the description given of the manuscripts of the plays in the preface to the folio edition of 1623. The editorial encomium was in these words : —

" His mind and hand went together; and what he thought, he uttered with that *easiness*, that we have scarce received from him a blot in his papers." [Italics our own.]

In this connection we reproduce the five autographs of Shakspere, the only acknowledged specimens of his penmanship in existence, in *fac-simile*.[1]

IV. No letter written by him has come down to us, and but one (soliciting a loan of money) addressed to him. An inspection of his autograph is alone sufficient to explain the paucity of his correspondence, if not its absolute non-existence.

slight respect from that of the actor. The true explanation, however, may lie deeper than this. In Grecian mythology, Pallas Athene (the Roman Minerva) was the goddess of wisdom, philosophy, poetry, and the fine arts. Her original name was simply Pallas, a word derived from πάλλειν, signifying " to brandish or shake." She was generally represented with a spear. Athens, the home of the drama, was under the protection of this Spear-shaker.

In our age such a signature would be understood at once as a pseudonym.

[1] The Public Library of the City of Boston contains a volume of North's Plutarch of 1603, in which is inscribed on a fly-leaf the name of " *Wilm. Shakspeare.*" Concerning this signature the following statement is made in one of the official bulletins of the association :

" The field of comparison of the library signature with the known originals is narrow, being limited to those written between 1613 and 1616, all of which show such a lack of facility in handwriting as would almost preclude the possibility of Shakespeare's having written the dramas attributed to him." — *Mellen Chamberlain, Librarian*, 1889.

V. In the dedication of the 'Venus and Adonis,' published in 1593, Shakespeare calls that poem the "first heir" of his invention. This makes it ante-date the Plays. Accordingly Richard Grant White sets it down as written in 1584-5, before Shakespeare left Stratford. Gervinus, also, assigns it to the same early date.

The 'Venus and Adonis' is a product of the highest culture. It is prefixed with a Latin quotation from Ovid,[1] and is written throughout in the purest, most elegant and scholarly English of that day. Hazlitt compares it to an ice-house, "almost as hard, as glittering, and as cold." Is it possible that in a town where six only of nineteen aldermen and burgesses could write their names, where the habits of the people were so inconceivably filthy that John

---

[1] "Taken from a poem of which there existed at the time no English version." — *Prof. Baynes in Fraser's Mag.*, 1880.

"It is hardly possible that the *Amores* of Ovid, whence he derived his earliest motto, could have been one of his schoolbooks." — *Halli-well-Phillipps.*

Shakspere, father of William, was publicly prosecuted on two occasions for defiling the street in front of his house, where the common speech was a *patois* rude to the verge of barbarism, and where, probably, outside of the school and church, not a half-dozen books, as White admits, were to be found among the whole population, — is it possible that in such a town a lad of twenty composed this beautiful epic?

"The 'Venus and Adonis' and the 'Lucrece' bear palpable tokens of college elegance and predilection, both in story and in treatment. The air of niceness and stiffness, peculiar to the schools, invests these efforts of the youthful genius with almost unmistakable signs of having been written by a schoolman."— *Charles and Mary Cowden Clarke.*

"It is extremely improbable that a poem so highly finished and so completely devoid of *patois* as the 'Venus and Adonis' could have been produced under the circumstances of his then domestic surroundings." — *Halliwell-Phillipps.*

"There was a grammar school in Stratford; but the idea of anybody being taught English grammar in an English grammar school (let alone the English language) in those days, is utterly inconceivable. There was no such branch, and mighty little of anything in its place except birchen rods, the church catechism, the criss-cross row, and a few superfluous Latin declensions out of Lily's Accidence. Nor did Shakespeare hear the limpid, urban English of the poems and sonnets at home or in Stratford streets. . . . Members of Parliament could not understand each other's rustic *patois*, says Mr. White. Even the soldiers in Elizabeth's army could not comprehend the word of command, unless given by officers of their own county or shire town. . . . But Shakespeare, uncouth rustic as he was, writes, as the 'first heir' of his invention, the most elegant, sumptuous, and sensuous verses that English literature possesses to-day." — *Appleton Morgan.*[1]

[1] It is well known that Dr. Morgan, after writing 'The Shakespearean Myth,' repudiated the conclusions to which that book natur-

SIGNATURES OF ALDERMEN AND BURGESSES OF STRATFORD-
UPON-AVON, 1565.

" When at twenty-two years of age he fled from Stratford to London, we may be sure that he had never seen half-a-dozen books other than his horn-book, his Latin Accidence, and a Bible. Probably there were not half-a-dozen others in all Stratford." — *Richard Grant White.*

" There were certainly not more than two or three dozen books, if so many, in the whole town." [1] — *Halliwell-Phillipps' Outlines.*

ally leads. He is now the orthodox president of a Shakespeare Society in New York, still asserting, however, that he knows of no misstatement of fact in the work above mentioned.

Of the curriculum of the Stratford Grammar School in the sixteenth century there is no record. We can judge of it only by the intellectual light which it shed upon the people around it, most of whom, as a matter of fact, could not read or write. Speculations drawn from the study of other schools of the same grade in more favored parts of the kingdom, such as Professor Baynes indulges in, are of little value.

[1] Here are two views of Stratford : —

1. The ideal :

" As his [Shakspere's] stout gelding mounted Edgehill [on the road to London], and he turned in his saddle to take a parting look at the familiar landscape he was leaving, he would behold what Speed, in his enthusiasm, calls ' another Eden.' " — *Prof. Baynes in Encyc. Brit.,* XXI. 739.

2. The real :

" A dirty village. . . . The streets foul with offal, mud, muckheaps, and reeking stable refuse." — *Richard Grant White.*

" Shakespeare's home was in the vicinity of middens, fetid watercourses, mud walls, and piggeries." — *Halliwell-Phillipps.*

" The most dirty, unseemly, ill-paved, wretched-looking town in all Britain." — *David Garrick,* 1769.

" Stratford was a perfect hot-bed of religious and domestic strife." — *C. Elliot Browne in Fraser's Mag.,* 1874.

As a specimen of the popular style in which the life of Shakspere is often written, we append the following : —

" Four years were spent by Shakespeare [after leaving London] in this dignified retirement, and the history of literature scarcely presents another such picture of calm felicity and satisfied ambition." — *Cleveland's Compendium of English Literature for the Use of Schools and Colleges,* p. 129.

VI. It is believed that Shakspere left his home in Stratford and went to London some time between 1585 and 1587. He was then twenty-one to twenty-three years of age. One of the first of the " Shakespeare" Plays to be produced on the stage was 'Hamlet,' and the date not later than 1589.[1] It was founded on a foreign tragedy of which no translation then existed in English. As first presented, it was probably in an imperfect form, having been subsequently rewritten and enlarged into what is now, perhaps, the greatest individual work of genius the human mind has produced.[2] To assume that Shak-

---

[1] In an epistle to university students, published in Greene's 'Menaphon' in 1589, Thomas Nash refers to 'Hamlet' as a play then familiar to them. That this early 'Hamlet' was Shake-speare's there can be no reasonable doubt, for we can trace it in contemporary notices all along from the time of its production in Oxford and Cambridge to its appearance in the Shake-speare quarto of 1603, where we read on the title-page that the play had often been acted in the presence of the two universities. In 1591 Nash alludes to the famous soliloquy, " To be or not to be," and says that it had been a subject of declamation on the public stage for five years preceding, or since 1586. Gabriel Harvey, writing in 1598, distinctly ascribes the 'Venus and Adonis' and 'Lucrece' and the play of 'Hamlet' to the same person. The most striking feature of the play from the first is the part taken by the ghost; this was not in the original legend, and is so extraordinary that, wherever it appears, we must ascribe it to the creative genius of Shake-speare himself. The play was therefore written in 1585-6, probably before William Shakspere left Stratford. Bacon was then about twenty-five years of age, had been highly educated at home and abroad, and was a briefless barrister at Gray's Inn.

[2] It has rivals for this honor : —
" Othello is, perhaps, the greatest work in the world." — *Macaulay.*
" King Lear, the most wondrous work of human genius." — *Richard Grant White.*
" Macbeth, perhaps the greatest tragedy of ancient or modern times." — *E. P. Whipple.*

THE
Tragicall Historie of
HAMLET
Prince of Denmarke

By William Shake-speare.

As it hath beene diuerse times acted by his Highnesse ser-
uants in the Cittie of London : as also in the two V-
niuersities of Cambridge and Oxford, and else-where

At London printed for N.L. and Iohn Trundell.
1603.

spere, under the circumstances in which he was then placed, at so early an age, fresh from a country town where there were few or no books, and from a family circle whose members could not read or write, was the author of this play, would seem to involve a miracle as great as that imputed to Joshua, — in other words, a suspension of the laws of cause and effect.

VII. His residence in London extended over a period of twenty-five years, during which time, according to popular belief, he wrote thirty-seven dramas, one hundred and fifty-four sonnets, and two or three minor poems, besides accumulating a fortune the income of which has been estimated at £400 (equivalent in our time and in our money to $24,000) per annum.[1] Such an instance of mental fecundity the world has never seen, before or since.

At the same time, he was personally unknown in literary and political circles.

"Of his eminent countrymen, Raleigh, Sydney, Spenser, Bacon, Cecil, Walsingham, Coke, Camden, Hooker, Drake, Hobbes, Inigo Jones, Herbert of Cherbury, Laud, Pym, Hampden, Selden, Walton, Wotton, and Donne may be properly reckoned as his contemporaries, and yet there is no evidence whatever that he was personally known to either of these men, or to any others of less note among the statesmen, scholars, soldiers, and artists of his day, excepting a few of his fellow-craftsmen." — *Richard Grant White's Memoirs of William Shakespeare*, p. cxi.

"The prose works published in the latter part of the sixteenth and the early part of the seventeenth centuries contain abundant notices of every poet of distinction save Shakespeare, whose

---

[1] "The relative value of money in Shakespeare's time and ours may be roughly computed at one-twelfth in articles of trade, and one-twentieth in landed or house property." — *Halliwell-Phillipps.*

name and works are rarely and only slightly mentioned. . . .
It is plain that the bard of our admiration was unknown to the
men of that age." — *Ingleby.*

"Since the constellation of great men who appeared in
Greece in the time of Pericles, there was never any such society; yet their genius failed them to find out the best head in
the universe." — *Emerson.*

Imagine the inhabitants of Lilliput paying no attention to Gulliver!

VIII. The end of his career was as remarkable as
its beginning. In 1610 or thereabouts, while he was
still comparatively young (at the age of forty-six),
he retired from London and passed the remainder of
his days among his old neighbors in Stratford,[1] loan-
ing money and brewing beer for sale.[2] His intellectual life seems to have terminated as abruptly as it
had begun. The most careful scrutiny fails to show
that he took the slightest interest in the fate of the
plays left behind him, or in his own reputation as the
author of them. Some of these productions were
still in manuscript, unknown even to the stage, and
not given to the public, either for fame or profit, till

---

[1] "Could go down to Stratford and live there for years, only col-
lecting his dividends from the Globe Theatre, lending money on
mortgage, and leaning over his gate to chat and bandy quips with
neighbors." — *Lowell's Among My Books*, p. 172.

"At a period of life when Chaucer began to write the 'Canterbury
Tales,' Shakspere, according to his biographers, was suddenly and
utterly to cease to write. We cannot believe it." — *Charles Knight.*

[2] Evidently a wholesale business, for a bill against a single person
for malt delivered within the space of about two months, called for
one pound nineteen shillings and ten pence, an amount equivalent
now to one hundred and twenty dollars. This bill, including an item
of two shillings, money loaned, was put in suit in 1604, the year in
which the perfected ' Hamlet ' was published.

Mark-signatures of William Shakspere's father and mother.

Mark-signature of William Shakspere's daughter Judith, at the age of twenty-six.

Mark-signatures of Fulk Sandells and John Richardson, subscribers to William Shakspere's marriage-bond.

Ignorance is the curse of God;
Knowledge the wing wherewith we fly to heaven.

2 HENRY IV.

The common curse of mankind, folly and ignorance.

TROILUS AND CRESSIDA.

There is no darkness but ignorance.

TWELFTH NIGHT.

O thou monster ignorance, how deformed dost thou look!

LOVE'S LABOR'S LOST.

thirteen years after his retirement. Such indifference to the children of his brain, and so complete a seclusion in the prime of his manhood from the refinements of life, present to us a picture, not only painful to contemplate, but one that stultifies human nature itself.

IX. He was exceedingly litigious. He brought suits against several persons for money loaned, in one instance for a sum as small as two shillings, and in another, failing to recover from the debtor, he relentlessly pursued the debtor's bondsman for a year. He was also plaintiff in an action against the town of Stratford in the matter of the tithes. There is reason to believe that he kept an attorney constantly beside him, domiciled in his house.[1]

"The biographer must record these facts, because the literary antiquaries have unearthed, produced, and pitilessly printed them as new particulars in the life of Shakespeare. We hunger and we receive these husks; we open our mouths for food, and we break our teeth against these stones." — *Richard Grant White's Memoirs of Shakespeare,* p. 88.

X. We have conclusive evidence that he was ambitious for a title, and that for the purpose of acquiring one for his father, and indirectly for himself, he made representations to the Herald's College which were not only false but ridiculous. The grant was refused.

"Toward the close of the year 1599 a renewed attempt was made by the poet to obtain a grant of coat-armor to his father. It was now proposed to impale the arms of Shakespeare with

[1] Thomas Greene, attorney, "residing under some unknown conditions at New Place." — *Halliwell-Phillipps.*

those of Arden, and on each occasion ridiculous statements were made respecting the claims of the two families." — *Halli-well-Phillipps' Outlines*, p. 87.

The officer at the head of the college, Sir William Dethick, was charged with connivance at the forgery under the influence of a bribe.

XI. He was also hard and unfeeling towards the poor. A conspiracy having been formed by a few interested persons in Stratford for enclosing the commons, he was induced by secret means to favor the movement, although the authorities of the town in a letter to him protested against it as unjust and oppressive to the poorer classes.

" It is certain that he was in favor of the enclosures." — *Halliwell-Phillipps' Outlines*, p. 168.

XII. Our surprises do not cease at his death. On the heavy stone slab that marks his grave in the old church at Stratford, visitors read the following inscription : —

" Good friend, for Jesus' sake forbear
To dig the dust enclosed here :
Blest be the man that spares these stones,
And cursed be he that moves my bones."

These lines are evidently his own,[1] for the imprecation contained in them prevented his wife, who survived him, from being laid at rest by his side.[2]

[1] " The rudeness of the verses seems to us a proof of authenticity." — *Lowell's Among My Books*, p. 17.

[2] " He was buried in the chancel of the church, because that locality was the legal and customary burial place for owners of the tithes." — *Halliwell-Phillipps.*

BUST OF SHAKSPERE AT STRATFORD-UPON-AVON.

XIII. Shakspere made no mention of any literary property in his will. He was careful to specify, among other bequests, his "second-best bed," but not a book, not one of his own books, not even a manuscript, though one-half of all the works that bear his name, including the immortal dramas of 'Macbeth,' 'The Tempest,' and 'Julius Cæsar,' were unpublished, and some of them even unknown, at the time of his death.[1]

"He had no books. His will shows the fact. He leaves houses, lands, messuages, orchards, gardens, wearing apparel, furniture, a sword, a silver and gilt punch-bowl, a second-best bed for his wife — no books. He had twenty thousand dollars a year, and not a volume. The man who wrote 'Love's Labor's Lost,' so learned, so academic, so scholastic in expression and allusion that it is unfit for popular representation, the man whose ample page is rich with the transfigured spoils of ages, that man lived without a library!" — *O'Connor's Hamlet's Note Book*, p. 75.

XIV. We have two portraits of Shakspere, each possessing historically some claims to our confidence. One is the famous bust in the church at Stratford, placed there within seven years after Shakspere's

[1] "It is simply silly to talk, as the commentators will, of Shakespeare's omitting to mention them in his testaments because his copyrights had expired, or because he or his representatives had sold them to the Globe Theatre. . . . These plays had been entered on the Stationers' books, and, once so entered, it was impossible to alienate them to the Globe Theatre or to any other purchaser, except by registry of later date. . . . The record of alienation could have been made in but one place, and it was never made there." — *Appleton Morgan.*

The cicerone at Stratford informs visitors that the wicked manuscripts were destroyed, after Shakspere's death, by his puritanical children!

death. This is, in all probability, a correct likeness. That it was not set up, however, by any one in Stratford is evident from the fact that Shakspere's body is said in one of the inscriptions to be "within this monument," whereas we know that the body was buried under the floor of the chancel, at some distance from the bust, and with one other grave intervening between them.[1] Concerning the bust itself we quote as follows : —

"What a painful stare, with its goggle eyes and gaping mouth! The expression of the face has been credited with humor, bonhommie, hilarity, and jollity. To me it is decidedly clownish." — *Norris' Portraits of Shakespeare*, p. 18.

"No one can look upon its manifest defects without wishing to know if he who wrote for all time did really inhabit such a body as this." — *Ibid.*

"The skull has the smoothness and roundness of a boy's marble, and about as much individuality or expression. . . . The cheeks are puffy and spiritless; the mustaches are curled up in a manner never found except on some city exquisite ; . . . finally, the expression of the eyes, so far as they have any, is simply that of easy, rollicking good nature, not overburdened with sense or intellect." — *Prof. J. S. Hart in Scribner's Monthly*, July, 1874.

" It has no more individuality or power than a boy's marble."— *Friswell's Life Portraits of Wm. Shakespeare*, p. 10.

Malone's work, in covering the bust with a coat of white paint, " did not altogether obliterate the semblance of an intellectual human being, and this is more than can be said of the miserable travesty which now distresses the eye of the pilgrim." — *Halliwell-Phillipps.*

" The painted figure-head-like bust is hideous." — *Richard Grant White.*

---

[1] " It is not likely that these verses [under the bust] were composed by a Stratfordian." — *Halliwell-Phillipps' Outlines*, I. 285.

Droeshout Portrait of Shakspere.

The other portrait is the Droeshout engraving on the title-page of the first folio, than which it would be impossible, we think, to imagine anything more hideous. It is, without doubt, a caricature. For once the critics are agreed : —

" A hard, wooden, staring thing." — *Richard Grant White.*

" Even in its best state, it is such a monstrosity that I, for one, do not believe that it had any trustworthy exemplar." — *Ingleby's The Man and the Book.*

" It is not known from what it was copied, and many think it unlike any human being." — *Norris' Portraits of Shakespeare,* p. 18.

" The hair is straight, combed down the sides of the face, and bunched over the ears; the forehead is disproportionately high; the top of the head bald; the face has the wooden expression familiar in the Indians used as signs for tobacconists' shops, accompanied by an idiotic stare that would be but a sorry advertisement for the humblest establishment in that trade." — *Appleton Morgan.*

Of the new portrait of Shakspere, found in the house of the Town Clerk of Stratford in 1861, and preserved among the treasures of the birthplace, Mr. Friswell says : —

" As a suggestion of the face of Shakspere it would be very good, save for the weakness, want of power, and, indeed, vacuity which is to be seen in it." — p. 57.

" I have very little, if any, doubt that this portrait was copied from the bust, at the very earliest, some time in the first half of the last century, but more probably about the time of the jubilee in 1769." [1] — *Halliwell-Phillipps.*

---

[1] The number of different portraits of Shakspere in existence exceeds three hundred, all of them, with the exception of those above mentioned, purely ideal. It is worthy of remark, however, that out of these has come, by a kind of evolution, a type which not only is

XV. So far as we know, Shakspere never claimed the authorship of the plays.[1] He permitted his name to be used, doubtless for good and sufficient reasons, and in accordance with a not unusual custom at that period,[2] on the title-pages of fourteen of them printed in his lifetime, though they were all (thirty-seven in number) ascribed to him unmistakably in the collective editions that appeared after his death.[3] His

characteristic and popular, but which bears a singular resemblance to the features of Francis Bacon. It would seem as though artists were unconsciously striving to get the two heads, as Mr. Donnelly says, "under one hat."

[1] "Shakespeare never claimed the plays as his own. . . . He was unquestionably indifferent about them, and died without seeing the most remarkable series of intellectual works that ever issued from the brain of man in the custody of type." — *The Athenæum* (London), Sept. 13, 1856.

"I pretend to no special erudition in English literature, but have read from boyhood that Shakespeare never claimed the tragedies as his, nor kept any copy of them." — *Prof. Francis W. Newman in The Echo*, Dec. 31, 1887.

"Here are plays constantly pirated, and yet it is impossible to discover that anybody, or a legal representative of anybody, named Shakespeare, ever set up a claim to proprietorship in any of these works." — *Appleton Morgan.*

[2] John Rogers published an edition of the Bible in 1537 with the statement that it was "truly and purely translated into English by Thomas Matthew." The name of Thomas Matthew was a fictitious one, the work itself being substantially a reprint from Tyndale and Coverdale. It is still known, however, as Matthew's Bible.

[3] It has been suggested that Bacon could not have voluntarily deprived himself of the honor of having written the plays, if he were the author of them; this is exactly what astonishes us in Shakspere.

"But for them [Heminge and Condell] it is more than likely that such of his works as had remained to that time [1623] unprinted, would have been irrecoverably lost, and among them were 'Julius Cæsar,' 'The Tempest,' and 'Macbeth.'" — *Lowell's Among My Books*, p. 167.

With Shakspere, the choice would have lain between fame as a reticence on the subject, especially after his retirement to Stratford, is itself significant. His fellow-townsmen, it is probable, never witnessed one of these productions on the stage. Neither his local fame (if he had any) as a dramatist, nor the influence of his wealth and position (if exerted by him) overcame their repugnance to theatrical representations, for in 1602 the board of aldermen prohibited any performance of the kind in the town under a penalty of ten shillings. In 1612, when Shakspere's reputation among his neighbors should have been at its zenith, the penalty was increased to ten pounds. The key to the situation lies in his stolidity or in his sense of honor.

XVI. The references to Shakspere, direct and indirect, in contemporaneous literature (1592–1616), have been carefully collated and published. They number (reckoning all that have been claimed, some of which are undoubtedly spurious, and only eighteen refer to Shakspere by name) one hundred and twenty-seven, and may be classified as follows : —

Those made to his works, one hundred and twenty; those made to him as a man, seven.[1] The citations in the first class are, of course, irrelevant to our purpose. In the second, we find statements from the following named persons: Thomas Nash, 1589;

dramatist and oblivion; with Bacon, between fame as a dramatist and fame as a statesman, the still greater one (in his own estimation) of a philosopher being assured.

[1] For the testimonies of Heminge, Condell, and Leonard Digges, given in 1623, see page 148 *et seq.* These ten contemporaries comprise the whole number of those whose references to Shakspere personally have come down to us, — seven during his lifetime, and three after his death. For Chettle's alleged testimony, see p. 150.

Robert Greene, 1592; John Manningham, 1601; two anonymous writers, about 1605; Thomas Heywood, 1612; and Ben Jonson, 1616. Nash calls Shakspere an idiot; Greene, a Jack-at-all-trades; Manningham makes him the hero of an amour; the anonymous writers refer to his wealth, to his landed proprietorship, and (one of them) to his aspirations for a title; Heywood is indignant because two of his own poems had been published by a piratical printer as Shakspere's, although (he affirms) without the latter's consent; and Ben Jonson caricatures him as a Poet-Ape.

With the exception of Manningham and Heywood, who make no reference to the subject, all these writers concur in attributing some sort of imposture to Shakspere. They seem to recognize in him a pretence of authorship which excites their contempt. Greene makes his statement from a dying bed, addressing it to the playwrights Marlowe, Nash (or Lodge), and Peele, as though they also were familiar with the truth of what he writes. Greene's sincerity cannot be successfully impugned.[1] We quote these testimonials as follows : —

A. "Amongst this kind of men that repose eternity in the mouth of a player [as distinguished from plays in print] I can but engross some deep-read schoolmen or grammarians [persons educated at grammar-schools] who have no more learning in their skull than will serve to take up a commodity [to keep a

---

[1] It is painful to read the harsh criticisms on Robert Greene's character made with one consent by all Shakspereans. Greene differed from his associates, so far as we can see, chiefly in one particular, viz.: he repented of his follies and with his dying breath tried to induce others to follow his example. But then, at the same time, he pronounced Shakspere an impostor. *Hinc illæ lacrymæ!*

tradesman's books] nor art in their brains ; " "idiot art-masters, who think to outbrave better pens with the swelling bombast of bragging blank verse, . . . and translate two-penny pamphlets from the Italian, without any knowledge even of its articles. . . . It may be the ingrafted overflow of some kill-cow conceit." — *Nash's Letter prefixed to Greene's 'Menaphon,'* 1589.

For interpretation of the above, we quote from a noted Shaksperean : —

" Nash was in demand for his style, and his business was to reduce to pointed form the matter furnished him by others. Hence his publications of 1589 must be supposed to represent, not the fruits of his own experience, but the ideas decanted into him. Greene may be assumed to have crammed him with what had to be said as introduction to *Menaphon ;* and the identity of idea, as well as of phrase, between Nash's epistle and things which Greene subsequently wrote will prove this assumption to be correct. We shall see that the actor-author, here attacked by Nash, is assailed in the same phrases as the one attacked by Greene three years later, in his ' Groatsworth of Wit.' But in the latter case it is Shakspere who is thus assailed. Therefore it is probably, also, Shakspere in the former case." — *Simpson's School of Shakspere*, II. 355.

The following specifications, drawn from points in Nash's epistle, will make this clearer : —

1. *Eternity in the mouth of a player*, and not in printed plays.

The plays of " Shake-speare " had then been coming out on the stage for several years, but not one of them had been printed. The earliest quarto edition of a " Shake-speare " play, of which we have any record, bears date 1591.

2. *I can but engross some deep-read schoolmen or grammarians*, that is, persons educated at grammar-schools.

Shakspere had had no opportunity to acquire an education beyond that afforded by the grammar-school of his native village.

3. *The swelling bombast of bragging blank verse.*

" Shake-speare," not Marlowe, was the first to introduce blank verse on a large scale into the English drama. Not only was Marlowe three years younger, but he began to write five years later, than " Shake-speare." It is time that the contrary opinion, a well-worn fiction, should be set at rest.

4. *Translate two-penny pamphlets from the Italian, without any knowledge even of its articles.*

The plays drawn from Italian sources or laid in Italian scenes and antedating Nash's letter, were ' The Comedy of Errors,' ' The Taming of a Shrew,' and ' The Two Gentlemen of Verona.'

5. *The ingrafted overflow of some kill-cow conceit.*

To kill the cow or the calf was, in the slang phrase of the day, to make extemporary speeches during a performance on the stage. It was said of Shakspere, by a ridiculous introversion of facts, that in his younger days, when apprenticed as a butcher to his father, " he would kill a calf in high style."

The whole gravamen of Nash's charge is that some contemporary playwright, having no education beyond that of a " country grammar-school," unable to read Italian or " even latinize his neck-verse," an idiot art-master, was endangering university scholarship by fraudulent pretences.[1]

---

[1] The prominent dramatists of the Elizabethan age were university men. Marlowe, Greene, Nash, Fletcher, and Heywood were educated at Cambridge ; Chapman, Peele, Daniel, Beaumont, Lodge, Lyly, Drayton, Ford, and Massinger, at Oxford. Ben Jonson received

B. " An upstart crow, beautified with our feathers, that, with his tiger's heart wrapped in a player's hide, supposes he is as well able to bombast out a blank verse as the best of you, and, being an absolute *Johannes Factotum*, is, in his own conceit, the only Shake-scene in a country." — *Greene's Groatsworth of Wit* (1592).[1]

"Throughout we see Greene's determination not to recognize Shakspere as a man capable of doing anything by himself. . . . He will not own that the man is capable of having really done that which passes for his." — *Simpson's School of Shakspere* (1878), II. 389.

C. " Thou shalt learn to be frugal, . . . to feed upon all men, . . . and, when thou feelest thy purse well lined, buy thee some place in the country." — *Ratsie's Ghost* (anon.), 1605.

D. " With mouthing words that better wits have framed,
They purchase lands and now esquires are made."[2]
Return from Parnassus (anon.), 1606.

E. " Poor Poet-Ape, that would be thought our chief,
Whose works are e'en the frippery of wit,
From brokerage is become so bold a thief
As we, the robbed, leave rage and pity it.
At first he made low shifts, would pick and glean,
Buy the reversion of old plays. Now grown
To a little wealth and credit in the scene,
He takes up all, makes each man's wit his own,

classical instruction at the famous Westminster school, supplemented, it is believed, by a course at Cambridge.

[1] In 1587 Greene wrote as follows of the author of ' Fair Em,' an anonymous production once attributed to Shakspere : —
" The ass is made proud by this underhand brokery. And he that cannot write true English, without the help of clerks of parish churches, will needs make himself the father of interludes." — *Preface to ' Farewell to Folly.'*
" Greene probably did not mean to accuse Shakespeare of theft, but only to charge him, a mere actor and an uneducated peasant, with intruding among authors." — *Richard Simpson.*

[2] No other actor is known at that time to have possessed large landed property, or aspired to any mark of social distinction.

And told of this, he slights it. Tut, such crimes
  The sluggish, gaping auditor devours ;
He marks not whose 't was first, and after times
  May judge it to be his, as well as ours."
                                        Ben Jonson.

This famous epigram, by Ben Jonson, was first
printed with many others of his in 1616, but was
written several years earlier, perhaps, as Mr. Thomas
W. White in ' Our English Homer ' conjectures, in
1598. That Shakspere is meant appears not only
from other and similar references to him from the
same pen (to be cited hereafter) [1] but also from the
following considerations : —

1. This " Poet-Ape " masqueraded as the " chief "
dramatist of the age.

2. He had acquired wealth.

3. He had the habit of appropriating to his own
use, freely and unscrupulously, the writings of others.

We add one more testimony of the same tenure.
We omitted it from our computation, given above,
for the reason that it is not personal enough to fall
directly within the scope of our argument. Never- ·
theless, it confirms in an unmistakable manner the
existence at that time of some great imposture on the
stage : —

F. "Our age doth produce many such, one of the greatest
being a stage-player, a man with sufficient ingenuity for imposi-
tion." — *Confessio Fraternitatis*, Chap. XII. (anon. 1615).[2]

---

[1] See pp. 93-108.

[2] It has been contended by a German writer that the person referred to as a stage-player by the author of the *Confessio* was one
Heinrich Khunrath ; but Khunrath was not a stage-player and, at
the time when the *Confessio* was published, had been dead fourteen

Excepting some further statements made by Ben Jonson (which we shall give in their proper place), and apart from the official records of baptism, marriage, and death, of transfers of property, of suits at law, and of two fraudulent and abortive applications for a title, these are all the references to be found in contemporaneous literature to William Shakspere, the man. Every one of them implies that he was an impostor. Not a word, not the remotest hint from friend or foe within the circle of his acquaintance, of a transcendent genius, or, indeed, of any literary ability whatever !

"I cannot marry this fact to his verse." — *Ralph Waldo Emerson.*

"A mere fabulous story, a blind and extravagant error. — *Schlegel.*

"To this individuality we tack on a universal genius, which is about as reasonable as it would be to take the controlling power of gravity from the sun and attach it to one of the asteroids." — *Whipple's Literature of the Age of Elizabeth*, p. 36.

"A miraculous [*sic*] miracle." — *Richard Grant White.*

"What ! are we to have miracles in sport ? . . . Does God choose idiots by whom to convey divine truth to man ? " — *Coleridge.*

years. The theory seems to be utterly without foundation. It appears, also, that in the next edition of the book this passage was omitted, as though some one, influential in Rosicrucian circles, considered it dangerous, even in its obscurity.

III.

FRANCIS BACON.

" If there was a Shakespeare of earth, as I suspect, there was also one of heaven; and it is of him that we desire to know something." — HALLAM.

" Shakespeare is a voice merely; who and what he was that sang, that sings, we know not." — RALPH WALDO EMERSON.

" The apparition known to moderns as Shakespeare." — JAMES RUSSELL LOWELL.

I. SETTING aside Shakspere, Francis Bacon was the most original, the most imaginative, and the most learned man of his time.

" The most exquisitely constructed intellect that has ever been bestowed on any of the children of men." — *Macaulay.*

" The great glory of literature in this island, during the reign of James, was my Lord Bacon." — *Hume.*

" Lord Bacon was the greatest genius that England, or perhaps any other country, ever produced." — *Pope.*

" One of the most colossal of the sons of men." — *G. L. Craik.*

" Crown of all modern authors." — *George Sandys.*

" He possessed at once all those extraordinary talents which were divided amongst the greatest authors of antiquity. He had the sound, distinct, comprehensive knowledge of Aristotle, with all the beautiful lights, graces, and embellishments of Cicero. One does not know which to admire most in his writ-

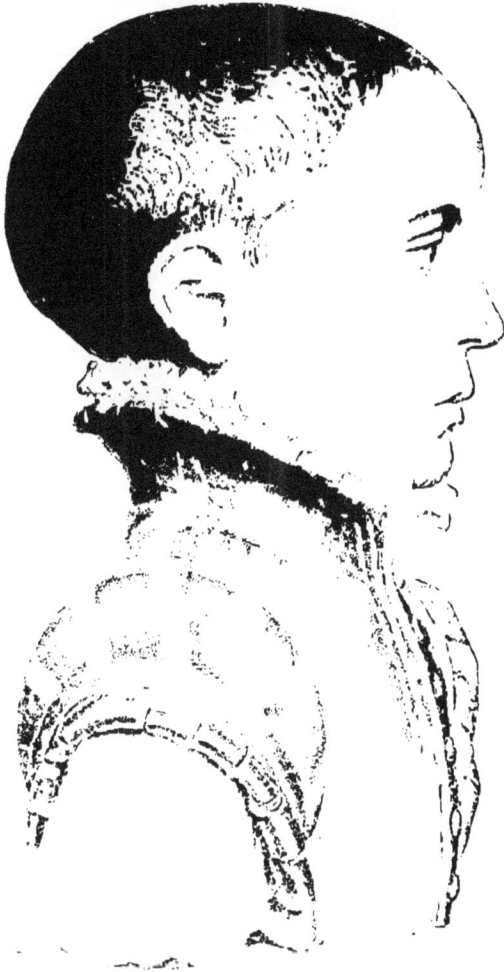

FRANCIS BACON AT THE AGE OF NINE.

ings, the strength of reason, force of style, or brightness of imagination." — *Addison.*

" Next to Shakespeare, the greatest name of the Elizabethan age is that of Bacon. Undoubtedly, one of the broadest, richest, and most imperial of human intellects." — *E. P. Whipple.*

"If we compare what may be found in the sixth, seventh, and eighth books of the ' De Augmentis,' in the ' Essays,' the ' History of Henry VII.,' and the various short treatises contained in his works on moral and political wisdom, and on human nature, with the rhetoric, ethics, and politics of Aristotle, or with the historians most celebrated for their deep insight into civil society and human character, — with Thucydides, Tacitus, Philippe de Comines, Machiavel, Davila, Hume, — we shall, I think, find that one man may almost be compared with all of these together." — *Hallam.*

" The wisest, greatest of mankind." — *Ibid.*

" Columbus, Luther, and Bacon are, perhaps, in modern times the men of whom it may be said with the greatest probability that, if they had not existed, the whole course of human affairs would have been varied." — *Edinburgh Review.*

" When one considers the sound and enlarged views of this great man, the multitude of objects to which his mind was turned, and the boldness of his style which unites the most sublime images with the most rigorous precision, one is disposed to regard him as the greatest, the most universal, and the most eloquent of philosophers." — *D'Alembert.*

" His imagination was fruitful and vivid ; a temperament of the most delicate sensibility, so excitable as to be affected by the slightest alterations of the atmosphere." — *Montagu.*

" He belongs to the realm of the imagination, of eloquence, of jurisprudence, of ethics, of metaphysics; his writings have the gravity of prose, with the fervor and vividness of poetry."— *Prof. Welsh.*

" Who is there that, hearing the name of Bacon, does not instantly recognize everything of genius the most profound, of literature the most extensive, of discovery the most penetrating, of observation of human life the most distinguishing and refined ? " — *Edmund Burke.*

"Shakespeare and the seers do not contain more expressive or vigorous condensations, more resembling inspiration; in Bacon, they are to be found everywhere." — *Taine.*

"No other author can be compared with him, unless it be Shakespeare." — *Prof. Fowler.*

"He was a genius second only to Shakespeare." — *Prof. Church.*

"Bacon little knew or suspected that there was then existing (the only one that ever did exist) his superior in intellectual power." — *Walter Savage Landor.*

Addison, referring to a prayer composed by Bacon, says that "for elevation of thought and greatness of expression it seems rather the devotion of an angel than that of a man."

Prof. Fowler pronounces this prayer "the finest bit of composition in the English language."

II. Bacon came of a family eminent for learning. His father, Nicholas Bacon, was Lord Chancellor and Keeper of the Great Seal under Elizabeth; his mother, daughter of Sir Anthony Cooke, tutor of Edward VI.

Of Bacon's mother, Macaulay writes : —

"She was distinguished both as a linguist and a theologian. She corresponded in Greek with Bishop Jewell, and translated his 'Apologia' from the Latin so correctly that neither he nor Archbishop Parker could suggest a single alteration. She also translated a series of sermons on fate and free-will from the Tuscan of Bernardo Ochino. Her sister, Katherine, wrote Latin hexameters and pentameters which would appear with credit in the 'Musæ Etonenses.' Mildred, another sister, was described by Roger Ascham as the best Greek scholar among the young women of England, Lady Jane Grey always excepted."

III. Bacon had a strong desire for public employment, due, it is fair to infer, to the consciousness that he possessed exceptional powers for the service of the state. It was a creditable ambition, though the methods then in vogue to gratify it would, according to modern standards, hardly be deemed consistent with personal honor. It is certain that the reputation of being a poet, and particularly a dramatic poet, writing for pay, would have compromised him at court.[1] In those days play-acting and play-writing were considered scarcely respectable. The first theatre in London was erected in 1576, ten or twelve years only before the earliest production of ' Hamlet.' The Government, in the interest of public morals, frowned upon the performances. The Lord Mayor, in 1597, at the very time when the greatest of the "Shake-speare" Plays were coming out, denounced the theatre as a "place for vagrants, thieves, horse-stealers, contrivers of treason, and other idle and dangerous persons." One man published a book entitled "A Pleasant Invective against Poets, Pipers, Players, Jesters, and such like caterpillars."[2] Another lamented because the people were given over to playing and dancing, instead of those exercises of the olden times, when "they went naked and were good soldiers; when they fed upon roots and barks of trees, and could stand up to the chin many days in marshes without victuals."

---

[1] It is only in recent times that a professional author has come, under the most favorable circumstances, to be considered in England a gentleman. To look to any kind of literary composition for a revenue was, in the time of Bacon, sufficient to degrade any man from that rank in which, according to Blackstone, no one was tolerated who could not "live idly and without manual labor." — *Commentaries,* I. 406.

[2] The author of this book, Stephen Gosson, is commended for it by Mr. Allibone in his ' Dictionary of Authors.'

Taine speaks of the stage in Shakespeare's day as
" degraded by the brutalities of the crowd, who not
seldom would stone the actors, and by the severities
of the magistrates, who would sometimes condemn
them to lose their ears." He thus describes the play-
house, as it then existed : —

" On a dirty site on the banks of the Thames rose the principal theatre, the Globe, a sort of hexagonal tower, surrounded
by a muddy ditch. Over it was hoisted a red flag. The common people could enter as well as the rich ; there were six-
penny, two-penny, even penny seats ; but no one could gain
admittance without money. If it rained (and it often rains in
London), the people in the pit — butchers, mercers, bakers,
sailors, apprentices — received the streaming rain upon their
heads. I suppose they did not trouble themselves about it ;
it was not so long since that they had begun to pave the
streets of London, and when men like these have had experience of sewers and puddles, they are not afraid of catching
cold.

" While waiting for the piece, they amuse themselves after
their fashion, — drink beer, crack nuts, eat fruits, howl, and
now and then resort to their fists ; they have been known to
fall upon the actors and turn the theatre upside down. At
other times, when they were dissatisfied, they went to the tavern
to give the poet a hiding, or toss him in a blanket. When the
beer took effect, there was a great upturned barrel in the pit, a
peculiar receptacle for general use. The smell rises, and then
comes the cry, ' Burn the juniper ! ' They burn some in a plate
on the stage, and the heavy smoke fills the air. Certainly, the
folk there assembled could scarcely get disgusted at anything,
and cannot have had sensitive noses."

It may easily be imagined that Bacon, considering
his high birth, aristocratic connections, and aspirancy
for official honors, and already projecting a vast
philosophical reform for the human race, would have

shrunk from open alliance with an institution like this.[1]

IV. To his confidential friend, Sir Toby Matthew, Bacon was in the habit of sending copies of his books as they came from the press. On one of these occasions he forwards, with an air of mystery and half apologetically, certain works which he describes as the product of his " recreation," called by him, also, curiously, " works of the alphabet," upon which not even Mrs. Pott's critical acumen has been able to throw, from sources other than conjecture, any light.[2] In a letter addressed to Bacon by Matthew while abroad, in acknowledgment of some

[1] " It must be borne in mind that actors occupied an inferior position in society, and that even the vocation of a dramatic writer was considered scarcely respectable." — *Halliwell-Phillipps.*

" Lodge [a contemporary of ' Shake-speare '], who had never trod the stage, but had written several plays, speaks of the vocation of the playmaker as sharing the odium attaching to the actor. At this day we can scarcely realize the scorn which was thrown on all sides upon those who made acting a means of livelihood." — *Dr. Ingleby.*

Under a law enacted in 1572, any person, exercising the profession of an actor without license from two justices or the written protection of a nobleman, was liable to be arrested, to be whipped, and to have his right ear bored with a hot iron not less than one inch in circumference. Professional actors were forbidden even the rites of Christian burial.

[2] " In 1623, Bacon writes to Sir Tobie Matthew about putting the ' alphabet in a frame ; ' if this was their cipher, the frame was the 1623 folio. Such enigmatical talk between two friends is evidence that they were both interested in some secret which they would not openly refer to." — *Francis Fearon in Bacon Journal*, I. 57.

Printers lock up their type in a *frame.*

In still another letter to Matthew, written in 1604, at about the time that the great tragedies of ' Hamlet,' ' Macbeth,' ' King Lear,' and ' Othello ' were appearing, he apologizes for some neglect on the ground that his head had been " wholly employed upon invention," i. e. upon works of imagination.

"great and noble token and favor," we find this
postscript: —

" The most prodigious wit that ever I knew, of my nation and
of this side of the sea, is of your lordship's name, though he be
known by another.''

It has been plausibly suggested that the "token of
favor," sent to Matthew, was the folio edition of the
"Shake-speare" Plays, published in 1623. It is certain that Matthew's letter was written subsequently
to January 27, 1621.[1]

[1] Various attempts have been made to break the force of this testimony. It has been urged that, as Bacon had been raised to the peerage, he had acquired another name under which to publish his works.
This seems too frivolous for serious remark. It has also been conjectured that Matthew may have been in Madrid, where a certain
Francisco de Quevedo was writing under a pseudonym. Unfortunately for this theory, the Spaniard (who has never become distinguished, so far as we know, for "prodigious wit") retained the name
of Francisco, the only part that suggested Bacon's, in his pseudonym.
The simple truth is, Matthew's description exactly fits the " Shakespeare " Plays and Bacon's literary alias.
     Indeed, is it credible that Matthew would have written to Bacon,
the Lord Chancellor of England, author of the *Novum Organum*
(then published), and his benefactor, the only friend who stood by
him, in his apostasy to Rome, when all others, even his own father
and mother cast him off, that he had found on the Continent a person
(then and ever since unknown) bearing his lordship's name, but
superior to his lordship in learning or wit ? Is it necessary to impute
to Matthew so gross a violation of good taste, not to say a gratuitous
insult to his correspondent ? On the contrary, who does not see that
this same "most prodigious wit," the greatest (according to the postscript) of all the world, was at another time also described by Matthew
in the following words : —   -
     " A man so rare in knowledge, of so many several kinds, indued
with the facility and felicity of expressing it all in so elegant, significant, so abundant, and yet so choice and ravishing a way of words, of
metaphors and allusions, as perhaps the world has not seen since it

V. Bacon kept a commonplace book which he called a Promus, now in the archives of the British Museum. It consisted of several large sheets, on which from time to time he jotted down all kinds of suggestive and striking phrases, proverbs, aphorisms, metaphors, and quaint turns of expression, found in the course of his reading and available for future use. With the exception of the proverbs from the French, the entries, one thousand six hundred and fifty-five in number, are in his own handwriting. These verbal treasures are scattered, as thick as the leaves of Vallombrosa, throughout the Plays. Mrs. Pott finds, by actual count, four thousand four hundred and four instances in which they are reproduced there — some of them in more or less covert or modified form — over and over again. We can almost see the architect at work, imbedding these gems of beauty and wisdom in the wonderful structures to which, according to Matthew, he gave the name of another. While they appear to a limited extent in Bacon's prose works, they seem to have constituted a storehouse of materials for particular use in the composition of the Plays.

Two of these entries reappear in a single sentence in ' Romeo and Juliet.' One is the unusual phrase,

---

was a world." — *Address to the Reader, prefixed to Collection of English Letters,* 1660.

This, of course, was Francis Bacon. The two portraitures are identical.

An amusing discussion, prompted by Mr. Appleton Morgan, on this subject was published in *Shakespeariana* (VIII. 44) in 1891. In it two noted anti-Baconians endeavored to explain this postscript, but ended simply in refuting each other's theories. Our readers will find in this correspondence an addition to the comic literature of the age.

"golden sleep;" and the second, the new word,
" uproused," then added for the first time, like hundreds of others in the Plays, out of the same mint, to
the verbal coinage of the realm.

> " But where unbruisèd youth with unstuffed brain
> Doth couch his limbs, there golden sleep doth reign;
> Therefore, thy earliness doth me assure,
> Thou art uproused by some distemperature." — II. 3.

To one familiar with the laws of chance, these coincidences will fall little short of a mathematical
demonstration.

> " One of these entries would prove little or nothing, but any
> one, accustomed to evidence, will perceive that two constitute a
> coincidence, amounting almost to a demonstration, that either
> [1] Bacon and Shakespeare borrowed from some common and
> at present unknown source; or [2] one of the two borrowed
> from the other." — *E. A. Abbott, in his Introduction to Mrs.
> Pott's Edition of the Promus.*

Perhaps the most interesting feature of the Promus
is the group of salutatory phrases it contains, such as
good-morning, good-day, and *good-night,* which had
not then come into general use in England, but which
occur two hundred and fifty times in the Plays.
These salutations, however, were common at that
time in France, where Bacon, as attaché of the
British Embassy, had spent three years in the early
part of his life. To him we are doubtless indebted
for these little amenities of speech.[1]

---

[1] One or two specimens have been found in earlier literature, but
the statement in the text is substantially correct. These salutations
did not take root in English speech till they were implanted there by
the author of the Plays. Their presence in Bacon's scrap-book is
alone sufficient evidence that they were new.

Particular attention is called to the entry "good-dawning," a style of address which Bacon failed to make popular, and which is found but once in the whole range of English literature outside of the Promus, — in 'King Lear.'

The date of the Promus (a strictly private record, published for the first time in 1882) was 1594; that of the play, 1606. In one, the seed; the only plant from that seed, in the other.

"The phrase 'good-dawning' is found only once in Shakespeare, put into the mouth of the affected Oswald [Lear, II. 2], 'Good-dawning to thee, friend.' The quartos are so perplexed by this strange phrase that they alter 'dawning' into 'even,' although a little farther on Kent welcomes the 'comfortable beams of the rising sun.' Obviously 'dawning' is right; but did the phrase suggest itself independently to Bacon and Shakespeare?

"Again, Bacon has thought it worth while to enter the phrase 'good-morrow.' What does this mean? It is one of the commonest phrases in the plays of Shakespeare, occurring there nearly a hundred times; why, then, did Bacon take note of a phrase so noteworthless, if it were at that time in common use?" — *E. A. Abbott.*[1]

No dialogues are found in Bacon's acknowledged works, and yet the Promus abounds in colloquialisms, of which the following are specimens: —

What else?	You put me in mind
How now?	If that be so
Say that	Is it because
Peradventure, can you?	Nothing less
See, then, how	Much less
For the rest	If you be at leisure
Your reason	The rather because
O the	O, my lord, sir
Believe it	Believe it not
I would not you had done it	Never, may it please you
Repeat your reason	Come to the point

[1] Dr. Abbott makes these admissions while disavowing Mrs. Pott's theory.

Answer me directly	Hear me out
Answer me shortly	Let me make an end of the tale
What will you?	You take more than is granted
Is it possible?	That is not so, by your favor
You take it right	What shall be the end?
Let it not displease you	I object
I distinguish	I demand
You go from the matter	Well
Verily, by my reason it is so	You have forgot nothing

We mention one more entry, No. 1096: "law at Twickenham for the merry tales." Twickenham was a country-seat to which Bacon frequently retired, and where works of his " recreation" would naturally have been written. The plays in which legal principles are most frequently stated and applied were produced at or near the time of the Promus.[1]

Mr. Spedding published a few only of the Promus entries in his edition of Bacon's works, alleging that he could make nothing of them. And yet the Promus was the only extended work he found in Bacon's

---

[1] In regard to proverbs, Mrs. Pott makes the following computations: English proverbs in the Promus, 203 ; reproduced in the plays, 152. French, Italian, and Spanish proverbs in the Promus, 240; reproduced in the plays, 150. Latin [Erasmus] proverbs in the Promus, 225; reproduced in the plays, 218.

"It may be broadly asserted that the English, French, Italian, Spanish, and Latin proverbs, which are noted in the Promus and quoted in Shakespeare, are not found in other literature of the fifteenth, sixteenth, and seventeenth centuries." — *Preface to Bacon's Promus*, p. 84.

"There are about two hundred English terms of expression entered in the Promus. Of these, seventeen only have been discovered in works written between the fifteenth and eighteenth centuries, other than the prose works of Bacon and the plays." — *Ibid.*, p. 83.

own handwriting. If Mr. Spedding had failed to understand the 'Novum Organum,' would he have omitted that also?

" The real significance of the Promus consists in the enormous proportion of notes which Bacon could not possibly have used in his acknowledged writings; the colloquialisms, dramatic repartees, turns of expression, proverbs, etc. Any biographer of Bacon, whatever his notions as to the Shakespearean authorship, may be reasonably expected to offer some explanation of this queer assortment of oddments, and to find out, if possible, what use Bacon made of them; and then our case becomes urgent." — *R. M. Theobald.*

" Why Bacon wrote down phrases like this, here and there [in the Promus], seems inexplicable." — *Richard Grant White.*

VI. Other internal evidences also point unmistakably to Bacon's pen. Peculiarities of thought, style, and diction are more important in a contested case of authorship than the name on the title-page, for there we find the author's own signature in the very fibre of his work. We have only to hold the Plays, as it were, up to the light, to see the water-mark imprinted in them. To elucidate this point, we offer the following parallelisms : —

FROM SHAKESPEARE.	FROM BACON.
" There is a tide in the affairs of men Which, taken at the flood, leads on to fortune ; . . . . . And we must take the current when it serves, Or lose our ventures." *Julius Cæsar*, IV. 3.	" In the third place, I set down reputation, because of the peremptory tides and currents it hath, which, if they be not taken in their due time, are seldom recovered." — *Advancement of Learning.*

"To thine own self be true,
And it must follow, as the
night the day,
Thou canst not then be false
to any man."
        Hamlet, I. 3.

"Be so true to thyself as
thou be not false to others."
— *Essay of Wisdom.*

"That strain again; — it had
a dying fall :
O, it came o'er my ear like
the sweet south,
That breathes upon a bank
of violets,
Stealing and giving odor."
        Twelfth Night, I. 1

"The breath of flowers . . .
comes and goes like the war-
bling of music." — *Essay of
Gardens.*

"This majestical roof fretted
with golden fire."
        Hamlet, II. 2.

"For if that great work-
master had been of a human
disposition, he would have cast
the stars into some pleasant
and beautiful works and orders,
like the frets in the roofs of
houses." — *Advancement of
Learning.*

"By a divine instinct, men's
minds mistrust
Ensuing danger; as, by proof,
we see
The waters swell before
a boist'rous storm."
        Richard III., II. 3.

"As there are . . . secret
swellings of seas before a tempest, so there are in States." —
Essay of Sedition.

"Who having unto truth, by
telling of it,
Made such a sinner of his
memory,
To credit his own lie."
        Tempest, I. 2.

"With long and continual
counterfeiting and with oft
telling a lie, he was turned by
habit almost into the thing he
seemed to be ; and from a liar
to a believer." — *History of
Henry VII.*

"The ivy which had hid my princely trunk,
And sucked my verdure out on 't."
Tempest, I. 2.

"It was ordained that this winding-ivy of a Plantagenet should kill the tree itself." — *History of Henry VII.*

"Let him be his own carver."
Richard II., II. 3.

"You shall not be your own carver." — *Advancement of Learning.*

"I shall show the cinders of my spirits
Through the ashes of my chance."
Antony and Cleopatra, V. 2.

"The sparks of my affection shall ever rest quick under the ashes of my fortune." — *Letter to Falkland.*

"Lo! as at English feasts, so I regreet
The daintiest last, to make the end most sweet."
Richard II., I. 3.

"Let not this Parliament end like a Dutch feast in salt meats, but like an English feast in sweet meats." — *Speech in Parliament*, 1604.

"Nothing almost sees miracles
But misery."
King Lear, II. 2.

"Certainly, if miracles be the control over nature, they appear most in adversity." — *Essay of Adversity.*

"The rogue fled from me like quicksilver."
2 *Henry IV.*, II. 4.

"It was not long but Perkin, who was made of quicksilver (which is hard to imprison), began to stir; for, deceiving his keepers, he took to his heels, and made speed to the sea-coast." — *History of Henry VII.*

"When we our betters see bearing our woes,
We scarcely think our miseries our foes.
.   .   .   ."

"Amongst consolations it is not the least to represent to a man's self like examples of calamity in others. If our betters have sustained the like

" The mind much suffrance
doth o'erskip,
When grief hath mates, and
bearing fellowship.
How light and portable my
pain seems now,
When that which makes me
bend makes the king
bow."
King Lear, III. 6.

" My Dionyza, shall we rest
us here,
And, by relating tales of
other's griefs,
See if 't will teach us to forget our own ? "
Pericles, I. 4.

" Of comfort, no man speak, . . .
For God's sake, let us sit
upon the ground
And tell sad stories of the
death of kings." [1]
Richard II., III. 2.

" Honorificabilitudinitatibus."
Love's Labor 's Lost.

" Had I but served my God
with half the zeal

events, we have the less cause
to be grieved." — *Letter to
Bishop Andrews.*

" Honorificabilitudino." [2] —
*MS. Title-page of one of
Bacon's Works.*

" Cardinal Wolsey said that
if he had pleased God as he

---

[1] It will be observed that this is not the commonplace sentiment
respecting companions in misery, but an opinion continually crop-
ping out in Bacon and " Shake-speare," that one may find consolation
in any misfortune by calling to mind similar experiences in the lives
of others, particularly of those who in times past have done great
deeds for humanity.

[2] This word is found in these two places only in all the world's
literature.

I served my king, he would
not in mine age
Have left me naked to mine
enemies."
Henry VIII., III. 2.

had pleased the king, he had
not been ruined."—*Letter* [*first
draft*] *to King James.*

"Ere my tongue
Shall wound mine honor with
such feeble wrong,
Or sound so base a parle, my
teeth shall tear
The slavish motive of recant-
ing fear,
And spit it bleeding, in his
high disgrace,
Where shame doth harbor, even
in Mowbray's face."
Richard II., I. 1.

"What a proof of patience
is displayed in the story told
of Anaxarchus, who, when
questioned under torture, bit
out his own tongue (the only
hope of information) and spat
it into the face of the tyrant."
—*De Augmentis.*

"*Viola.* 'T is poetical.
Olivia. It is the more likely
to be feigned."
Twelfth Night, I. 5.

"Poetry is feigned history."
—*Advancement of Learning.*

"How shall we stretch our
eye when capital crimes, chew'd,
swallow'd, and digested, appear before us?"—*Henry V.,*
II. 2.

"Some books are to be
tasted, others to be swallowed,
and some few to be chewed
and digested."—*Essay of
Studies.*

"I saw him run after a gilded
butterfly; and, when he caught
it, he let it go again; and after
it again."[1]—*Coriolanus,* I. 3.

"To be like a child following a bird, which, when he is
nearest, flyeth away and 'light-
eth a little before: and then
the child after it again."—*Letter to Greville.*

[1] Professor Nichol refers to this extraordinary parallelism in his
Biography of Bacon, showing by date that Bacon could not have
copied from "Shake-speare," nor "Shake-speare" from Bacon. The
sentence from Bacon is found in a private letter, written in 1595, but
not made public till 1657. The production of 'Coriolanus' is assigned to a date not earlier than 1610. The play was first printed in 1623.

" I do much wonder that one man, seeing how much another man is a fool when he dedicates his behaviors to love, will, after he has laughed at such shallow follies in others, become the argument of his own scorn by falling in love." — *Much Ado About Nothing,* II. 3.

" Amongst all the great and worthy persons whereof the memory remaineth, there is not one that hath been transported to the mad degree of love; which shows that great spirits and great business do keep out this weak passion." — *Essay of Love.*

"*Sil.* Do you change color? *Val.* Give him leave, madam ; he is a kind of chameleon."
Two Gentlemen of Verona, II. 4.

" If he be laid upon green, the green predominates ; if upon yellow, the yellow ; laid upon black, he looketh all black. Some that have kept chameleons a whole year together could never perceive that they fed upon anything but air." — *Syl. Syl.*

" *King.* How fares our cousin Hamlet? *Hamlet.* Excellent, i' faith ; of the chameleon's dish ; I eat the air."
Hamlet, III. 2.

" The moon sleeps with Endymion."
Merchant of Venice, V. 1.

" The moon of her own accord came to Endymion as he was asleep." — *De Augmentis.*

" So we grew together, Like to a double cherry."
Midsummer Night's Dream, III. 2.

" There is a cherry-tree that hath double blossoms." — *Syl. Syl.*

" Have you a daughter? . . . Let her not walk i' th' sun." —
Hamlet, II. 2.

" Aristotle dogmatically assigned the cause of generation to the sun." — *Novum Organum.*

Of Julius Cæsar:
"The foremost man of all
this world."
Julius Cæsar, IV. 3.

"The most excellent spirit,
his ambition reserved, of the
world." — *Imago Civilis Julii
Cæsaris.*

"The noblest man
That ever lived."—*Ibid.*, III. 1.

"A man of a great and noble
soul." — *Ibid.*

"I am constant as the northern star,
Of whose true fixed and rest-
ing quality
There is no fellow in the firmament.
The skies are painted with un-
number'd sparks;
They are all fire, and every
one doth shine;
But there's but one in all doth
hold his place.
So in the world; 't is furnished
well with men,
And men are flesh and blood,
and apprehensive;
But in the number I do know
but one
That, unassailable, holds on
his rank,
Unshaked of motion." — *Ibid.*

"He [Julius Cæsar] referred
all things to himself, and was
the truest centre of his own
actions. — *Ibid.*

"When we were boys,
Who would believe that there
were mountaineers
Dew-lapped like bulls, whose
throats had hanging at 'em
Wallets of flesh?"
Tempest, III. 3.

"The people that dwell at
the foot of snow mountains,
or otherwise upon the ascent,
especially the women, by drinking snow-water, have great bags
hanging under their throats."
— *Natural History.*

"Idle weeds that grow
In our sustaining corn."
King Lear, IV. 4.

"There be certain corn-
flowers which come seldom or
never in other places unless
they be set, but only amongst
corn." — *Ibid.*

"Ill mayst thou thrive, if thou grant any grace."
Richard II., V. 3.
"What! wouldst thou have a serpent sting thee twice?"
Merchant of Venice, IV. 1.

" He who shows mercy to his enemy denies it to himself." —
Advancement of Learning.

"Go thou, and, like an executioner,
Cut off the head of too-fast-growing sprays,
That look too lofty in our commonwealth."
Richard II., III. 4.

" Periander, being counselled with how to preserve a tyranny newly usurped, went into his garden and topped all the highest flowers, signifying that it consists in the cutting off and keeping low of the nobility and grandees." — *Ibid.*, Book II.

"*Bir.* By Jove, I always took three threes for nine.
Cost. O Lord, sir, it were pity you should get your living by reckoning, sir."
Love's Labor 's Lost, V. 2.

"Philip of Macedon, when he would needs overrule and put down an excellent musician in an argument touching music, was well answered by him again. " God forbid, sir," saith he, "that your fortune should be so bad as to know these things better than I." — *Ibid.*, Book VII.

" It was to show my skill,
That more for praise than purpose meant to kill.
And. out of question, so it is sometimes;
Glory grows guilty of detested crimes,

" I am of his opinion that said pleasantly that it is a shame to him that is a suitor to the mistress to make love to the waiting woman."[1] — *The Apology.*

---

[1] It is every one's duty, Bacon often said, to cultivate virtue, not for fame or praise, but for virtue's own sake. He makes a note of this in the Promus, where he calls praise the handmaid (waiting woman), and virtue the mistress. The two forms of expression, quoted above, constitute a binary star.

When for fame's sake, for
    praise, an outward part,
We bend to that the work-
    ing of the heart.
And I, for praise alone, now
    seek to spill
The poor deer's blood, that
    my heart means no ill."
Love's Labor 's Lost, IV. I.

" But sweetest things turn sour-
    est by their deeds ;
Lilies that fester smell far
    worse than weeds."
    Sonnet XCIV.

" The best things are in their
corruption the worst; the sweetest wine makes the sharpest
vinegar." — *Charge against
Robert, Earl of Somerset.*

" This is th' imposthume of
    much wealth and peace,
That inward breaks, and
    shows no cause without
Why the man dies."
    Hamlet, IV. 4.

" He that turneth the humors
back and maketh the wound
bleed inwards endangereth ma-
lign ulcers and pernicious im-
posthumations." — *Essay of
Seditions.*

" I am never weary when I
    hear sweet music.
The reason is, your spirits
    are attentive."
Merchant of Venice, V. I.

" Some noises help sleep, as
— soft singing; the cause is,
they move in the spirit a gentle
attention."— *Natural History.*

" To take arms against a sea
    of troubles,
And, by opposing, end
    them." [1]
    Hamlet, III. 4.

" He came with such a sea
of multitude upon Italy." —
Apothegm, No. 242.

[1] This singular metaphor has caused commentators great perplexity. The sight of a man advancing against ocean waves with a sword
or needle gun would not be, it must be confessed, an edifying spec-
tacle. Pope, therefore, proposed to read a *siege* of troubles ; Forest
so rendered it on the stage. Another commentator preferred an
assail of troubles. It requires, however, but a glance at Bacon's writings, in which the word *sea* is used over and over again for *host* or
multitude, to redeem the passage. Bacon evidently adopted it from
the Greek, κακῶν πέλαγος.   5

"Sense sure you have, Else could you not have motion." [1]

Hamlet, III. 4.

[So in the quarto, 1604; omitted in the folio, 1623.]

"Some of the ancient philosophers could not conceive how there can be voluntary motion without sense." — *De Augmentis.*

"There 's a divinity that shapes our ends."

Ibid.

"I cannot forget that the poet Martial saith, 'What divinity there is in chance!'" [2] — *Letter to King James.*

"Advantage is a better soldier than rashness."

Henry V., III. 6.

"If time give his Majesty the advantage, what need precipitation to extreme remedies?" — *Letter to Villiers.*

"With taper light To seek the beauteous eye of heaven to garnish, Is wasteful and ridiculous excess."

King John, IV. 2.

"But this work, shining in itself, needs no taper." — *Amendment of Laws.*

[1] The commentators can make nothing of these lines also. One of them suggests that for "motion" we substitute *notion;* another, *emotion.* Others still contend that the word "sense" must be understood to mean *sensation* or *sensibility.* Dr. Ingleby was certain that Hamlet refers to the Queen's wanton impulse. As to the omission in the folio, not even the most daring commentator has ventured to offer a remark. In Bacon's prose, however, we find not only an explanation of the passage in the quarto, but the reason why it was excluded from the folio. The 'Advancement of Learning' was published in 1605, the year after the quarto, but it contains no repudiation of the ancient doctrine that everything which has motion has sense. Indeed, Bacon had a lingering opinion that the doctrine is true, even as applied to the planets in the influence which they were supposed to exercise over the affairs of men. But in 1623 he published a new edition of the 'Advancement' under the title of *De Augmentis Scientiarum,* and therein expressly declared that the doctrine is untrue; that there is motion in inanimate bodies without sense, but with what he called a kind of perception. The Shake-speare folio came out in the same year, and the passage in question, no longer harmonizing with the author's views, dropped out.

[2] "O quantum est casibus ingenium."

" Brother, you have a vice of
mercy in you,
Which better fits a lion than
a man."
Troilus and Cressida, V. 3.

" To be wise and love exceeds
man's might; that dwells
with gods above."
Ibid., III. 2.

" Court holy-water in a dry
house is better than this
rain-water out o' door."
King Lear, III. 2 [1606].

" Like bright metal on a sullen
ground,
My reformation, glittering
o'er my fault,
Shall show more goodly, and
attract more eyes,
Than that which hath no
foil to set it off."
1 *Henry IV.,* I. 2.

" I know he would not be
a wolf,
But that he sees the Romans
are but sheep."
Julius Cæsar, I. 3.

" Being seldom seen, I could
not stir
But, like a comet, I was wondered at."
1 *Henry IV.,* III. 2.

" For of lions it is a received
belief that their fury ceaseth
toward anything that yieldeth
and prostrateth itself." [1] — *Of
Charity.*

" It is impossible to love and
be wise." — *Essay of Love.*

" He was no brewer of holy
water in court." [1592.]
" Your lordship is no dealer
of holy water, but noble and
real." — *Letter to Salisbury*
[1607].

" We see in needle-works
and embroideries it is more
pleasing to have a lively work
upon a sad and solemn ground
than to have a dark and melancholy work upon a lightsome
ground." — *Essay of Adversity.*

" Cato, the censor, said that
the Romans were like sheep."
— *Advancement of Learning.*

" Wonder is the child of rarity." [2] — *Val. Ter.*

---

[1] In this instance, as in many others, it requires Bacon's prose to
explain " Shake-speare's " poetry.

[2] This conception of wonder, as a state of mind produced by anything (whether extraordinary or not) that is rare, was a favorite one

" Love   " Love must creep where it
Will creep in service where cannot go." — *Letter to King*
it cannot go."   *James.*
Two Gentlemen of Verona,
IV. 2.

" O great corrector of enor- " I account no state flourish-
mous times,   ing but that which hath neither
Shaker of o'er-rank states, civil wars nor too long peace.
thou grand decider
Of dusty and old titles, that
heal'st with blood
The earth when she is sick
and cur'st the world
O' the pleurisy of people." [1]
Two Noble Kinsmen, V. 1.

" The cankers of a calm world "States corrupted through
and a long peace." wealth and too great length of
1 *Henry IV.,* IV. 2. peace." — *Letter to the Earl
of Rutland.*

with Bacon. We find it repeatedly in his prose works. We find it
also in many of the plays. Henry IV. tells his son to keep himself as
much as possible out of the people's sight in order that, whenever he
is seen, he may excite greater applause. It is, at least, remarkable
that a causal relation of so subtle a nature should occur over and over
again in both sets of works.

[1] " I believe that Shakespeare has expressed the true philosophy
of war [!] in those magnificent verses in the ' Two Noble Kinsmen,'
which are as unlike Beaumont and Fletcher as Michael Angelo's char-
coal head on the wall of Farnesia is unlike Raphael." — *James Russell
Lowell.*

" We cannot escape from a certain truth in Shakespeare's view of
war that it is the great corrector of enormous times." — *Pearson's National Life and Character,* p. 140.

We must add that the sentiment itself, pardonable perhaps in the
seventeenth century but not in this, is as barbarous as it is illogical.
Force has no moral quality. As well expect an earthquake to disturb
a theorem in Euclid, or the guns of an iron-clad to shake the rule of
three.

" To be or not to be, that is the question."
Hamlet, III. 1.

" To be or not to be, that is the alternative." — *Parmenides.*[1] [Specially commended by Bacon.]

" *Boult.* I warrant you, mistress, thunder shall not so awake the beds of eels." — *Pericles*, IV. 2.

" Upon the noise of thunder . . . fishes are thought to be frayed [terrified]." — *Natural History.*

" As the mournful crocodile With sorrow snares relenting passengers."
2 *Henry VI.*, III. 2.

" It is the wisdom of crocodiles, that shed tears when they would devour." — *Essay of Wisdom.*

" *Soothsayer* :
Therefore, O Antony, stay not by his side :
Thy dæmon, that 's thy spirit which keeps thee, is
Noble, courageous, high, unmatchable,
Where Cæsar is not; but near him thy angel
Becomes a Fear, as being overpowered : therefore,
Make space enough between you."
Antony and Cleopatra, V. 2.

" There was an Egyptian soothsayer that made Antonius believe that his genius, which otherwise was brave and confident, was, in the presence of Octavius Cæsar, poor and cowardly; and therefore he advised him to absent himself as much as he could, and remove far from him."[2] — *Natural History.*

---

[1] Not translated from the original Greek into any other language till more than two hundred years after ' Hamlet ' was written.

We give the original, and also a Latin version published at Amsterdam in 1835 : —

" Οὕτως ἤ πάμπαν πελέναι χρέων ἐστὶν οὐχί."
" Ergo vel esse omnino vel non esse necesse est."

[2] The ' Natural History ' was not printed till eleven years after Shakspere's death. It is clear, then, that Shakspere did not take the story from Bacon. It is almost equally clear that Bacon

"It is so very very late   "It is not now late but
That we may call it early."   early." — *Essay of Death*.
Romeo and Juliet, III. 4.

It may be interesting, also, to compare some of the
entries in Bacon's scrap-book with passages in the
plays, as follows : —

FROM "SHAKE-SPEARE."	FROM BACON'S PROMUS.
"One fire drives out one fire; one nail, one nail." *Coriolanus*, IV. 7.	"To drive out a nail with a nail."
"Losers will have leave To ease their stomachs with their bitter tongues." *Titus Andronicus*, III. 1.	"Always let losers have their words."
"Happy man be his dole." *Merry Wives*, III. 4.	"Happy man, happy dole."
"Pardon is still the nurse of second woe." *Measure for Measure*, II. 1.	"He that pardons his enemies, the amner [bailiff] shall have his goods."
"Of sufferance comes ease." 2 *Henry IV.*, V. 4.	"Of sufferance cometh ease."
"Call me not fool, till heaven hath sent me fortune." *As You Like It*, II. 7.	"God sendeth fortune to fools."
"Thou bear'st thy heavy riches but a journey." *Measure for Measure*, III. 1.	"Riches, the baggage of virtue."

did not take it from "Shake-speare," for he adds a particular which
is not in the play. viz.: "The soothsayer was thought to be suborned
by Cleopatra to make Antony live in Egypt and other places remote
from Rome."

" So the maid that stood in the way for my wish shall show me the way to my will."
Henry V., V. 2.

" He had rather have his will than his wish."

" Seldom cometh the better."
Richard III., II. 2.

" Seldom cometh the better."

" Frost itself as actively doth burn."
Hamlet, III. 4.

"*Frigus adurit.*" [Frost burns.]

" The dissembler is a slave."
Pericles, I. 1.

" He who dissembles is not free."

" A fool's bolt is soon shot."
Henry V., III. 7.

" A fool's bolt is soon shot."

" Deceive more slyly than Ulysses could.'
3 *Henry VI.*, III. 2.

" Ulysses, sly in speech." [1]

" The mild glance which sly Ulysses lent."
Lucrece.

" Give sorrow leave awhile to tutor me."
Richard II., IV. 1.

" Our sorrows are our school-masters."

" For loan oft loses both itself and friend."
Hamlet, I. 3.

" He who lends to a friend loses double."

" I 'll devil-porter it no further."
Macbeth, II. 3.

" He is the devil's porter who does more than what is required of him."

---

[1] Dr. Theobald calls attention to the fact that this entry in the Promus is the sole instance in Bacon's prose works in which Ulysses is spoken of as *sly*, though in " Shake-speare " he is never alluded to otherwise. The entry seems to have been made with exclusive reference to dramatic use.

" Goodness, growing to a pleurisy,
Dies in his own too much."
Hamlet, IV. 7.

" So good that he is good for nothing."

" All 's well that ends well."
All's Well that Ends Well,
IV. 4.

" All is well that ends well."

" Pride must have a fall."
Richard II., IV. 5.

" Pride will have a fall." [1]

" Love moderately; long love doth so."
Romeo and Juliet, II. 6.

" Love me little, love me long."

" Two, together weeping, make one woe."
Richard II., V. 1.

" Make not two sorrows of one."

" Every Jack became a gentleman."
Richard III., I. 3.

" Every jack would be a lord."

" Your words and your performances are no kin."
Othello, IV. 2.

" Saying and doing are two things."

" The latter end of a fray and the beginning of a feast."
1 *Henry IV.*, IV. 2.

" Better come to the ending of a feast than to the beginning of a fray."

" Good wine needs no bush."
As You Like It.

" Good wine needs no bush."

" Thy nature,
It is too full o' the milk of human kindness
To catch the nearest way."
Macbeth, I. 4.

" In ways, commonly the nearest is the foulest."

[1] It should be borne in mind that many words, phrases, and sentiments, now familiar to us, have been made so by " Shake-speare." Their simultaneous admission into Bacon's memorandum-book sufficiently attests the fact that they were then new to English readers. The above entry is a mere paraphrase of a biblical proverb.

" The inaudible and noiseless foot of time."
All 's Well, V. 3.

" The gods have woollen feet."

" The ripest mulberry."
Coriolanus, III. 2.

" Riper than a mulberry."

" Do we must what force will have us do."
Richard II., III. 3.

" They that are bound must obey."

" To hazard all our lives in one small boat."
1 *Henry VI.,* IV. 6.

" You are in the same ship."

" Let him not know 't, and he 's not robb'd at all."
Othello, III. 3.

" What the eye seeth not, the heart rueth not."

" Must bend his body,
If Cæsar carelessly but nod on him."
Julius Cæsar, I. 2.

" A beck is as good as a *dieu vous garde.*"

" Dieu vous garde, monsieur."
Twelfth Night, III. 1.

" Your bait of falsehood takes this carp of truth."
Hamlet, I. 2.

" Tell a lie to know a truth."

" The strings of life Began to crack."
Lear, V. 3.

" At length the string cracks."

" Thou hast quarrelled with a man for coughing in the street."
Romeo and Juliet, III. 1.

" A cough cannot hide itself."

" Ay, sir, but ' while the grass grows ' — the proverb is something musty."
Hamlet, III. 2.

" While the grass grows, the horse starveth."

"Out of heaven's benedic-
tion
To the warm sun."
　　　　Lear, II. 2.

"Out of God's blessing into
the warm sun."

"The world on wheels."
Two Gentlemen of Verona,
III. 1.

"The world runs on wheels."

"Thought is free."
　　　　Tempest, III. 2.

"Thought is free."

"To seek the beauteous eye of
heaven to garnish."
　　　　King John, IV. 2.

"To help the sun with lan-
terns."

"You go not, till I set you up
a glass
Where you may see the in-
most part of you."
　　　　Hamlet, III. 4.

"There is no better glass
than an old friend."

"You shall not gauge me
By what we do to-night."
Merchant of Venice, II. 2.

"Evening's speech is very
different from the morning's."

"Fortune . . . doth ebb and
flow like the sea, being governed, as the sea is, by the
moon."
　　　　1 *Henry IV.*, I. 2.

"Fortune changes like the
moon."

"A giving hand, though foul,
shall have fair praise."
Love's Labor 's Lost, IV. 1.

"Food is wholesome which
comes from a dirty hand."

"As if increase of appetite
had grown
By what it fed on."
　　　　Hamlet, I. 2.

"If you eat, appetite will
come."

"If the cat will after kind,
So be sure will Rosalind."
　　　As You Like It, III. 2.

"It is the cat's nature and
the wench's fault."

He woo'd in haste and means to wed at leisure.
Taming of the Shrew, III. 2.

" He that resolves in haste repents at leisure."

" I am quickly ill, and well, So Antony loves."
Antony and Cleopatra, I. 3.

"A woman is ill whenever she wishes, and whenever she wishes, she is well."

" I am giddy; . . . I do fear That I shall lose distinction in my joys."
Troilus and Cressida, III. 2.

"When one good follows another, a man loses his balance."

" Make use of thy salt hours."
Timon of Athens, IV. 3.

" Life is a little salt-cellar."

"When the sea is calm, all boats alike
Show mastership in floating."
Coriolanus, IV. 1.

" Any one can be a pilot in fine weather."

" Beggars cannot choose."
Taming of the Shrew, Ind.

" Beggars should be no choosers."

" Teach me to forget."
Romeo and Juliet, I. 1.

" The art of forgetting."

" *Cres.* Well, well.
Pan. ' Well, well ' ! "
Troilus and Cressida, I. 2.

" Well." [1]

" That is all one."
Merry Wives, I. 1.

" All is one."

" Can so young a thorn begin to prick ? "
Henry VI., V. 5.

" A thorn is gentle when it is young."

---

[1] " The peculiarity of the use of this word consists in the fact that Shakespeare uses it both as continuing a conversation and as *concluding* it ; other authors, previous and contemporary, in the first manner only." — *Mrs. Pott's Edition of the Promus*, page 168.

" Coal black is better than another hue,
In that it scorns to take another hue."
Titus Andronicus, IV. 2.

" Black will take no other hue."

" Not to be abed after midnight is to be up betimes ; and *diluculo surgere*, thou knowest." — *Twelfth Night*, II. 3.

" *Diluculo surgere salubrium* " [sic].

" Romeo.
Good morrow.
What early tongue so sweet saluteth me ?

" Romē.
Good morrow.
Sweet, for speech in the morning [i. e. morning speech is to be noted as sweet].

So soon to bid good morrow to thy bed.

Early rising.

Where care lodges, sleep will never lie.

Lodged next.

There golden sleep doth reign.

Golden sleep.

Thou art uproused by some distemperature." [1]
Romeo and Juliet, II. 3.

Uprouse." [2]

The foregoing lists might be extended almost indefinitely ; but enough is given to show that on

[1] The above disconnected sentences from ' Romeo and Juliet ' are taken from within a space of eleven consecutive lines. The corresponding entries in the Promus were also made substantially at one time ; they are found very near together. We find the earliest notice of the play to have been under date of 1597, or immediately after this curious preliminary study for a part of it was recorded by Bacon in his private memorandum book. It seems to us as undeniable as any theorem in Euclid that the writer of the Promus had something to do with the composition of ' Romeo and Juliet.'

[2] This was the first (private) appearance of this word in the English language ; its second (public) appearance was two or three years later — in the play.

SIGNATURES OF FRANCIS BACON AND OTHERS.

these two minds (if there were two) fell the light of intelligence, in repeated flashes, at the same exact angle. The cumulative force of these examples, taken in connection with the solid prejudice against which, in some instances, they break in vain, reminds us of the charge of the Old Guard at Waterloo, the "irresistible meeting the immovable."[1]

" It is safe to say that no such list can be produced from the writings of any other two authors of that age or of any age; no similarity of life, genius, or studies ever produced an identity like this. . . . The coincidences are not merely such as might be attributed to the style and usage of that time; they extend to the scope of thought, the particular ideas, the modes of thinking and feeling, the choice of metaphors, the illustrative imagery, and those singular peculiarities, oddities, and quaintnesses of expression and use of words which everywhere and at all times mark and distinguish the individual writer." — *Holmes' Authorship of Shakespeare.*

If we consider, also, the difference between the two men in birth, education, and mode of life, these similarities become, on the commonly accepted theory, absolutely inexplicable. In any view, however, they are so extraordinary that John Weiss (who has produced the ablest argument against the Baconian theory we have ever read) is compelled to admit that the two authors were probably close companions in literary work.

" Does any one dare to say that Shakespeare and Bacon did not compare notes upon many subjects? Many of the reputed parallelisms are indirect traces of such an intercourse. — *Wit, Humor, and Shakespeare*, p. 261.

"When we come to internal evidences, afforded by a comparison of what Bacon has written and what Shakespeare wrote, some quoted coincidences are assuredly very striking. Enough of unimpeachable force has been got together to disclose a really remarkable similarity of phrase, of metaphor, of

---

[1] The number of parallelisms similar to the above, already found in these two sets of works, exceeds a thousand.

opinions, and of inferred attainments. What perhaps affords the nearest approach to a convincing argument for a common authorship, is the use of the same out-of-the-way quotations and the reproduction of precisely the same errors." — *The [London] Standard*, May 1, 1888.

"Some of these parallelisms are not coincidences, but something like identities." — *Appleton Morgan.*

7. Bacon's love of flowers perfumed his whole life. It was to him, as he said, "the purest of human pleasures." Of the thirty-five species of garden plants mentioned in the Plays, he enumerates thirty-two in his prose works, bending over them, as it were, lovingly, and, like the dramatist, noting the seasons in which they bloom. In both authors, taste and knowledge go hand in hand.

This point will bear elaboration, for the two methods of treatment seem to be mutually related, like the foliage of a plant and the exquisite blossom. Bacon says: "I do hold it, in the royal ordering of gardens, there ought to be gardens for all the months of the year, in which severally things of beauty may be then in season;" and with this end in view, he proceeds to classify plants according to their periods of blooming.

"Shake-speare," on his part, introduces to us a beautiful shepherdess distributing flowers among her friends, — to the young. the flowers of spring; to the middle-aged, those of summer; while the flowers that bloom on the edge of winter are given to the old. What is still more remarkable, the groupings in both are substantially the same. One commentator has even proved the correctness of a disputed reading in the play by reference to the corresponding passage in the essay.

We present the two lists, side by side, for comparison, as follows: —

FROM SHAKESPEARE.

" Now, my fair'st friend,
I would I had some flowers o'
th' spring, that might
Become your time of day; and
yours; and yours,
. . . . *daffodils,*
That come before the swallow
dares, and take
The winds of March with
beauty; *violets,* dim,
But sweeter than the lids of
Juno's eyes,
Or Cytherea's breath ; pale
primroses,
That die unmarried ere they
can behold
Bright Phœbus in his strength,
a malady
Most incident to maids; bold
ox lips and
The crown imperial; *lilies of
all kinds,*
The *flower-de-luce* being one.

" Sir, the year growing ancient —
Not yet on summer's death,
nor on the birth
Of trembling winter — the fairest flowers o' th' season
Are our *carnations* and
streaked *gilliflower.*
. . . . .
Hot *lavender,* mint, savory,
marjoram ;

FROM BACON.

" There followeth, for the latter part of January and February . . . crocus vernus, both
the yellow and the gray ; *Primroses,* anemones, the early tulip,
the hyacinthus orientalis. For
March, there come *violets,* especially the single blue, which
are the earliest ; the yellow
daffodil, the daisy. In April,
follow the double white *violet,*
the wall-flower, the stock gilliflower, the *cowslip, flower-de-luces,* and *lilies of all natures ;*
rosemary-flowers, the tulip,
the double peony, the pale
daffodil, the French honeysuckle."

" In May and June, come
pinks of all sorts, specially
the blush-pink ; roses of all
kinds, except the musk, which
comes later ; honeysuckles, the
French *marigold,* flor-Africanus, vine flowers, *lavender* in
flowers, the sweet satyrian. In
July, come *gilliflowers* of all
varieties, musk-roses."

6

The *marigold*, that goes to bed
with th' sun,
And with him rises, weeping ;
these are flowers
Of middle summer, and I think
they 're given
To men of middle age.

" Reverend sirs,
For you there 's *rosemary* and
rue ; these keep
Seeming and savor all the win-
ter long."
Winter's Tale, IV. 3.

" For December and Janu-
ary and the latter part of November, you must take such
things as are green all winter :
holly, ivy, *rosemary*, lavender,
periwinkle, and sweet marjoram."[1] — *Essay on Gardens.*

The essay was first printed in 1625, nine years after Shakspere's death. It seems reasonable to conclude that Bacon
[who had made a study of gardens all his life], either borrowed
from Shakspere or wrote the play.

" It is not probable that Bacon would have anything to learn
of William Shakespeare concerning the science of gardening."
— *Spedding.*

VIII. In 1867 there was discovered in a private
library in London a box of old papers, among
which were some manuscripts of Francis Bacon,
bound together in the form of a volume. In the
table of contents on the title-page, among the names
of other compositions known to be Bacon's, but not
in his handwriting, appear those of two of the
" Shake-speare " plays, — Richard II. and Richard
III., — though the plays themselves have been ab-
stracted from the book.[2] Judge Holmes adds the

[1] Trees and fruits only omitted.

[2] In the table of contents we find, also, the title of one of Nash's
plays, 'The Isle of Dogs,' never published. But Nash did not write
the whole of this play. He complained that several scenes in it had

following piece of information in regard to this discovery: —

" The blank space at the side and between the titles is scribbled all over with various words, letters, phrases, and scraps of verse in English and Latin, as if the copyist were merely trying his pen, and writing down whatever first came into his head. Among these scribblings, beside the name of Francis Bacon several times, the name of William Shakespeare is written eight or nine times over."

It is a singular coincidence that the extraordinary word, " honorificabilitudino," found here, occurs with a slight change of ending in ' Love's Labor's Lost.' Also, the line, " revealing day through every cranny peeps," from the " Shake-speare " poem, ' Lucrece,' appears among the scribblings.[1]

The best experts assign the date of these pen performances, in which the names of Bacon and Shakespeare flowed so naturally, and, on the part of the writer, so unconsciously and spontaneously, to the age of Elizabeth.

" The only place in the world where we may be sure the manuscript of a " Shake-speare " play once existed is Bacon's portfolio." — *R. M. Theobald.*

been interpolated by another. The presence of the MS. among Bacon's papers sufficiently indicates whose hand had supplemented the author's. Furthermore, following the title of this play, appears the abbreviated word, "frmnt" (fragment), as though the interpolated part only had been included in the collection.

[1] The line in ' Lucrece ' is as follows : —
" Revealing day through every cranny spies."
As this does not end so happily as the line in the scribblings, it has been suggested that the latter may represent the form as first presented to the mind of the poet, if not so written, but subsequently changed under the exigency of rhyme.

Mr. Francis Bacon

of tribute or giving what is due.

The Praise of the worthiest Virtue
The Praise of the worthiest Affection
The Praise of the worthiest Power

Anthony   The Praise of the worthiest Person

Mr. Francis

Francis Bacon

Multis annis jam transactis   *Francis*
Nulla fides est in pactis,
Mell in ore, verba lactis ;   Earl of Arundell's letter to the Queen
Fell in corde, fraus in factis.   Speeches for my lord of Essex at the tilt.

A Speech for my lord of Sussex tilt.

honorificabilitudino   Leicester's Commonwealth, Incerto auth.

Orations at Gray's Inn Revels

Bacon

By Mr. Francis Bacon

Essays by the same author

William Shakespeare

Baco   Richard the Second.   *Shakespeare*

Richard the Third

Bacon   Asmund and Cornelia

Asmund and Cornelia Isle of Dogs, frmnt.

speare *revealing*
          day through   by Thomas Nash.

every cranny   *William Shakespeare*
peeps   *Sh   hakespeare*
Shak   *William Shakespeare*
Sh   Shak   *William Shakespeare*
                                        Shakespeare
                    willi   william

IX. At the death of Queen Elizabeth, John Davies, the poet and courtier, went to Scotland to meet James I. To him, while on the journey northward, Bacon addressed a letter, asking kind intercession in his behalf with the king, and expressing the hope, in closing, that he (Davies) would be " good to concealed poets." This expression indicates that Bacon's acknowledged writings do not reveal the whole man.[1] Something in him of a poetic nature was unquestionably hid from the mass of his contemporaries. John Aubrey, Milton's friend, who was born the year after Bacon's death, and who derived his knowledge of Bacon from those who knew the chancellor personally, states that " his lordship was a good poet, but concealed."[2]

We find a similar hint in Florio's 'World of Words,' published in 1598. Florio was a learned Italian, and a familiar figure in the literary and court circles of London. He is now known to fame as translator of Montaigne's Essays into English. That he was on terms of intimacy with Bacon is now a known fact, for in some of the Pembroke MSS., recently pub-

[1] " The allusion to ' concealed poets ' I cannot explain." — *Spedding's Life of Bacon*, Vol. III. p. 190.

[2] As usual, critics differ in their estimates of Aubrey : —

" His character for veracity has never been impeached ; and as a very diligent antiquary his testimony is worthy of attention." — *Malone.*

" He was a very honest man, and most accurate in his account of matters of fact." — *Toland.*

" A shiftless person, roving, and magotie-headed, and sometimes little better than crazed." — *Anthony Wood.*

" Aubrey thought little, believed much, and confused everything." — *Gifford.*

lished, he figures as a member, with Herbert, Hobbes, and Jonson, of Bacon's literary bureau at Gorhambury. In the preface to the above-mentioned work, Florio commends a certain sonnet, written, as he says, by a "friend" of his, "who loved better to be a poet than to be counted so." Professors Minto and Baynes, judging from internal evidences, concur in opinion that the author of the "Shake-speare" plays wrote this sonnet.[1]

[1] Edward Arber, in the preface to his valuable edition of Bacon's Essays, says that Anthony Bacon visited Bordeaux and contracted a friendship with Montaigne in 1582, two years after the first publication of Montaigne's Essays. "Without doubt," he adds, "this acquaintanceship resulted in these French Essays being early brought under [Francis] Bacon's notice." We know that the author of 'The Tempest' was familiar with them, as the following close parallelism will show : —

"For no kind of trafic Would I admit; no name of magistrate; Letters should not be known; riches, poverty, And use of service, none; contract, succession, Bourn, bound of land, tilth, vineyard, none; No use of metal, corn, or wine, or oil; No occupation; all men idle.... All things in common."
The Tempest, II. I.

"It is a nation that hath no kind of trafic; no knowledge of letters; . . . no name of magistrate; . . . no use of service, of riches, or of poverty; no contracts, no successions, no dividences; no occupations, but idle; no respect of kindred, but common; no manuring of lands; no use of wine, corn or metal." — *Montaigne's Essays*, I. Chap. XXX.

The above passage from 'The Tempest' is plainly taken from Montaigne's Essays. "The identity of phrase in the play and the Florio translation indicate the latter as the source." — *R. G. White*, *Shakespeare*, II. 88.

It may be pertinent to remark, in this connection, that the alleged autograph of Shakspere in a copy of Florio's 'Montaigne,' now in the British Museum, is beyond doubt a forgery.

X. With the exception of a brief but brilliant career in Parliament, and an occasional service in unimportant causes as attorney for the crown, Bacon seems to have been without employment from 1579, when he returned from France at the age of eighteen, to 1597, when he published his first volume of Essays. Here were nearly twenty of the best years of his life apparently run to waste. The volume of Essays was a small 12mo, containing but ten out of the fifty-eight sparkling gems which subsequent editions gave to the admiration and delight of posterity. His philosophical works, excepting a slight sketch in 1585, did not begin to appear till several years later. From 1597 to 1607, when he was appointed Solicitor General, he was again, so far as we know, substantially unemployed, — a period of ten years, contemporaneous with the appearance of the great tragedies of Hamlet (rewritten), Julius Cæsar, King Lear, and Macbeth. In the mean while he was hard pressed for money, and, failing to get relief (unhappily before the days of Samuel Weller) in a vain effort to marry a wealthy widow, he was twice actually thrown into prison for debt.[1]

That he was idle all this time, under great pecuniary pressure, his mind teeming with the richest fancy, it is impossible to admit. Such a hypothesis is utterly inconsistent with the possession of those

---

[1] On one of these occasions the debt was due to a Jewish money-lender, and was paid by Anthony, Francis' brother, who mortgaged his property for the purpose. At about that time appeared the great drama, 'The Merchant of Venice,' in which a money-lending Jew is pilloried for all time, and the debtor's friend, who also placed his property under mortgage on the occasion, was named *Antonio*.

fixed, almost phenomenal habits of industry with
which he afterward achieved magnificent results. On
this point, indeed, we have interesting testimony
from his mother. A woman of deep piety, mindful
of the proprieties of her station in life, she evidently
became alarmed over some mystery connected with
her son. Probably she had a suspicion of its nature,
for not even the genius that created 'Hamlet' could
subdue maternal instincts. In a letter to Anthony,
under date of May 24, 1592, she expresses her solici-
tude, as follows : —

> "I verily think your brother's weak stomach to digest hath
> been much caused and confirmed by untimely going to bed, and
> then musing *nescio quid* when he should sleep." [1]

At another time, when the two brothers were
together at Gray's Inn, and full of enthusiasm, as
she knew, for the wicked drama, she wrote, begging
them —
> "Not to mum, nor mask, nor sinfully revel."

It may be added that with his appointment to high
office and advent into public life the production of
the "Shake-speare" plays, for several years at least,
suddenly terminated.[2]

---

[1] Aubrey says it was his lordship's "working fancy" that kept him
awake.

[2] What a crushing argument our friends on the other side would
have made against Scott's authorship of the Waverly novels, had a
kind Providence sent them into the world fifty years earlier! Scott
was a great poet, and previously to the publication of 'Waverly,' in
the forty-third year of his age, he had never written a romance in
prose. In 1814, at which time 'Waverly' made its mysterious appearance, Scott published in two volumes a work on 'Border An-
tiquities,' contributed articles on 'Chivalry' and the 'Drama' to the

BEN JONSON.

XI. Ben Jonson was at one time Bacon's private secretary, and presumably in the secret, if there were any, of his employer's literary undertakings. In this fact we find the key to the exquisite satire of the inscription, composed by him and printed opposite "Shake-speare's" portrait in the folio of 1623, of which the following, in reference to the engraver's art, is an extract: —

> " Oh, could he but have drawn his wit
> As well in brasse as he hath hit
> His face, the print would then surpass
> All that was ever writ in brasse."

The portrait is "a hard, wooden, staring thing" (Richard Grant White), stupid, inane, hideous, with

Encyclopædia Britannica, and edited the ' Life and Works of Dean Swift.' The latter publication, comprising nineteen volumes, was issued in the same week with ' Waverly.' In the following year, ' Guy Mannering' appeared; and also, from Scott, the two poems, ' Lord of the Isles' and ' Field of Waterloo.' In 1816 came in quick succession from the Great Unknown the ' Antiquary,' ' Black Dwarf,' ' Old Mortality,' and ' Tales of My Landlord,' first series; and in the same year from Scott's pen, ' Paul's Letters to his Kinsfolk' and the ' Edinburgh Annual Register.' The poem ' Harold the Dauntless' was published in January, 1817, preceded within thirty days by three of the above-named works of fiction.

During all this time Scott was keeping " open house at Abbotsford in the old feudal fashion, and was seldom without visitors, entirely occupied to all outward appearance with local and domestic business and sport, building and planting, adding wing to wing, acre to acre, plantation to plantation, with just leisure enough for the free-hearted entertainment of his guests and the cultivation of friendly relations with his humble neighbors."

He even mystified some of his most intimate friends by reviewing one of his own novels in the ' Quarterly,' going so far as to claim that " the characters of Shakespeare are not more exclusively human, not more perfectly men and women as they live and move, than those of this mysterious author."

straight hair, while the bust at Stratford has curls.
Is this a work so extraordinary that we must sigh
because the artist did not depict the mind as well as
the face of his subject ?   Such a sentiment was very
appropriate under Bacon's beautiful likeness, taken at
the age of seventeen, *where Jonson found it*,[1] but
what a satire under Shakspere's !   No wonder he
added, —

> " Look,
> Not on his picture, but his book."

Indeed, it requires just this view of Jonson in his
relations with the mysterious author of the plays to
vindicate his character.   We want a stroke of lightning to clear the atmosphere around him.   Down to
the time of Gifford, a period of nearly two hundred
years, his insincerity towards the reputed dramatist
was a matter of almost universal comment among
scholars.   Dryden, Malone, Steevens, Chalmers, and
others looked upon him for this reason as almost
a monster of ingratitude and jealousy.   In 1816,
however, Gifford came to Jonson's defence with all
the resources of his practised pen, and, if he did not
succeed in driving his antagonists wholly from the
field, he had the satisfaction, at least, of stretching
several of them at full length upon it.

It is the old story of the quarrel between two
parties who were looking each upon a different side
of the same shield.   Jonson's testimony is self-contra-
dictory.   In the early part of his career he took one

---

[1] A miniature painted by Hilliard in 1578, and bearing the words,
Si tabula daretur digna, animum mallem : " If one could but paint his
mind ! "

view of " Shake-speare "; later on, another and a very
different one. The dividing line may be drawn at or
near the year 1620. Previous to that date Shakspere
was to him, as to all other contemporaries who give
us any glimpse of the man, an impostor, or, in the
words of Richard Simpson, an " uneducated peasant,"
masquerading as a dramatist. Accordingly, his references to Shakspere during this period were caustic
and bitter in the extreme. They were such as almost
to preclude the possibility of any friendship between
them.[1] We have already cited the well-known epigram to Poet-Ape ;[2] we purpose now to give two
other extracts from Jonson's works, written at this
time of his life, and to give them *in extenso*, in order
that our readers may judge fairly and intelligently of
the use we shall make of them.

The first is from the epilogue to ' Every Man in
his Humor,' printed in 1616. The play was produced
on the stage in 1598.

> " Though need make many poets, and some such
> As art and nature hath not bettered much,
> Yet ours for want hath not so loved the stage,
> As he dare serve the ill customs of the age,
> Or purchase your delight at such a rate,
> As, for it, he himself must justly hate :

---

[1] The tradition that Shakspere was the means of securing for
Jonson an introduction to the stage is unsupported by historical evidence. Gifford rejects the story as apocryphal.

" It is my fixed persuasion (not lightly adopted, but deduced from a
wide examination of the subject) that Jonson never received either
patronage, favor, or assistance from Shakespeare." — *Gifford's Preface
to Jonson's Works*, p. ccli.

[2] Page 35.

> To make a child now swaddled, to proceed
> Man, and then shoot up, in one beard and weed,
> Past threescore years ; or, with three rusty swords,
> And help of some few foot and half-foot words,
> Fight over York and Lancaster's long jars,
> And in the tyring-house bring wounds to scars."

That two of the historical plays of " Shake-speare " and ' The Winter's Tale ' are slightingly alluded to in the above can hardly be questioned. The reference to Perdita in the comedy is unmistakable. To represent a babe in one act, grown to sweet sixteen in the next, was the most conspicuous violation of the Greek unities on the English stage at that time. Blinded by a very natural prejudice against the reputed author of the play, Jonson failed to see the exquisite beauties of the play itself. He declared that he would have hated himself, had he been the author of it.[1]

'The Poetaster' was produced in 1601. The leading personage in it is Crispinus, a famous caricature, in which the use of uncouth words derived from the Latin, on the part of one or more of Jonson's rivals, is severely ridiculed. At the instance of Horace, who complained that many of these words were stolen from him, Crispinus is finally arrested and brought to trial before a Roman court, Julius Cæsar himself being present and taking part in the proceedings. The indictment is read, and then the fol-

---

[1] In his conversations with Drummond he again returned to the attack on the ' Winter's Tale.' " Shakespeare wanted art," he said, instancing the sea-coast of Bohemia as a proof, though he must have known that " Shake-speare " simply retained that much-abused item in geography from the novel on which the play was founded. See further on same subject, p. 101.

lowing paper, duly acknowledged by defendant to be
of his composition, is put in evidence : —

> " Ramp up my genius, be not retrograde ;
> But boldly nominate a spade a spade.
> What, shall thy lubrical and glibbery muse
> Live, as she were defunct, like punk in stews !
> Alas ! that were no modern consequence,
> To have cothurnal buskins frighted hence.
> No, teach thy Incubus to poetize,
>
> .　.　.　.　.　.　.　.
>
> Upon that puft-up lump of balmy froth,
> Or clumsie chilblained judgement; that with oath
> Magnificates his merit; and bespawls
> The conscious time, with humorous foam and brawls,
> As if his organons of sense would crack
> The sinews of thy patience.　Break his back,
> O poets, all and some !　For now we list
> Of strenuous vengence to clutch the fist."

Then comes the following remarkable scene : —

Cæs. " Here be words, Horace, able to bastinado a man's ears.
Hor. Ay.
　　　Please it, great Cæsar, I have pills about me,
　　　Mixt with the whitest kind of hellibore,
　　　Would give him a light vomit, that should purge
　　　His brain and stomach of those tumorous heats,
　　　Might I have leave to minister unto him.
Cæs. O, be his Æsculapius, gentle Horace !
　　　You shall have leave, and he shall be your patient.
　　　Virgil,
　　　Use your authority, command him forth.
Virg. Cæsar is careful of your health, Crispinus ;
　　　And hath himself chose a physician
　　　To minister unto you ; take his pills.
Hor. They are somewhat bitter, sir, but very wholesome.
　　　Take yet another ; so ; stand by, they 'll work anon.

.　.　.　.　.　.　.　.　.　.　.

Crisp. O ——!

Tib. How now, Crispinus?

Cris. O, I am sick ——!

Hor. A basin ! a basin ! quickly ; our physic works. Faint not, man.

Cris. *Retrograde — reciprocal — incubus.*

Cœs. What 's that, Horace ?

Hor. *Retrograde, reciprocal,* and *incubus* are come up.

Gal. Thanks be to Jupiter !

Cris. O — *glibbery* — *lubrical* — *defunct* — O — !

Gal. They come up easy.

Cris. O — O — !

Tib. What 's that?

Hor. Nothing yet.

Cris. *Magnificate* —

Mac. *Magnificate !* That came up somewhat hard.

Cris. O! I shall cast up my — *spurious* —

Hor. Good. Again.

Cris. *Chilblain'd* — O — O — *clumsie* —

Hor. That *clumsie* stuck terribly.

Gal. Who would have thought there should have been such a deal of filth in a poet?

. . . .

Cœs. Now all 's come out, I trow. What a tumult he had in his belly !

Hor. No, there 's the often *conscious damp* behind still.

Cris. O — *conscious* — *damp.*

Hor. It is come up, thanks to Apollo and Æsculapius; yet there 's another.

You were best take a pill more.

Cris. O, no; O — O — O — O — O — !

Hor. Force yourself then a little with your finger.

Cris. O — O — *prorumpt.*

Tib. *Prorumpt !* What a noise it made !

As if his spirit would have prorumpt with it.

Cris. O — O — O !

Virg. Help him, it sticks strangely, whatever it is.

Cris. O — *clutcht.*

Cæs. *Clutcht!* it is well that's come up; it had but a narrow passage.

Cris. O —— !

Virg. Again! hold him! hold his head there.

Cris. O — *obstupefact.*

Tib. Nay, that are all we, I assure you.

Hor. How do you feel yourself?

Cris. Pretty and well, I thank you.

Virg. These pills can but restore him for a time,
Not cure him quite of such a malady.
'T is necessary, therefore, he observe
A strict and wholesome diet. Look you take
Each morning of old Cato's principles
A good draught next your heart. That walk upon,
Till it be well digested; then come home,
And taste a piece of Terence; but, at any hand,
Shun Plautus and Ennius; they are meats
Too harsh for a weak stomach. Use to read
(But not without a tutor) the best Greeks.

. . . .

Now dissolve the court.

Cæs. It is the bane and torment of our ears,
To hear the discords of those jangling rhymers,
That with their bad and scandalous practices
Bring all true arts and learning in contempt.

Blush, folly, blush; here's none that fears
The wagging of an ass's ears.
Detraction is but baseness' varlet,
And apes are apes, though clothed in scarlet."

It is admitted that Jonson intended this satire for
the benefit of more than one of his contemporaries,
— for Marston, among others; but that Shakspere
was his principal target is fully apparent: —

1. At the opening of the above scene the name of
Crispinus is given with a hyphen; thus, Cri-spinus.

2. Crispinus was also an actor, for Cæsar expressly

states that, " though clothed in scarlet," he will still be an ape.[1] A scarlet dress was the badge of the profession. When Shakspere's company marched through the streets of London on the day of the king's coronation, each member of it was presented with four and one-half yards of red or scarlet cloth. No other person whom Jonson could have had in mind ever trod the boards. Marston and Dekker were playwrights only.

3. Crispinus had no classical education, for he is advised, when studying the Greek dramatists, to employ a tutor. This could not have been said of Marston, who was an accomplished Oxford scholar.

4. The father of Crispinus was a " man of worship." John Shakspere, father of William, had been bailiff of Stratford, and entitled to the designation of " worship."

5. Crispinus possessed a coat-of-arms. Shakspere had applied for one, and on that account was called " gentle."

" The very character of the arms attributed to Crispinus is exactly that of Shakspere's fraudulent coat; it belongs to the canting department of heraldry, and is merely an emblematic pun upon the name. The *shake* of Shakspere is represented by the crest. — a falcon flapping his wings; the *speare*, by a spear in a bend upon the shield. Such was Crispinus' canting coat: the *cry*, by a face crying; the *spinas*, by three thorns. There is no suggestion that Marston's arms warranted any such satire.

" It was not against the misfortune of hereditary gentility

---

[1] The word " Ape " seems to have been Jonson's favorite appellation for Shakspere previously to 1620. It is the exact word to express his contempt for a great literary imposture.

that Jonson directed his satire; it was against the folly, as he considered it, of a peasant seeking to improve his social status by obtaining a grant of arms." — *R. Simpson, No. Brit. Review,* July, 1870, p. 413.

6. The charge of using outlandish terms is applicable to " Shake-speare" as well as to Marston. The first word to " come up" in the presence of the Court was *retrograde*, " recently used," says Mr. Morley (English Writers, Vol. X. p. 392), " by Shakespeare in Hamlet": —

" It is most retrograde [1] to our desire." — I. 2.

Several others in the list, including the one that Cæsar thought so fortunately delivered, were also taken from " Shake-speare." Mr. Donnelly gives the following kindred specimens found in the plays: —

Rubrous	Evitate
Deracinate	Imbost
Cantelous	Disnatured
Recordation	Inaidable
Enwheel	Oppugnancy
Armipotent	Enskied
Unsuppressive	Legerity [2]

7. This was also the opinion of contemporaries, for the anonymous author of 'The Return from Parnassus,' published in 1606, refers to this caricature in 'The Poetaster' as follows: —

---

[1] Bacon used the word once in his prose works before it was caricatured by Jonson. He called special attention to it as, on the occasion, very apt and expressive.

[2] *The Great Cryptogram*, p. 24.

"Oh, that Ben Jonson is a pestilent fellow, for he brought up Horace giving the poets a pill; but our fellow Shakespeare hath given him a purge that made him beray his credit." [1]

'Bartholomew Fair' was acted in 1614; in the induction to that play we find the following: —

"If there never be a servant-monster in a fair, who can help it, he says, nor a nest of antiques! he is loth to make nature afraid in his plays, like those that beget tales, tempests,

---

[1] Mr. Nicholson, the latest editor of Jonson's works (II. 262) thinks that "Shake-speare" must have ridiculed Jonson "in a piece that has not come down to us" (at some time previously to the appearance of the Poetaster), "as a precedent for Horace's pills."

"Of the twenty-nine inculpated words, several either had been, or were immediately afterwards, used by Shakespeare, — such as retrograde, reciprocal, defunct, puff, damp, clutched.

"In the 'Troilus and Cressida' it is quite clear that Shakespeare, as if in express defiance of Jonson's criticism, laid himself out to adopt strange-sounding words into his language." — *R. Simpson, No. Brit. Review*, July, 1870.

Jacob Feis, author of 'Shakspere and Montaigne,' presents an additional reason for believing that Crispinus is a caricature of Shakspere. He says: —

"The full name given by Jonson to Crispinus is Rufus Laberius Crispinus. John Marston already, in 1598, designates Shakspere by the nickname of 'Rufus.' Every one can convince himself of this by reading first Shakspere's 'Venus and Adonis' and, immediately afterwards, John Marston's 'Pigmalion's Image.'

"The name of Rufus has two peculiarities which may have induced Marston to confer it upon Shakspere. First of all, like the English king of that name, Shakspere's pre-name was William. Secondly, the best-preserved portrait of Shakspere shows him with hair verging upon a reddish hue.

"Laberius (from *labare*, to shake ; hence Shak-erius, a name similar to Greene's *Shake-scene*) is clearly an indication of the Poet's [*sic*] family name." — p. 160.

Herr Feis also calls attention to the fact that Horace in the 'Poetaster' asks if the father of Crispinus be not dead; John Shakspere had just died in Stratford.

and such like drolleries, to mix his head with other men's heels." — *Ben Jonson.*

In explanation of the above we quote as follows :

"The mention of 'servant-monster' recalls Caliban in Shakespeare's 'Tempest,' and the expression 'to mix his head with other men's heels,' a scene in the play where Trinculo takes refuge from the storm under Caliban's gabardine. There can be no doubt that Jonson was alluding to the 'Tempest.'" — *Dr. Ingleby's Century of Praise,* p. 83.

"Our author [Jonson] is still venting his sneers at Shakespeare." — *Whalley's Edition of Jonson's Works,* III. 282.

In 1619, Jonson told Drummond of Hawthornden that " Shakespeare wanted art, and sometimes sense."

Now let us see what happened in 1620 or thereabouts for after that date we find in Jonson nothing but the most extravagant eulogy of " Shake-speare." A sudden and complete change of heart must be accounted for. We quote the following from Jonson's verses prefixed to the first " Shake-speare " folio of 1623 : —

" Soul of the age !
The applause ! delight ! the wonder of our stage !
My Shakespeare, rise ; I will not lodge thee by
Chaucer, or Spenser, or bid Beaumont lie
A little further. to make thee a room ;
Thou art a monument, without a tomb,
And art alive still. while thy book doth live,
And we have wits to read, and praise to give,

.   .   .   .

And tell, how far thou didst our Lily outshine,
Or sporting Kid, or Marlowe's mighty line.

And though thou hadst small Latin and less Greek,[1]
From thence to honor thee, I would not seek
For names : but call forth thundering Æschylus,
Euripides, and Sophocles to us,
Paccuvius, Accius, him of Cordova dead,
To life again, to hear thy buskin tread,
And shake a stage ;[2] or, when thy socks were on,
Leave thee alone, for the comparison
Of all that insolent Greece or haughty Rome
Sent forth."

During the latter part of his life, Jonson was in the habit of jotting down from time to time certain *memorabilia*, or disjointed remarks on persons and things which he deemed worthy of record, and which were published after his death under the title of 'Timber, or Discoveries made upon Men and Matter.' The collection contains (not without some admixture of facetiousness, however) an amiable sketch of the author of the plays. It is as follows : —

[1] This is evidently a humorous remark, called out by Bacon's well-known want of correctness in the use of these foreign tongues. Bacon was fully aware of his deficiency in this respect, for he once felicitated himself in a private letter upon the increased fluency with which he was writing Latin. The Promus notes in Latin are full of inaccuracies.

A contemporary thus criticises Bacon's use of Latin : " I come even now from reading a short discourse of Queen Elizabeth's life, written in Latin by Sir Francis Bacon. . . . I do not warrant that his Latin will abide test or touch." — *John Chamberlain*, Dec. 16, 1608.

[2] Another example of the vein of humor running through this whole performance. Greene's characterization of the reputed dramatist in 1592 as a " Shake-scene " is undoubtedly referred to.

Further on, Jonson again parodies the name, saying, —

" He seems to shake a lance,
As brandish't at the eyes of ignorance."

" I remember the players have often mentioned it as an honor to Shakespeare that in his writing, whatsoever he penn'd, he never blotted out a line. My answer hath been. ' would he had blotted a thousand ! ' — which they thought a malevolent speech. I had not told posterity this, but for their ignorance who choose that circumstance to commend their friend by wherein he most faulted ; and to justify mine own candor ; — for I loved the man, and do honor his memory, on this side idolatry, as much as any. He was, indeed, honest, and of an open and free nature ; had an excellent fantasy ; brave notions and gentle expressions, wherein he flowed with that facility that sometimes it was necessary he should be stopped ; — *sufflaminandus erat,* as Augustus said of Haterius. His wit was in his own power ; would the rule of it had been so too ! Many times he fell into those things could not escape laughter ; as when he said in the person of Cæsar, one speaking to him, — ' Cæsar, thou dost me wrong ; ' he replied, — ' Cæsar did never wrong but with just cause,' and such like ; which were ridiculous. But he redeemed his vices with his virtues. There was ever more in him to be praised than to be pardoned."

Considering the absurdity of the above criticism on the play of ' Julius Cæsar ' (explainable on the supposition that Shakspere the actor had made such a mistake in a recitation on the stage), we find ourselves entirely free to question the identity of this famous portraiture. It seems to carry with it a double implication, as though the artist had painted a picture with the eyes and nose of one man, and the mouth and chin of another. In these days of composite photography he would have focused the two heads together for a common likeness. As it is, we are sure only that all ill-nature toward Shakspere was now gone from the rival who had so often and, as the critics say, so malignantly persecuted him in the past as an impostor. To be sure, there is in the above little praise even now for anything in "Shake-speare" but his personal qualities; but those qualities receive at last from Jonson unstinted praise. The dramas are not changed, but a lovable author, instead of a "Poet-Ape," now stands behind them.

The following is a summary of Jonson's utterances concerning "Shake-speare": —

1598. He degrades the stage. He is ignorant of the ordinary rules of dramatization.

1601. He barbarizes the English language, and brings all arts and learning into contempt. He wags an ass's ears. He is an ape.

1614. His tales are but drolleries. He mixes his head with other men's heels.

1616. He is a poet-ape, an upstart, a hypocrite, and a thief. His works are but the frippery of wit.

1619. He wanted art and sometimes sense.

.   .   .   .   .   .

1623. The soul of the age; the greatest writer of ancient or modern times.

1637. I loved him this side idolatry as much as any.

The key to this paradox lies, without doubt, in the sudden intimacy which Jonson contracted with Francis Bacon in or about the year 1620. We hear of it for the first time after Jonson's long walk from London to Edinburgh in 1618–19, for we know that Bacon bantered him on the subject, protesting that poetry should go on no other feet than dactyls and spondees. Jonson soon afterwards took up his residence with Bacon at Gorhambury, and became one of the "good pens" which Bacon employed to translate the 'Advancement' and other philosophical works into Latin; and when the latter celebrated his sixtieth

birthday in January, 1621, Jonson was an honored
guest, making the occasion memorable by an epigram in which he invested the ancestral pile on the
Thames with some great mystery, and apostrophized
its owner in the following beautiful lines : —

" England's high Chancellor ! the destined heir,
In his soft cradle, to his father's chair ;
Whose even thread the Fates spin round and full
Out of their choicest and their whitest wool."

This conclusion becomes practically certain when
we note the following : —

1. In the preface to the Shake-speare folio Jonson
pronounced the works of Shake-speare superior to

" All that insolent Greece or haughty Rome sent forth."

A few years afterwards, in his ' Discoveries,' he
declared that Bacon's works were to be —

" preferred either to insolent Greece or haughty Rome."

Evidently, in genius and therefore in personality,
the two, as Jonson now viewed them, had become one.

2. In the ' Discoveries ' Jonson made a list of the
great men he had known, thirteen in number. In
this list Shakspere's name is not mentioned, but
Bacon's is put at the head. Bacon is called the
" mark and *acme* of our language." This is indubitable proof that Jonson was not sincere in his contribution to the preliminary matter of the Shake-speare
folio. Those famous verses were exoteric only.

3. Jonson also asserted that Bacon had " filled all
numbers."

" He [Bacon] hath filled up all numbers, and performed that
in our tongue which may be compared or preferred to insolent
Greece or haughty Rome ; . . . so that he may be named the
mark and acme of our language." — *Discoveries.*

To " fill all numbers " is a Latinism, signifying *to
have every perfection.* In early times, however, it was
used as an expression for poetry, as the following
examples will show : —

> " These numbers will I tear, and write in prose."
> > *Love's Labor 's Lost,* IV. 3.

> " And now my gracious numbers are decayed,
> And my sick muse doth give another place."
> > *Shake-speare Sonnet,* LXXIX.

> " My early numbers flow."
> > *Milton.*

> " I lisped in numbers, and the numbers came."
> > *Pope.*

Finally, it is possible, perhaps even probable, that
Jonson referred to the secret, immediately after it
was revealed to him, in the epigram which he read
on the occasion of Bacon's sixtieth birthday in 1621.
We have already quoted a part of this production ;
we now present it entire : —

> " Hail, happy genius of this ancient pile !
> How comes it all things so about thee smile ?
> The fire, the wine, the men ! and in the midst
> Thou stand'st as if some mystery thou didst !
> Pardon, I read it in thy face, the day
> For whose returns, and many, all these pray ;
> And so do I.   This is the sixtieth year
> Since Bacon and thy lord was born, and here.
> Son to the grave wise keeper of the seal,
> Fame and foundation of the English weal.

What then his father was, that since is he,
Now with a title more to the degree.
England's high chancellor : the destined heir
In his soft cradle to his father's chair ;
Whose even thread the fates spin round and full,
Out of their choicest and their whitest wool.
'T is a brave cause of joy, let it be known,
For 't were a narrow gladness, kept thine own.
Give me a deep-crown'd bowl, that I may sing
In raising him the wisdom of my king."

The obvious or superficial explanation of these lines is this : Jonson, entering the time-honored mansion, sees on all sides around him unusual signs of rejoicing, which, for the moment, he pretends he does not understand. He invokes the presiding genius of the place, and demands to know the cause of so much gayety. Then he begs pardon, for he reads the answer in the spirit's face ; — it is the birthday of its lord, over whom Jonson at once pronounces a splendid panegyric. Finally, he declares that this is a secret which the spirit of no private mansion should keep to itself, and offers, if a well-filled bowl be given to him, to drink a bumper to the king in tribute to it.

It will be noticed, we think, that this paraphrase, while entirely faithful to the original, fails to do justice to the nature or magnitude of the mystery suggested by the poet. The "genius" of the place was making no effort to keep the birthday a secret; on the contrary, it was commemorating the event in a manner to give it the widest publicity. The real "cause of joy," which Jonson wanted divulged, was one that required some bravery, as he said, to di-

vulge it, but one, nevertheless, that would bring to his
friend, in spite of some fear to the contrary, only
honor and "gladness." That secret, it may safely
be assumed, was the authorship of the Shake-speare
plays.

> "'*Tis a brave cause of joy, let it be known,*
> *For 't were a narrow gladness, kept thine own.*"

"The statements of Ben Jonson [in the latter part of his life]
are quite compatible with his being in the secret." — *Chambers'
Edinburg Journal*, Aug. 7, 1852.

XII. With the exception of the isolated play of
'King John,' the series depicting English history extends from the deposition of Richard II. to the birth
of Elizabeth, in the reign of Henry VIII. In this
long chain there is one break, and one only, — the
important period of Henry VII., when the foundations
of social order, as we now have them, were firmly
laid. The omission, on any but the Baconian theory
of authorship, is inexplicable, for the dramatist could
hardly have failed, except for personal considerations,
to drop his plummet into the richest and most in-
structive experiences of political life that lay in his
path. The truth is, Bacon wrote a history of the
missing reign in prose which exactly fills the gap;
the one is tongued and grooved, as it were, into the
other.[1]

---

[1] This point was first brought out by Mr. William H. Smith, of
England, who enjoys the distinction, with Miss Delia Bacon and
Mrs. Constance M. Pott, of having been an independent discoverer
of the world's greatest dramatist. Miss Bacon made her public announcement in Putnam's Monthly (N. Y.), January, 1856; Mr. Smith,
in an open letter to Lord Ellesmere, President of the Shake-

It is noteworthy, also, that the events of this reign are admirably suited for dramatic representation. Indeed, we know of no subject for psychological study more attractive to such a pen as Shakespeare's than the king's hesitancy in crowning his royal consort. The marriage with Elizabeth was a political one; it united the Roses, but not the hearts of husband and wife. For several months the bridegroom was a curious prey to the conflicting sentiments of ambition and fear. It was in this reign, also, that Simnel and Perkin Warbeck headed their ridiculous insurrections, — the former personating an imprisoned earl, and the latter one of the princes murdered by Richard in the Tower, and both ending their respective careers on the gibbet and doing scullery work in the king's kitchen. To our minds, incidents such as these afford admirable materials for the stage, and may well require us to explain why they were ignored by " Shake-speare."

XIII. 'Troilus and Cressida' was published for the first time, without reservation, in 1609. A writer in

speare Society of London, in September following. Like Adams and Le Verrier in the case of the planet Neptune, neither knew at the time of the work, or even of the existence, of the other.

Mr. Smith is still living (1896), full of years and (Baconian) honor. He had passed the prime of life when he rocked the cradle of this *enfant terrible.*

The following notice of his book is interesting: —

" Mr. Smith denies the appropriation of Miss Bacon's theory, and assures us that he never heard the name of Miss Bacon until September, 1856. The question may be of slight importance *which* of two given individuals first conceived a crazy notion." — *The (London) Athenæum,* 1857.

Per contra, Ralph Waldo Emerson declared that Miss Bacon " has opened the subject so that it can never again be closed."

the preface claims special credit for the work on the ground that it had not been produced on the public stage, or (to use his own words) "never clapper-clawed with the palms of the vulgar," or "sullied with the smoky breath of the multitude." Then he thanks fortune that a copy of the play had escaped from "grand possessors."

Three inferences seem to be justifiable, viz.: 1. The author was indifferent to pecuniary reward;[1] 2. He was not a member of the theatrical profession; 3. He was of high social rank.

"We learn that the copy had an escape from some powerful possessors. It appears that these possessors were powerful enough to prevent a single copy of any one of the plays which Shakespeare produced in his noon of fame (with the exception of 'Troilus and Cressida' and 'Lear') being printed till after his death; and between his death in 1616, and the publication of the folio in 1623, they continued the exercise of their power, so as to allow only one edition of one play ('Othello') which had not been printed in his lifetime to appear." — *Charles Knight.*

XIV. The plays, as they came out, were first published anonymously. Several of them had been in the hands of the public for years before the name of " Shake-speare " appeared on a title-page. Other plays, not belonging to the Shakespearean canon, and most of them of very inferior merit, were also given to the world as " Shake-speare's." We have fourteen of these heterogeneous compositions attrib-

---

[1] At this time Bacon was in easy circumstances. By the death of his brother he had come into possession of Gorhambury and other remnants of the family estate; and he was in receipt of a salary from the government.

uted to the same "divine" authorship, — geese and eagles coming helter-skelter from a single nest, — at a time when Coke, the law officer of the government, declared poetasters and playwrights to be "fit subjects for the grand jury as vagrants." It was enough for the impecunious authors of these plays that Shakspere, manager and perhaps part proprietor of two theatres, and amassing a large fortune in the business, was willing, apparently, to adopt every child of the drama laid on his door-step. This accounts for Greene's characterization of him as "an upstart crow beautified with our feathers." It is evident, nevertheless, that "Shake-speare" was a favorite *nom de plume* with the dramatic wits of that time.[1]

XV. The first complete edition of the plays, substantially as we now have them, was the famous folio of 1623. Its titles number thirty-six, and for our present purpose may be classified as follows: Plays, previously printed in various quartos at dates ranging from 1597 to 1622, eighteen; those not previously printed, but known to have been produced on the stage, twelve; lastly, those, so far as we know, entirely new, six. Of the plays in the first class it is found, by comparison, that several had been rewritten, and in some cases greatly enlarged during the

---

[1] The following were published in Shakspere's lifetime, and subsequently incorporated in the third "Shake-speare" folio: —

The London Prodigal, "by William Shakespeare."
Sir John Oldcastle,   "   "   "
A Yorkshire Tragedy,   "   "   "
Thomas Lord Cromwell, "by W. S."
The Puritan,   "   "
Locrine,   " "

fourteen years or more subsequent to their first appearance. The same is probably true of some in the
second class, though on this point we are, naturally
enough, without means of verification. In any event,
however, it is certain that the compositions which
were new, together with those which, by changes and
accretions, had been made new, constitute no incon-
siderable part of the book. Who did this work?
Who prepared it for the press? Shakspere died in
1616, seven years before the folio was published, and
for several years before his death he had lived in
Stratford, without facilities for such a task, and in a
social atmosphere in the highest degree unfavorable
for it. On the other hand, Bacon retired to private
life in 1621, at the age of sixty, in the plenitude of
his powers, and under circumstances that would naturally cause him to roll this apple of discord, refined
into the purest gold, down the ages.[1]

[1] The most noteworthy examples under this head are the Second
and Third Parts of Henry VI. These plays were first published in
1594 and 1595, under the titles, respectively, of the First Part of the
Contention between the Two Famous Houses, York and Lancaster,
and the True Tragedy of Richard, Duke of York. They were re-
published in 1600, and again in 1619 (three years after Shakspere's
death), under the same general title, and in other respects, also, substantially as first printed. In the folio of 1623, however, they appear
under new titles, and largely rewritten. The Second Part (for instance), which had originally contained three thousand and fifty-seven
lines, suddenly comes out with fifteen hundred and seventy-eight lines
entirely new, and with about one-half of the remainder altered or
expanded from passages in the old.

'The Merry Wives of Windsor' was first published in quarto in
1602, and again, as a mere reprint, in 1619. In the folio it is nearly
twice as long as in the quartos, — the latter being, as Richard Grant
White says, "simply a sketch of the perfected play."

As printed in Shakspere's lifetime, 'Troilus and Cressida' had no

XVI. Other mysteries cluster around this edition. The ostensible editors were two play-actors, named Heminge and Condell, formerly connected with the company of which Shakespeare was a member. Heminge appears, also, to have been a grocer. In the dedication of the book they characterize the plays with singular, not to say suspicious, infelicity as " trifles." They astonish us still more by the use they make of Pliny's epistle to Vespasian, prefixed to his ' Natural History.' Not only are the thoughts of the Latin author most happily introduced, but they are amplified and fitted to the purpose with consummate literary skill.

Then follows a pithy address to the public, in which the editors seek to justify their revolutionary work, undertaken so long after Shakespeare's death, on the ground that all previous publications of the plays had been made from stolen copies, and were, therefore, inaccurate as well as fraudulent. A comparison of the two sets, however, discloses a state of things quite inconsistent with the sincerity of Messrs. Heminge and Condell. Some of the finest passages given in the Quartos are omitted in the Folio, — one particularly in ' Hamlet,' in which the genius of the author, as Swinburne asserts, " soars up to the very highest of its height, and strikes down to the very deepest of its depth."[1] In ' King Lear,' also, but for

prologue. It appeared with one in 1623, — a circumstance so extraordinary that commentators are vainly inquiring who wrote these introductory verses.

' Othello ' was first given to the world in quarto form in 1622, six years after Shakspere's death; and yet it received numerous and important emendations for the folio one year later.

[1] " Magnificent as is that monologue on suicide and doubt, it is ac-

8

the "stolen copies," the following description of Cordelia's sorrow, together with the whole scene containing it, would have been lost forever: —

> " You have seen
> Sunshine and rain at once; her smiles and tears
> Were like a better May; those happy smilets,
> That play'd on her ripe lip, seemed not to know
> What guests were in her eyes ; which parted thence,
> As pearls from diamonds dropp'd."

And who is not shocked at the statement in the folio that Desdemona, at one of her first interviews with the swarthy Moor, received the story of his life "with a world," not of sighs, but " of kisses ! "

" It can be proved to demonstration that several of the plays in the folio were printed from earlier quarto editions, and that in other cases the quarto is more correctly printed, or from a better MS., than the folio text, and therefore of higher authority. For example, in ' Midsummer Night's Dream' and in ' Richard III.' the reading of the quartos is almost always preferable to that of the folio ; and ' Hamlet,' where it differs from the quartos, differs for the worse in forty-seven places, while it differs for the better in twenty at most." — *The Cambridge Shakespeare*, Preface, p. xxvi.

The truth probably is that Heminge and Condell were merely nominal editors; that they loaned their names to some person or persons of high literary attainments, who wrote the introductory matter for them ; and that the introductory matter itself, with its absurd misrepresentation of facts, was intended to

tually eclipsed and distanced, at once on philosophical and on poetic grounds, by the later soliloquy on reason and resolution." — *Study of Shakespeare*, p. 166.

mystify and cajole the public. Of the body of the work there was evidently no intelligent supervision.[1]

[1] The book was entered for license at Stationers' Hall, Nov. 9, 1623; when it was printed is not known. Halliwell-Phillipps thought that a large part of it must have gone to press before August 6 of that year, the date of Mrs. Shakspere's death. Bacon was banished from the court and from London in 1621, and may not have had the opportunity, if he had wished, to supervise the publication. We know, however, that he was indifferent to the details of such an undertaking. He permitted the third edition of his Essays, printed in 1625, to go out so disfigured with excess of punctuation that it is to-day a typographical curiosity. It is literally cut into inch pieces with commas.

The printing of the " Shake-speare " folio, of one thousand pages, was undoubtedly a great achievement for those days. It was sufficient to tax the resources of any establishment then existing, or perhaps of several establishments combined. The book was probably set up and printed one page at a time, — a method generally pursued in the early stages of the art, and one that prevailed when the second (1632) and third (1664) editions of the folio went to press, causing that curious reproduction of page work about which so many conjectures have recently been made. As a rule, compositors were assigned each a page at a time for copy, evidently without much allowance, in the case of reprints, for changes introduced into the preceding parts of the book. The beginnings of the pages of the three editions of the " Shake-speare " folio would therefore be identical. Other irregularities may also be accounted for in this simple way. For instance, the typos were too independent of one another for any rigid system of paging. The first edition of the ' Paradise Lost ' (1667) was not paged at all. Bacon's 'Advancement of Learning' had the leaves, not the pages, numbered. Even then the pagination was exceedingly irregular, as the following consecutive examples from it, beginning with page 69, will show, — 69, 70, 70, 71, 70, 72, 74, 73, 74, 75, 69, 77, 78, 79, 80, 77, 74, 69, 69, 82, 87, 79, 89. The number on the last page is incorrect. (See *Shakespeariana*, III. 334.)

The 'Advancement of Learning' affords another proof of Bacon's inattention to such matters. In the first edition of that work occurred the word *dusinesse*, which, though evidently a misprint, the author did not correct. He left it to conjecture, under which a subsequent editor let it pass as *business*. It was not until Mr. Spedding, two hundred and fifty years afterwards, compared the original with the Latin version that the word was printed correctly, — *dizziness*.

XVII. It would be well-nigh miraculous if in all
these works, dealing as they do with so many kinds
and degrees of human vicissitude, we could not find
somewhere in them a trace of the author's own personality. Indeed, editors have been constantly
searching for it, even at the risk of converting ex-
egesis into biography. Two of them, for instance,
have surmised that the dramatist was educated at
Oxford or Cambridge, and afterward trained to law
at one of the Inns of Court, because Justice Shallow
recommended such a course of study (actually pursued by Bacon) in ' Henry IV.' It is not surprising,
therefore, that on the supposition of Bacon's authorship we should discover in two of the plays unmistakable marks of a great crisis in his life. These two
are ' Timon of Athens ' and ' Henry VIII.' They
seem to be filled, like ocean shells, with the dash and
roar of waves. They were both printed for the first
time in the folio of 1623, — the ' Timon ' having never
been heard of before, and the other also, almost as
certainly, a new production. An older play, entitled ' All is True,' based on unknown incidents of the
same reign, was on the boards of the Globe Theatre
on the night of the fire in June, 1613 ; but we have
no reason to believe that it was the magnificent
Shakespearean drama of ' Henry VIII.,' at least in
the form in which it was printed in the folio ten
years later.[1]

[1] " It is in the folio of 1623 that we hear, for the first time, of the
' Taming of the Shrew,' ' Henry VIII.,' ' All 's Well that Ends Well,'
' Julius Cæsar,' ' Timon of Athens,' and ' Coriolanus.' " — *Halliwell-
Phillipps' Outlines.*

" ' Henry VIII.,' as we have it, is not the play that was in action
at the Globe when that theatre was burned on Tuesday, 29th June,
1613." — *Fleay's Life of Shakespeare,* p. 250.

The catastrophe that overwhelmed Bacon in 1621 was one of the saddest in the annals of our race. No wonder Timon hurls invectives at his false friends, and Cardinal Wolsey utters his grand but pathetic lament over fallen greatness! Such storms of feeling, sweeping over a human soul, must have gathered their force among the mountains and valleys of a mighty personal experience.

"'Timon of Athens' forms the beautiful close of Shakespeare's poetical career. It reflects more clearly than any other piece the poet's consciousness of the nothingness of human life. No one could have painted misanthropy with such truth and force without having experienced its bitter agony." — *Ulrici's Dramatic Art of Shakespeare*, p. 244.

IV.

OBJECTIONS CONSIDERED.

As counsel for defendant may be disposed at this point to demur to the evidence, and thus take the case from the jury, we feel obliged to file a statement of facts and objections on the other side, arranged seriatim in the inverse order of their importance, as follows: —

I. From 1598, *when the publication of the plays ceased to be anonymous, to* 1848, *when Joseph C. Hart, an American, publicly initiated the doubt concerning their authorship* [1] *(a period of two hundred and fifty years), the whole world, nem. con., attributed them to William Shakspere.*

The plays came into existence in obscurity. No person appears to have taken the slightest interest in their putative author. His very insignificance saved him from prosecution when the play of 'Richard II.'

---

[1] Disraeli (Earl Beaconsfield) raised the question, it appears, in his novel, 'Venetia,' published in 1837. One of his characters, understood to personate Byron, is made to utter the following: —

"And who is Shakespeare? We know of him as much as we do of Homer. Did he write half the plays attributed to him? Did he write even a single whole play? I doubt it."

"Lord Byron is reported to have expressed similar sentiments, *in propria persona,* several years earlier." — *Medwin's Conversations with Lord Byron,* 1821.

Our attention was called to these interesting facts by Mr. W. H. Wyman, of Omaha, Nebraska.

was used by Essex for treasonable ends; and the same indifference to him continued for a long time after his death. Indeed, the critics were as blind to the character of these great works as they were, in the early part of the present century, to the merits of Wordsworth, whom the most eminent of them at one time flatly denounced as little better than an idiot. Wordsworth now ranks as third in the list of British poets.[1]

Dr. Appleton Morgan, in his brilliant contribution to the literature of this subject, reminds us of the general contempt in which the plays were buried at the time of Cromwell, and, to a certain extent, for more than a hundred years after the Restoration. In 1661 Evelyn reports that they " begin to disgust this refined age." Pepys preferred Hudibras to " Shake-speare," pronouncing ' Midsummer Night's Dream ' the " most insipid, ridiculous play," and ' Romeo and Juliet' the " worst," he had ever seen. He thought very well for a time of ' Othello,' but an unkind providence leading him to read the ' Adventures of Five Hours,' he immediately regarded ' Othello ' as " mean," and ' Twelfth Night ' (the perfection of English comedy) as " silly." In 1681 Tate, a poet who afterward wore the laurel, could find no epithet sufficiently opprobrious to express his aversion for ' King Lear,' and so he called it simply a " thing." In Hume's condemnation, " Shake-speare " and Bacon

---

[1] The next in rank had the same experience. The great critic, " Christopher North," did not hesitate to call Tennyson, on the appearance of the first book of his poems in 1830, " an owl," and to say, " All that he wants is to be shot, stuffed, and stuck in a glass case, to be made immortal in a museum."

were yoked together as wanting in simplicity and
purity of diction, " with defective taste and elegance."
Addison styled the plays " very faulty,"̀and Johnson
asserted, with his usual emphasis, that " Shakespeare " never wrote six consecutive lines " without
a fault." " Perhaps you might find seven," he added,
with grim humor, " but that does not refute my general assertion." He further declared that " Shakespeare " had not, perhaps, produced " one play which,
if it were now exhibited as the work of a contemporary writer, would be heard to the conclusion."
Margaret Cavendish, a voluminous author of the
seventeenth century, took her cue from no less a
person than Homer, who praised the valor of the
Trojans in order to make the victory of the Greeks
more glorious; she praised the wit of the plays, but
ended in a fine gush of conjugal loyalty by claiming
that her own husband was, in that respect at least,
superior to the creator of Falstaff. Dryden, though
not without lucid intervals of high appreciation, still
regarded " Shake-speare " and Fletcher as " below
the dullest writers of our own or any precedent age,"
full of " solecisms of speech," " flaws of sense," and
" ridiculous and incoherent stories meanly written."
He disapproved of " Shake-speare's " style, describing
it as " pestered with figurative expressions," " affected,"
and " obscure."

    In 1680 Otway stole the character of the nurse and
all the love-scenes in ' Romeo and Juliet,' and published them as his own, evidently under no fear of
detection.

    The author of the ' Tatler,' one hundred years after
" Shake-speare's " time, told the story of the ' Taming

of the Shrew' as though it were new to his readers; and having occasion to quote a few lines from 'Macbeth,' was content to receive them from a new version of that drama, in which, as Chalmers says, "almost every original beauty is either awkwardly disguised or arbitrarily omitted."

John Dennis, also, thought himself competent to rewrite the plays, and he actually put one or two of them, "revised and improved," on the boards in London, apparently without the least suspicion, on the part of the audiences that witnessed them, of any sacrilege. It was George Granville, however, who gave to "Shake-speare" the unkindest cut of all, for, having rewritten the 'Merchant of Venice,' he brought "Shake-speare's" ghost upon the stage, and made him say, —

> "The first rude sketches [my own] pencil drew,
> But all the shining master-strokes are new.
> This play, ye critics, shall your fury stand,
> Adorn'd and rescu'd by a faultless hand."

In this respect Davenant was the most persistent offender, for he remodelled 'Macbeth,' 'Measure for Measure,' 'Much Ado about Nothing,' and also (in conjunction with Dryden) 'The Tempest.'

In this latter play the treatment of Miranda, who had never seen a man, and of Hippolyto, a new character who had never seen a woman, is, as the work of two poets laureate, almost incredible. After Davenant's death, Dryden went on with the task of demolishing these edifices of marble and rebuilding them with brick.[1]

[1] "There was probably no man of his day better qualified to write sound criticism on the drama, as he knew it, than Dryden. Dryden

Thomas Rymer capped the climax. He was Historiographer Royal, and he left behind him works that constitute a small library. He said of Desdemona, " There is nothing in her which is not below any country kitchen-maid; no woman bred out of a pig-sty could talk so meanly." And of Othello, " There is not a monkey but understands nature better; not a pug in Barbary that has not a truer taste of things."

Steevens declared that only an act of Parliament could make any one read the sonnets.

On the other side, we have a stock quotation from Milton, as follows : —

> " Or sweetest Shakespeare, Fancy's child,
> Warble his native wood-notes wild," —

requiring a considerable stretch of the imagination to apply to the plays. Mr. White calls it " a petty, puling dribble of belittling, patronizing praise." [1]

tells us that he loved Shakespeare, and he says a great deal about Shakespeare that shows an appreciation unusual for those times ; but he confesses that he admired Ben Jonson more, and thought Beaumont and Fletcher superior for the construction of plots, for natural dialogue, for pathos, and for gayety. Even this might pass, but before he died, Dryden declared Congreve to be the equal of Shakespeare." — *Pearson's National Life and Character,* p. 306.

[1] " The boundless veneration for Shakespeare in the sonnet is, indeed, gone in this passage." — *Masson's Life of Milton.*

" Fond and belittling phrases, as little appropriate as would be the patronizing chatter of the planet Venus about the dear, darling Sun." — *Whipple's Literature of the Age of Elizabeth,* p. 37.

" No poet was ever less a warbler of 'wood-notes wild.' " — *Walter Savage Landor.*

" The slur, the gibe, and the covert satire are too obvious." — *Isaac Disraeli.*

" Milton's panegyric takes no notice at all of the tragedies. This

Milton was a Puritan, and probably never soiled his fingers with a copy of these wicked works. He had some knowledge of their character, to be sure, for he accused Charles I. of making them, and " other stuff of this sort," his daily reading. Evidently, in Milton's opinion, a king who read and admired ' Hamlet ' or ' Othello ' deserved to lose his head.[1]

With such sentiments as these in vogue regarding the plays themselves, how much value should we attach to the concurrent belief in the authorship of them? Why should men look upward for a star when they are content to see it reflected in the dirty puddles of the streets? And how natural, under a law of moral mechanics, the swinging of public opinion from blind detraction at one time to equally blind idolatry at another![2]

always suggested to me that he had no idea that the author of the songs had any hand in them." — *Prof. Francis W. Newman, Letter to the Echo,* Dec. 31, 1887.

In his Preface to the ' Samson Agonistes ' (1671), Milton refers to Æschylus, Sophocles, and Euripides as "the three tragic poets unequalled yet by any."

[1] In his youth Milton wrote a sonnet to Shakespeare, which is one of the finest in our language. It was prefixed to the folio edition of the plays published in 1632.

[2] As a specimen of the capacity of Shakespearean critics, exhibited one hundred years later still, we give the following facts : —

In 1795 a boy in London, seventeen years old and possessing no precocity but that of impudence, composed a play nearly as long as ' Hamlet,' which he undertook to palm upon the world as " Shakespeare's." The effect was electrical. Dr. Warton, Henry James Pye (poet laureate), Sir Isaac Heard, Dr. Parr, James Boswell, John Pinkerton, George Chalmers, and many others, commentators, students, and lovers of " Shake-speare," received the work with delighted credulity. Boswell gave thanks to God that he had lived to see it. Sheridan purchased the MS. for the Drury Lane Theatre, where the

" In the neighing of a horse, or in the growling of a mastiff, there is a meaning. there is as lively expression, and, I may say, more humanity, than many times in the tragical flights of Shakespeare." — *Rymer*,[1] 1693.

" The true restoration of a single line in Shakespeare is well worth the best volume of any other English writer." — *Halliwell-Phillipps*, 1850.

II. It is hardly conceivable that Bacon, if the author of these works, would not have claimed the credit of them before he died, or, at least, left posthumous proofs that would have established his title to them.

Bacon had one great aim in life, — an aim that, it seems to us, gave a fine consistency to all that he did. He sought to instruct in better ways of think-

wretched stuff was brought out to an overflowing house amid great excitement. The young man had the audacity even to produce a love-letter, purporting to have been written by Shakspere to Anne Hathaway, and containing a lock of red hair.

" All the critics of the land came to look upon the originals. Some went upon their knees and kissed them. Hard names were given and returned; dunce and blockhead were the gentlest vituperations. The whole controversy turned upon the color of the ink, the water-mark of the paper, the precise mode of superscription to a letter, the contemporary use of a common word, the date of the first use of promissory notes, the form of a mortgage. Scarcely one of the learned went boldly to the root of the imposture. and showed that Shakespeare could not have written such utter trash." — *Charles Knight*.

" The Irelands palmed upon literary critics a manuscript play of Shakespeare ; it was read, discussed ; an antiquarian or two said no ; most of the critics said yes, and fell upon their knees before the manuscript. It was put upon the stage : coal-heavers and apprentices set literary criticism right in ten minutes. Why ? The stuffed fish, thrown down on a bank, might pass for a live fish ; but put it in the water ! " — *Charles Reade*.

[1] Here are two opinions of Rymer : —

" One of the best critics we ever had." — *Pope*.

" The worst critic that ever lived." — *Macaulay*.

ing, not his own generation alone, but those that were to come after. " I feel myself born," he says in one of his letters, " for the service of mankind." Accordingly, we find him in his will bequeathing sets of his philosophical works and his essays to the chief public libraries of the kingdom. He even translated them into Latin, for the avowed reason that our modern languages are ephemeral, while Latin will last as long as human speech.[1] In his will, also, with the sublime confidence that is inseparable from genius, he left his name and memory to the " next ages."

At the same time he showed no anxiety for personal credit. His mind was bent on grander results. In the introduction to one of his books, unpublished at the time of his death, he asks his executors to leave some parts of it unprinted, in order that they might be passed in manuscript " from hand to hand." He had the curious conception that in this impersonal way certain truths might take deeper root. Then follow these noble words : —

" For myself my heart is not set upon any of those things which depend on external accidents. I am not hunting for fame. I have no desire to found a sect, after the fashion of the heresiarchs; and to look for any private gain from such an undertaking as this, I should consider both ridiculous and base. Enough for me the consciousness of well-deserving, and those real and effectual results with which fortune itself cannot interfere."

[1] Latin was at that time the common language of scholars throughout the civilized world. Bacon, who appreciated, perhaps more than any other man then living, the advantages of such a medium, thought it would remain so indefinitely. He failed to perceive that a language for scholars, *per se*, would retard not only the diffusion of knowledge but its advancement.

The ring of these words three centuries have not dulled. They will ring through all time, for they are of pure gold.

It should be remembered, too, that Bacon had an ambition to occupy his father's seat on the woolsack, and that to be known as a writer of plays for money would have been fatal to his advancement. After his downfall he had not the heart, if he had the will, for the exposure. He may well have hesitated to make another invidious confession in the face of a frowning world.[1]

" The question why Bacon, if he were the composer of the plays, did not acknowledge the authorship, is not difficult to answer. His birth, his position, and his ambition forbade him, the nephew of Lord Burleigh, the future Lord Chancellor of England, to put his name on a play bill. In the interest of his family and of his political career, the secret must be so strictly preserved that mere anonymity would not be sufficient. A live man-of-straw, a responsible official representative known to every one, was required. No person could be better fitted for such a purpose than an actor, wise enough to understand and appreciate what was to his own advantage. Perhaps this ' Johannes Factotum ' of Greene's did not know the name of his benefactor. But even if he did know the name, it was obviously to his interest to keep from the world, and particularly from his gossiping companions. a secret which brought him money and fame." — *Allgemeine Zeitung.*

[1] A French critic has conjectured that Bacon may have left instructions to his executors to divulge the secret at some opportune time after his death, but that the alarming growth of Puritanism, culminating in its complete ascendancy under Cromwell twenty-five years later, rendered such a step inexpedient. Holding his reputation in trust and knowing what a fierce popular storm the announcement would cause, they may have deemed it their duty to let the plays remain as " Mr. William Shakespeare's," until such time as these writings might reveal by their own light the name and genius of the author.

Sir Walter Scott kept his authorship of the Waverley Novels from the public for more than twelve years, because he deemed the writing of fiction beneath the dignity of a clerk of courts and of a landowner. Thirty-two persons shared the secret.

The letters of Junius are among the most celebrated of literary productions. In elegance of diction, in perspicuity and force of argument, in display of knowledge, in boldness and in high moral tone, they have seldom been surpassed; but the writer carried the secret with him to his grave. And we have no reason to believe that while indulging in this self-abnegation, he had any other title, as Bacon had, to immortal honor.

The popular ballad, 'Auld Robin Gray,' was disowned for a period of fifty years by the gifted woman who wrote it. It was not until some other person had claimed the authorship that the secret was disclosed.

It must not be supposed, for an instant, that if Bacon wrote the plays he did not appreciate them. He confessed to a correspondent that certain of his writings (not described by him, but, without doubt, like the Essays, literary in their character) might after all do more for his fame than those others upon which he was expending his greatest energies.[1] And yet it is equally certain that, if he then had the plays

---

[1] "As for my Essays and some other particulars of that nature, I count them but as the recreations of my other studies, and in that sort purpose to continue them; though I am not ignorant that that kind of writing would, with less pains and embracement, perhaps yield more lustre and reputation to my name than those other which I have in hand." — *Bacon to Bishop Andrews*, 1622.

in mind, he could not have anticipated for them the species of idolatry with which they are now regarded. No man can entirely dispossess himself of the prejudices of the age in which he lives. The moral atmosphere exerts a pressure upon the intellect as great as that of the physical upon the body. Bacon's mind was so filled with a sense of the infinite importance of his new method in philosophy that everything else "paled its uneffectual fires" in comparison.

Authors are very apt to misjudge the relative values of their different works. Galileo is said to have considered his theory of the tides (which was wholly erroneous) a more brilliant triumph of his skill than all his discoveries in the heavens.[1] Descartes subordinated his beautiful exposition of the rainbow to an absurd doctrine of planetary vortices. Milton thought his 'Paradise Regained' a finer poem than the 'Paradise Lost.' Wellington would never admit that Waterloo was his greatest battle. Is it, then, extraordinary that Francis Bacon, contemplating the vast results which he knew would follow, and which actually did follow, the appearance of his 'Instauratio Magna,' neglected other compositions upon which he had spent only his recreative hours, which nearly every one about him despised, which a great essayist quoted from, one hundred years later, as though they were then unknown, and over which David Garrick, fifty years later still, created a sensation among his fellow-actors

---

[1] Galileo strangely assumed that tides ebb and flow but once in twenty-four hours.

in London by using the text as it had come from the author, instead of one from scribblers and mountebanks to which they had become accustomed?

III. The plays contain anachronisms and other errors which Bacon, "who took all knowledge for his province," could not have committed.

Chief among the errors in question, of sufficient importance to be noted here, are the following: —
1. The famous one in the quotation from Aristotle:[1] —

> " Young men, whom Aristotle thought
> Unfit to hear moral philosophy."
> > *Troilus and Cressida*, II. 2.

It was *political* philosophy that Aristotle referred to; but Bacon makes the same mistake. He quotes the Greek as saying, —

> " Young men are no fit auditors of moral philosophy."

Even in their blunders our two authors were not divided.

2. The curious conception of heat in its " mode of motion," one flame pushing another by force out of its place.
Shakespeare: —

> " Even as one heat another heat expels,
> Or as one nail by strength drives out another."
> > *Two Gentlemen of Verona*, II. 4.

> "One fire drives out one fire; one nail, one nail."
> > *Coriolanus.*

---

[1] " Διὸ τῆς πολιτικῆς οὐκ ἔστιν οἰκεῖος ἀκροατὴς ὁ νέος." — *Nicomachean Ethics*, I. 3.

Bacon : —

" Flame doth not mingle with flame, but remaineth contiguous." — *Advancement of Learning.*

" Clavum clavo pellere " (To drive out a nail with a nail). — *Promus.*

The materiality of heat was a dogma of the ancients. It held almost absolute sway over mankind till long after the time of Francis Bacon ; but this nail illustration, found in Bacon's intellectual workshop and reproduced in the plays, is startling. It may fairly be said to clinch the argument.

3. Mark Antony tells the Romans that he comes

" To bury Cæsar, not to praise him,"

notwithstanding the fact that the Romans did not bury the bodies of their dead.

The play was written for an English stage, and for an audience to whom cremation was practically unknown. The reference to burial indicates the art, rather than the ignorance, of the dramatist. What would our critics say of a famous actor of modern times who always armed the Roman guard in the play with Springfield muskets !

" Shakespeare turns his Romans into Englishmen, and he does right, for otherwise his nation would not have understood him." — *Goethe.*

4. A Trojan hero quotes Aristotle, Cleopatra plays billiards, and a clock strikes the hours in ancient Rome.

Historical perspective is not necessary to the drama. The poet sees the world reflected on a retina that ignores time and place. He idealizes facts.

The Globe

GLOBE THEATRE.

Egypt, Greece, Rome, Pericles, Cæsar, are so many stars set in his firmament, and shining apparently in one plane. This illusion extended even to the accessories of the stage in Shake-speare's day. There was no scenery to help the spectators.[1] Imagination was left to its own unaided wings, with nothing but the atmosphere of the play to sustain it. At the call of the magical flute piping through the Globe, billiards, clocks, churchyards, seaports, Ilium, all local and temporary objects of sense, " shot madly from their spheres," in blind obedience to the melody.[2]

[1] The want of scenic effects is thus portrayed by Sir Philip Sidney : —

" You shall have Asia of the one side and Africa of the other, and so many other under kingdoms that the player, when he comes in, must ever begin with telling where he is. . . . Now, you shall have three ladies walk to gather flowers, and then you must believe the stage to be a garden ; by and by, we have news of a shipwreck in the same place, and we are to blame if we accept it not for a rock. Upon the back of that comes a hideous monster, with fire and smoke, and the miserable beholders are bound to take it for a cave ; while, in the mean time, two armies fly in, represented with four swords and bucklers, and then what hard heart will not receive it for a pitched field ? "

[2] It may be well to add, on this subject of anachronisms, that the game of billiards was known to the ancients before the time of Cleopatra, and that the boundaries of Bohemia, it is said, once extended to the sea-coast. These facts, however, are immaterial. Is it possible to conceive that the author of ' Coriolanus,' ' Julius Cæsar,' ' Anthony and Cleopatra,' ' Timon of Athens,' and ' Troilus and Cressida,' whoever he was, did not know that Aristotle lived hundreds of years after the time of Hector ?

It was one of the rules laid down by Lessing, perhaps the ablest literary critic that ever lived, that dramatic art should represent not what men have done, but what under given circumstances, without regard to actual occurrences, men would do ; not historical truth, but the laws and principles of human nature. Goethe followed this rule in the composition of his ' Egmont,' making Machiavelli Margaret of Parma's secretary, though Machiavelli died fifty years before Mar-

" Poesy is feigned history, which, not being tied to the laws of matter, may at pleasure join that which nature hath severed, and sever that which nature hath joined, and so make unlawful matches and divorces of things." — *Bacon.*

" There is no reason why an hour should not be a century in the calenture of the brains that can make the stage a field." — *Dr. Johnson.*

Numerous other errors of a minor character are found in the plays, though, like the spots on the sun's disk, they are lost to all but professional observers in the radiance that envelops them. Paradoxical as it may seem, however, these very blemishes are a distinct indication of Bacon's authorship. We find the same in his prose works. The great philosopher, notwithstanding his industry and his learning, was singularly careless in some of the minutiæ of his work. The sublime confidence with which he employed his mental powers often made a " sinner of his memory." It was simply impossible, in the multiplicity and magnitude of his productions, particularly if the plays be superadded, to prevent

garet's time, and assigning for the conduct of his hero motives which we know did not exist. In the ' Lay of the Last Minstrel ' the author introduces Sir Michael Scott, a wizard who flourished four hundred years before.

To Lessing belongs the honor of having been first in the world to appreciate and expound the true genius of " Shake-speare." In defiance of the whole school of French critics, by the members of which " Shake-speare " was regarded as an "inspired idiot " or " drunken savage," he declared that not only was the Englishman superior to Corneille, Racine, and Voltaire, but that he was the originator of a new method of writing tragedy, destined to overthrow the tyranny of the Greek. That is to say, " Shake-speare " repudiated the ancient models for dramatization. precisely as Bacon did for science, and with equal claims to a complete mastery.

unimportant errors from creeping in. In no other way can we account for the false quotation from Solomon in the " Essay of Revenge," or that from Tacitus in the " Essay of Traditions." The grammatical mistakes in the Latin entries of the Promus, written with his own hand, would send a school-boy to the bottom of his class, but they put a tongue in every wound of syntax found in the plays.

In this connection it may not be amiss to quote a few of Bacon's " Apothegms," with Devey's notes (Bohn's standard edition) appended to them, as follows : —

" Michael Angelo, the famous painter, made one of the damned souls in his portraiture of hell so like a cardinal, his enemy, as everybody at first sight knew it. Whereupon the cardinal complained to the Pope, humbly praying it might be effaced. The Pope said to him, ' Why, you know very well I have power to deliver a soul out of purgatory, but not out of hell.' "

The victim was not a cardinal, but the Pope's master of ceremonies.

" A king of Hungary took a bishop in battle, and kept him prisoner. Whereupon the Pope writ a monitory to him, for that he had broken the privilege of holy church and taken his son. The king, in reply, sent the armor wherein the bishop was taken, and this only in writing, ' Know now whether this be thy son's coat?' "

It was Richard Cœur de Lion who did this, and not a king of Hungary.

" Antigonus, when it was told him the enemy had such a volley of arrows that they did hide the sun, said : ' That falls out well, for it is hot weather, and so we shall fight in the shade.' "

This was a speech, not of Antigonus, but of a Spartan, previously to the battle of Thermopylæ.

"One of the seven was wont to say that laws are like cobwebs, where small flies are caught, but the great break through."

This was said, not by a Greek, but by Anacharsis, the Scythian.

"An orator of Athens said to Demosthenes, 'The Athenians will kill you if they wax mad.' Demosthenes replied, 'And they will kill you if they be in good sense.' "

This retort was made to Demosthenes by Phocion.

"Demetrius, King of Macedon, had a petition offered him divers times by an old woman, and answered that he had no leisure. Whereupon the woman said aloud, 'Why, then, give over to be king.' "

This happened, not to Demetrius, but to Philip.

"A philosopher disputed with Adrian, the emperor, and did it but weakly. One of his friends, that stood by, afterwards said to him: 'Methinks you were not like yourself in argument with the emperor. I could have answered better myself.' 'Why,' said the philosopher, 'would you have me contend with him that commands thirty legions?' "

This took place, not under Adrian, but under Augustus Cæsar.

"Chilon said that kings' friends and favorites are like counters, that sometimes stand for one, sometimes for ten, and sometimes for an hundred."

This was a saying of Orontes.

"Alexander, after the battle of Granicum, had very great offers made to him by Darius; consulting with his captains concerning them, Parmenio said: 'Sure, I would accept these offers, if I were Alexander.' Alexander answered: 'So would I, if I were Parmenio.'"

This happened after the battle of Issus.

The above are gross blunders, and, being in the domain of history, they are far more astonishing than any found in the dramas of " Shake-speare." Abbott testifies on this point as follows : —

"We have abundant proof that he [Bacon] was eminently inattentive to details.[1] His scientific works are full of inaccuracies. King James found in this defect of his chancellor the matter for a witticism, — '*De minimis non curat lex.*'"[2]
"Inexhaustible constructiveness, — that, and not scientific patience or accuracy, was his characteristic." — *Prof. Minto's English Prose Composition*, p. 241.
" Bacon, always in the ancient sense a magnificent, was never an exact man." — *Nichol's Life of Bacon*, p. 171.

IV. " Shake-speare " and Bacon were of essentially different types of mind, the ' Novum Organum ' and the conception of ' Falstaff ' being respectively at opposite poles, and wholly beyond the range of one man's powers.[3]

Bacon's mind had as many facets as a diamond; turn it whichever way you will, it gives a flash. No feature of it was more conspicuous, in the eyes of his contemporaries, than his wit. Indeed, his wit was simply prodigious. Macaulay asserts that in this respect he "never had an equal."

[1] " It has been said of Shakespeare that he had a fine contempt for details." — *Quarterly Review*, April, 1894.
[2] The law takes no notice of trifles.
[3] We state this objection substantially as given to us by the late Francis Parkman.

" He possessed this faculty, or this faculty possessed him, in a morbid degree. When he abandoned himself to it without reserve, as he did in 'Sapientia Veterum,' or at the end of the second book of 'De Augmentis,' the feats which he performed were not only admirable, but portentous, and almost shocking. On those occasions we marvel at him, as clowns on a fair-day marvel at a juggler, and can hardly help thinking that the devil must be in him." — *Macaulay.*

Bacon had also a sense of humor that must have been extraordinary, for, according to Ben Jonson, he could with difficulty, even on solemn occasions, " spare or pass by a jest." We find some admirable specimens of it in the reports of his conversations with the Queen, — his powers of repartee sometimes proving more than a match for her imperious will.

It seems like piling Ossa on Pelion to add that the world's most famous jest-book we owe to Francis Bacon, dictated by him from a sick-bed, entirely from memory, in one day.[1] No wonder the portly Falstaff sprang, full-grown, from such a brain!

V. The author of the 'Essay on Love' could not have written 'Romeo and Juliet.'[2]

The two productions are certainly widely dissimilar. In one, the tender passion is a flower in bloom, exquisitely sweet and beautiful; in the other, it is torn up by the roots and analyzed scientifically, not to say contemptuously. Indeed, Bacon quotes with

---

[1] " The best jest-book ever given to the public." — *Edinburgh Review.*

" The best collection of jests in the world." — *Macaulay.*

[2] Especially urged against us by Mr. Goldwin Smith.

approval an old saying, that a man cannot love and be wise.[1]

We have no direct evidence to show that the author of the essay did not possess a susceptible heart. To be sure, he was married late (at the age of forty-five), and was unfortunate in losing the affections of his wife before he died. It may be worthy of note, also, that the play was written several years before, and the essay several years after, his marriage. We cannot admit, however, in any view of his matrimonial adventure, that he was disqualified to write the garden scene in ' Romeo and Juliet.' It is not necessary to possess a trait in order to depict it. "Shakespeare's admiration of the great men of action is immense," says Professor Dowden, "because he himself was primarily not a man of action." We instinctively see and appreciate what is exactly opposite to us in mental aptitudes. Human nature makes an uncon-

---

[1] Shake-speare makes the same quotation : —

> " To be wise and love
> Exceeds man's might; that dwells with gods above."
> *Troilus and Cressida*, III. 2.

" The tendency of love, of which Bacon speaks, to ' trouble a man's fortunes, and make him untrue to his own ends,' is most forcibly illustrated in the character of Proteus, who contrasts his slavery as a lover with Valentine's freedom as a student, thus : —

> ' He after honor hunts, I after love ;
> He leaves his friends to dignify them more,
> I leave myself, my friend, and all for love.
> Thou, Julia, thou hast metamorphosed me,
> Made me neglect my studies, lose my time,
> War with good counsel, set the world at naught,
> Made wit with musing weak, heart sick with thought.' "
> *Two Gentlemen of Verona*, I. 1.
> *R. M. Theobald.*

scious effort in this way to round itself out into the
complete and perfect. The theory of complementary
colors is based on this tendency. Unity in diversity
is the ideal of married life. Tom Hood was the wittiest of men, and at the same time one of the most
melancholy. The president of a New England theological seminary, who was very penurious, preached
the ablest sermon of his life on charity. The people
of Scotland are notoriously intemperate every Saturday night; it is said that thirty thousand persons get
drunk at that time in the city of Glasgow alone; and
yet the finest idyl in our language, consecrated to the
domestic peace and religious sanctity of that season,
we owe to a Scottish poet, himself in full accord with
the habits of his countrymen.

" In ' Venus and Adonis ' the goddess, after the death of her
favorite, utters a curse upon love which contains in the germ,
as it were, the whole development of the subject as Shakespeare
has unfolded it in the series of his dramas." — *Gervinus.*

" Shakespeare manifests a total insensibility to the gross
passion of love. In descriptions of Platonic affection and con-
ventional gallantry he is unsurpassed; but when he essays to
be personally tender his muse becomes tediously perfunctory,
as we see it in ' Hamlet.' Then his intense abhorrence of in-
temperance and personal defilement is another proof of super-
animal organization, in which he seems to stand alone. In
what other author of the time do we read anything like his
intense loathing of them which we find in ' Antony and
Cleopatra ' ? —

> ' To sit
> And keep the turn of tippling with a slave !
> To reel the streets at noon, and stand the buffet
> With knaves that smell of sweat.' — I. 4.

" It may be said that his love of music, of flowers, and of
perfume was a wholly sensuous love; but he associates it

with sublime ideas, which animal natures never do, as in the
following:—

> 'That strain again; it had a dying fall.
> O! it came o'er my ear like the sweet south
> That breathes upon a bank of violets,
> Stealing and giving odor.'— *Twelfth Night,* I. 1."
>
> *Thomas W. White's Our English Homer*, p. 123.

"Shake-speare's" ability to assume any character
—a Romeo, a Falstaff, an Iago — without regard to
his own private sentiments, itself deprives the above
objection of pertinency and force.

*VI. The author of the plays had a thorough practical
knowledge of dramatic art that could have been derived, in
part at least, only from experience in stage management.*

We are now on William Shakspere's own ground;
for not only did he tread the boards himself, but he
was a successful manager of one or two theatres.
That Francis Bacon also had a *penchant* for the business will appear from three considerations, to wit:

1. He possessed the temperament that fits one for
it. On this point we summon a pen-and-ink artist of
exceptional abilities to testify, as follows:—

"Slight in build, rosy and round in flesh, dight in a sumptuous suit; the head well-set, erect, and framed in a thick starched
fence of frills; a bloom of study and travel on the fat, girlish
face, which looks far younger than his years; the hat and
feather tossed aside from the broad, white forehead, over which
crisps and curls a mane of dark, soft hair; an English nose,
firm, open, straight: mouth, delicate and small,—a lady's or
a jester's mouth,—a thousand pranks and humors, quibbles,
whims, and laughters, lurking in its twinkling, tremulous lines:
such is Francis Bacon at the age of twenty-four." — *Dixon's
Personal History of Lord Bacon*, p. 25.

2. Bacon was prominent in the dramatic revels at Gray's Inn and before the Court. According to Chamberlain (who wrote in 1613), he was the "chief contriver" of them. Anthony's tastes in this direction were so strong that he removed his residence to the neighborhood of the Bull Inn for better opportunities to gratify them.[1] That his brother shared the same indulgence we cannot doubt, for the two were involved in a common censure from their mother on account of it; and when Francis rode in state through the streets to take his seat for the first time on the woolsack, the players turned out *en masse* to do him honor.

" It is said that William Shakespeare once played before Queen Elizabeth. There is no record of it in the Court minutes, though we cannot find that any of that period have been lost. There 's a record, however, that Francis Bacon did. Feb. 8, 1587, certain gentlemen of Gray's Inn, Bacon among them, performed before Her Majesty a play called ' The Misfortunes of Arthur,' which surely no one can read without being impressed with its resemblance to what men call, nowadays, the Shakespearean gait and movement." — *Appleton Morgan.*

" There is one play, ' The Misfortunes of Arthur,' in the production of which there can be no doubt that Francis Bacon had a share. In the old record of this play he is only credited with having contributed the ' dumb shows; ' but in certain passages and scenes there appear the same peculiarities of expression and thought as have been found to connect the Shakespeare plays with entries in the Promus. It seems easy to distinguish the pages which have been illuminated and beautified by his hand." — *Mrs. Henry Pott, Promus,* p. 90.

" Unless we much mistake, there is a richer and nobler vein of poetry running through it than is to be found in any previous work of the kind." — *J. P. Collier.*

[1] The " Shake-speare " plays were then running there.

3. Bacon regarded the drama as an educational instrumentality of the highest value. He says of it : —

" Although in modern states play-acting is esteemed but as a ludicrous thing, except when it is too satirical and biting, yet among the ancients it became a means of forming the souls of men to virtue. Even the wise and prudent, and great philosophers, considered it to be, as it were, the *plectrum* of the mind. And most certainly, what is one of the secrets of nature, the minds of men, when assembled together, are more open to affections and impressions than when they are alone."

In the second book of the ' Advancement of Learning,' he recommends that dramatic art be included in the regular curriculum of schools.

After all, the plays are not such as a business manager, intent on making money and indifferent to literary fame, would write for his theatre. Some of them are impracticable on account of their length ; they always have to be cut for public use. Others are too philosophical. How long would the gods of the pit endure ' Troilus and Cressida,' full as it is of the profoundest wisdom, and wholly unsuited even now for popular presentation? Others, still, are the outcome of successive revisions, growing more and more fitted for the closet, less and less for the stage. Taken together, these writings seem to be the productions of a man who had high subjective ideals, who sought relief in them from severer studies, and who made pecuniary results a secondary consideration.

" Every genuine work of art has as much reason for being as the earth and the sea. The Iliad of Homer, the songs of David, the odes of Pindar, the tragedies of Æschylus, the Doric

temples, the Gothic cathedrals, the plays of Shakespeare, all
and each were made not for sport, but in grave earnest, in tears
and smiles of suffering and loving men." — *Emerson's Essay
on Art.*

The opposite view, that the plays were written solely
for the theatre and for money, leads Richard Grant
White to the following *reductio ad absurdum :* —

"All that we know of his [Shakspere's] life and of his
domestic career leaves us no room for doubt that, if his public
had preferred it, he would have written thirty-seven plays like
'Titus Andronicus,' just as readily, though not as willingly,
as he wrote 'As You Like It,' 'King Lear,' 'Hamlet,' and
'Othello.' " — *Shakespeare Studies,* p. 20.

"He wrote what he wrote merely to fill the theatre and his
own pockets." — *Ibid.,* p. 209.

We find the same degrading sentiment in one who
was still more unjust to Bacon : —

> "For gain, not glory, wing'd his roving flight,
> And grew immortal in his own despite."
>
> *Pope.*

"It has been frequently observed that, if this view be accepted, it is at the expense of investing him [Shakespeare] with
a mean and sordid disposition." — *Halliwell-Phillipps.*

Such is the inevitable consequence of attempting
to make the facts of Shakspere's life fit the writings of
" Shake-speare." Messrs. White and Halliwell-Phillipps are, perhaps, our two best authorities on the
Shakspere side of the question, and they would have
us believe that the noblest productions of the human
mind are the offspring of vulgarity as well as of
ignorance.

But there is still a deeper depth of absurdity, and
Mr. White does not hesitate to make the plunge : —

" He had as much deliberate purpose in his breathing as in his play-writing." — *Studies in Shakespeare*, p. 209.

No wonder that Mr. White pronounces Shakspere a "miraculous miracle," or, in other words (as carefully defined by him), a miracle that is not a miracle! It is almost shocking to see an able man driven by inexorable logic to such an extremity.

VII. The author of the plays had intimate knowledge of persons and localities in the neighborhood of Stratford, and of certain peculiarities of speech prevailing there.

The local references, on which the first part of the above statement is based, are mostly found in the Induction to the play of ' The Taming of the Shrew.' The localities mentioned there are Wincot and Burton-Heath. The former is probably Wilmecote, a hamlet near Stratford, and the latter, Barton-on-the-Heath, a small town in the extreme southwestern part of the county. There are other Wincots in England, but the one distinguished as having been the residence of Marian Hacket can hardly be mistaken, on account of its comparative proximity to Sly's birthplace. The tradition that Shakspere was accustomed to make the buxom ale-wife's premises his favorite place of resort required two hundred years to get itself into print, and is doubtless apocryphal.

These local allusions are explainable on one of two grounds, to wit : —

1. In 1598 Bacon rendered a great service to the crown. He introduced into the House of Commons, of which body he was the acknowledged leader, a bill to arrest decay of tillage, by requiring all land-

owners to restore to the plough, within eighteen
months from the date of the passage of the act, every
acre of land that had been taken from it and given
to pasturage since the beginning of the Queen's
reign, a period of forty years. The bill itself was
a high-handed procedure, in clear violation of the
principles of political economy as now understood,
but made necessary at that time in order to counter-
act the influence of another absurd piece of legisla-
tion, under which products of pasturage could be
exported for sale, while those of tillage could not.
The Commons supported Bacon enthusiastically, but
the Lords, Essex among them,[1] resisted. A parlia-
mentary battle followed, with Coke at the head of the
barons and Bacon at the head of the burgesses. The
result was the triumphant passage of the bill, and a
royal grant to its champion of a valuable lease at
Cheltenham, twenty-five miles from Stratford, and
twenty from Barton-on-the-Heath.

Furthermore, in 1606, Bacon married a step-daugh-
ter of Sir John Packington, whose residence was
within an easy drive in another direction from Stratford. He was also connected by marriage with Sir
Thomas Lucy of Charlecote, in the immediate vicinity
of Stratford. It would be very remarkable if under
these circumstances Bacon did not become familiar
with the valley of the Avon, in the branches of which
all the above-mentioned places, with the exception
of Barton-on-the-Heath, are situated.

2. 'The Taming of the Shrew' is one of those

---

[1] Essex took great pains to place himself in opposition to Bacon,
coming to London expressly for the purpose. The breach between
them had been widening for two or three years.

plays in the Shakespearean canon with the composition of which "Shake-speare" himself is generally
considered to have had little to do. The question is
an open one. Critics divide on it, not only as to
what part of it he actually wrote, but whether he
wrote any part whatever. Richard Grant White sums
up the case as follows : —

> " In my opinion it is the joint production of Greene, Mar-
> lowe, and possibly Shakespeare, who seem to have worked
> together for the Earl of Pembroke's servants during the first
> three years of Shakespeare's London life. Much the greater
> part of it appears to have been the work of Greene; Marlowe
> probably but little, and Shakespeare, if at all, much less." —
> *Ed. of Shakespeare's Works*, IV. 391.

The nativity of the author has also been inferred
from the use in the plays of words peculiar to the
dialect of Warwickshire. Mr. Wise devoted a chapter to this subject in his book ' Shakespeare : his
Birthplace and its Neighborhood; ' but Professor
Langlin, whose scholarly criticism in this field of research commands our confidence, has published the
following conclusions in a review of it : —

> " I have been led to examine his [Wise's] list of alleged pro-
> vincialisms of Shakespeare, and am much surprised to find how
> very uncertain is their evidence as to the actual locality in
> which the writer really lived. Wise's argument proves too
> much, and therefore, in my opinion, proves nothing." — *Shake-
> speariana*, I. 185.

A partial glossary of Warwickshire provincialisms
has been compiled by Dr. Appleton Morgan, and
subjected to a critical analysis in the columns of the
"London Daily Telegraph" by Mrs. Henry Pott, with
results as follows : —

1. " Of the 518 words enumerated, there are 46 only which are not so current in Surrey, Kent, Sussex, Wiltshire, Hampshire, Lincolnshire, and Leicestershire (and perhaps in any other English county) as they are in Warwickshire."

2. " Of the 46 which we do not recognize as common to the southern and eastern counties, not one is to be found in Shakespeare."

VIII.   Contemporaneous testimony establishes the identity of Shakspere the actor and " Shake-speare " the dramatist.

Under this head four persons only can be summoned as witnesses. They are John Heminge, Henry Condell, Leonard Digges, and Ben Jonson.[1] The first two were fellow-actors with Shakspere on the stage. They were also beneficiaries under his will, receiving each a ring. In strict accord with these known facts, and in flat contradiction to our theory of the origin of the plays, they declare, in the preface to the first folio (of which they were at least nominal editors), that the author was their friend, and that he was not then living. Unfortunately for their reputation for sincerity, however, they also declare, in the ' Address to Readers ' which follows the preface, that they had in their hands the author's own manuscripts (the appearance of which they describe), and that they were thus enabled to substitute, for the stolen and mutilated individual quartos, a collective version absolutely perfect in all its parts. Everybody knows

---

[1] " I own at once that those evidences are scanty; . . . there are but four [contemporaries] who directly identify the man or the actor with the writer of the plays." — *Ingleby's Essays*, p. 24 (1888).

In this list we substitute Digges for Chettle, for reasons which will fully appear in the text.

that these last statements are untrue. The book they printed contains on an average about twenty errors to the page, or twenty thousand in all. In some places poetry is printed as prose; in others, gems, sparkling with thought in the quartos, are omitted; in others still, names of actors are given instead of those of the *dramatis personæ*, showing that in such cases they followed copies that had been previously used in the theatre, and followed them, too, "out of the window." On the ground of insincerity, therefore, we must ask Messrs. Heminge and Condell to step down from the witness-stand; we cannot accept their testimony even under oath.

" I suppose that I must, in the next place, cite the ostensible editors of the first collection of Shakespeare's works, . . . but, unfortunately for their credit and our own satisfaction, their prefatory statement contains, or at least suggests, what they must have known to be false." — *Dr. Ingleby.*

The next witness is Leonard Digges, also one of the immortal few who helped, with poetic lubrications, to launch the first folio upon the public. He testifies distinctly that the author of the plays had had a monument erected to his memory at Stratford:

"Shake-speare, at length thy pious fellows give,
The world thy works; thy works, by which, out-live
Thy tomb, thy name must; when that stone is rent.
And time dissolves thy Stratford monument,
Here we alive shall view thee still. This book,
When brass and marble fade, shall make thee look
Fresh to all ages."   *Leonard Digges.*

The following verses, written by Digges, were also intended, it is said, to accompany the above in the

introduction to the first folio, but are found prefixed
to a volume of the Shake-speare poems printed in
1640: —

> " Next, Nature only helped him ; for look thorough
> This whole book, thou shalt find he doth not borrow
> One phrase from Greeks, nor Latins imitate,
> Nor once from vulgar languages translate,
> Nor, plagiary-like, from others glean,
> Nor begs he from each witty friend a scene
> To piece his acts with : all that he doth write
> Is pure his own ; plot, language exquisite."

Mr. White, who was an unmitigated Shaksperean,
stands aghast at these lines, wholly unable to account
for what he calls the "sad blunder" in them. Was
the witty Digges really so ignorant ? [1]

It will be noticed that the entire quartette of these
witnesses including Ben Jonson)[2] were engaged,
either as editors or contributors, in the printing of the
first folio. *It is impossible to name a single person,
taking no part in this symposium of wit, who can be
quoted as authority on the point at issue.*

We are well aware that Henry Chettle is said by
all but two of the Shaksperean commentators of
the last one hundred years to have testified to the
literary ability of Shakspere the actor, and thus indirectly identified him with the dramatist. The facts
of the case do not warrant any such conclusion.
Chettle was editor of a posthumous pamphlet, entitled a 'Groatsworth of Wit,' by Robert Greene.
He was also author of 'Kind Heart's Dream,' a book
published later in the same year (1592). In the

---

[1] Digges was known as a " wit of the town."

[2] For a discussion of Jonson's testimony, see p. 91 *et seq.*

preface to the latter work he apologizes to some one who had taken offence at certain personal allusions in Greene's pamphlet, and held him, as editor, responsible for them.

We quote from the pamphlet as follows : —

"To those gentlemen, his quondam acquaintance, that spend their wits in making plays, R. G. wisheth a better exercise and wisdom to prevent his extremities. . . . Base-minded men, all three of you, if by my misery you be not warned ; for unto none of you (like me) sought those burrs to cleave ; those puppets, I mean, that speak from our mouths, those antics garnished in our colors. . . . Yes, trust them not ; for there is an upstart crow, beautified with our feathers, that, with his *tiger's heart wrapped in a player's hide*, supposes he is as well able to bombast out a blank verse as the best of you, and being an absolute *Johannes Factotum*, is, in his own conceit, the only *Shake-scene* in a country."

That the putative author of the "Shake-speare" dramas is referred to in the closing sentence of the above, there can be little doubt; because of the parody, not only on the name, but also on a line in the third part of 'King Henry VI., " *O tiger's heart, wrapped in a woman's hide !* " It is conceded, also, that the character of the reference was such as would naturally cause offence. But was Shakspere one of those whom Chettle represents as offended, and to whom, as the biographers claim, he apologizes in commendatory terms? On this point we quote from Chettle himself, in the preface above mentioned: " Among others his ' Groatsworth of Wit,' in which a letter, written to divers play-makers, is offensively by one or two of them taken." One or two of whom? Evidently, of the play-makers (Marlowe, Nash or

Lodge, and Peele, it is said), who had been addressed by Greene, who had been warned against the *Johannes Factotum*, and who had themselves been characterized elsewhere in the pamphlet, one as an atheist and another as a blasphemer and drunkard. Chettle then goes on to say : —

" With neither of them that take offence was I acquainted, and with one of them I care not if I never be ; the other whom at that time I did not so much spare as since I wish I had . . . because myself have seen his demeanor no less civil than he, excellent in the quality he professes ; besides, divers of worship have reported his uprightness of dealing, which argues his honesty, and his facetious grace in writing that approves his art."

It is very remarkable that of all the biographers of Shakspere, so far as noted, Frederick Gard Fleay alone states this matter correctly, thus : —

" In December, Chettle issued his ' Kind Heart's Dream,' in which he apologizes for the offence given to Marlowe in the ' Groatsworth of Wit,' ' because myself have seen his demeanor,' etc. To Peele he makes no apology, nor indeed was any required. Shakespeare was not one of those who took offence ; they are expressly stated to have been two of the authors addressed by Green : the third (Lodge) not being in England." — *Chronicle History of the Life and Works of William Shakespeare*, p. 111.

Even Dr. Ingleby admits that Chettle's commendatory words cannot be applied to Shakspere without a violation of the text. It is necessary, he says, to interpolate a few words, to the effect that Greene wrote his letter *to* divers playwrights, his friends and associates, and *against* another, his avowed enemy, and that two of these, *including the latter*, took offence !

That is to say, for the purpose of saving Chettle's testimony to Shakspere, he would not only fabricate proofs in support of it, but reduce the whole passage to nonsense. This would only add another, however, to the fourteen deliberate forgeries already uttered at various times in behalf of the legendary dramatist. No wonder that Dr. Ingleby finally confesses, in despair, that contemporary evidence on this point is " contemporary rumour," and that he attaches " little weight" to it!

For further elucidation of this subject, see 'The Athenæum,' Feb. 7, 1874. An intelligent writer, himself a Shaksperean, there contends that the two who took offence were Marlowe and Nash. It is certain, he says, that "Shakespeare was not one of them."

IX. The theory of composite authorship can alone account for the wide diversity of talents exhibited in the plays.

The objections to the above are twofold : —

1. It has no external evidence, direct or circumstantial, in its favor.

The difficulty of believing that one man could have written the plays and been restrained by prudential considerations from acknowledging them, even with the concession that he had other and, in his own opinion, higher claims to fame, is very great; but it vanishes in the light of this composite theory. That so important a secret should have been shared on equal terms by several persons, and no hint of it escape in any direction, while then, as now, every friend had a friend, and every friend's friend had a friend, is simply incredible.

2. The theory is inconsistent with the unique character of the plays.

The Shake-spearean "gait and movement," wherever it may be found, is unmistakable. Indeed, if the pages of the first folio were so many stone slabs taken from an ancient river-bed, they could not bear clearer marks of the stride of a colossus. No play in the canon is without these giant footprints.

" The stamp of a mighty genius is impressed on them all."— *Schlegel.*

"No one ever yet produced one scene conceived and expressed in the Shakespearean idiom." — *Coleridge's Table-Talk*, p. 214.

" He is not only superior in degree, but he is also different in kind. . . . We never saw a line in any modern poet that reminded us of him." — *Lowell's Among My Books*, p. 180.

" Upon the most insignificant of Shakespeare's beauties there is an impress stamped which to all the world proclaims, · I am Shakespeare's.' " — *Lessing.*

What is it, then, that the advocates of this composite theory ask us to believe? It is this: that there lived at one time, in one country and in intimate personal association, several poets, not only greater than any that lived in the world before them, and greater than any that have lived since, but so similar in literary style, in character, and in intellectual development that it is impossible to distinguish one from another in their work. Not only this, but we must also believe that these men, while exhibiting transcendent powers of genius in dramas which they published under the common pseudonym of " Shakespeare," were all of them at the same time writing

and publishing over their own names other poetical
works which James Russell Lowell declared to be in
every instance "immeasurably inferior" to those
known as "Shake-speare's." Juliet's prayer that
Romeo at his death might be cut out in little stars
and

"make the face of heaven so fine
That all the world will be in love with night,"

was an extravagant hyperbole; but what shall we
say of those who, out of "Shake-speare," would
create blazing suns?

*X. Shakspere's life furnishes the key to the writings that
bear his name.*

Critics who take this view simply hug their chains
to keep them from clanking. Coleridge, Emerson,
Schlegel, Whipple, Hallam, Furness, all substantially
agree that (in the language of one of them) the life
of William Shakspere and the writings ascribed to
him cannot be brought "within a planetary space of
each other." Professor Swing was convinced that
Shakspere must, at least, "have kept a poet."

If we come to particulars, the case is even worse.
Everybody admits that in or about the year 1600 a
change came over the dramatist's spirit. He then
sought, as Professor Dowden remarks, to "appre-
hend life adequately." He fell "into the shadow of
some of the deep mysteries of human existence."
"Somehow," a new relation "between his soul and
the dark and terrible forces of the world" began to
exist. How can this be explained from anything in

the life of the man Shakspere? How can we account, consistently with what we know of him, for this sudden and stupendous sweep of mind from Falstaff and Romeo to ' Othello,' [1] ' Macbeth,' and ' Lear'? " Shakspere had by this time," we are told, " mastered the world from a practical point of view; he was a prosperous and wealthy man." Yes, he was buying houses and lands, bringing suits against debtors, scheming for a title, and preparing to settle down for the remainder of his days in a town where but few of his prospective neighbors could read or write, where there were no books, and where his domestic surroundings would be fetid watercourses, stable refuse, mud-walls, and piggeries. Without ambition for anything higher or better, with no calamity of any kind to disturb the easy current of his thoughts, it is simply inconceivable that he could at that time have taken the new departure which Professor Dowden ascribes to him.[2] It is only in the "whine

[1] " The tragedy of 'Othello,' Plato's records of the last scenes of the career of Socrates, and Isaac Walton's Life of George Herbert are the most pathetic of human compositions." — *William Wordsworth*.

[2] Our friends on the other side have not overlooked this difficulty ; with what success they have met it, the following, perhaps the best adventure of the kind, may show. We beg to assure our readers that it was not intended as a caricature : —

" There were outward causes and reasons enough ; . . . He was doomed to look on, while that on which he had spent all his mental energy was profaned and blackened by rude hands ; he was doomed to see genuine poetry, and with it *the deep seriousness of the Christian view of life*, banished from the age. It was, therefore, but natural that he should have had misgivings, *lest his name and all his labors would be soon forgotten*, perhaps, forever. . . . Well, then, might the tone of his mind have sunk into the harsh dissonance which he seems to have labored to embody in his last works, in order to shake it off from his

of poets," says James Russell Lowell, that the " outward world was cold to him."

Turning now to Bacon, all difficulty vanishes.
To him life had suddenly become very dark. The
execution, however merited, of Essex, his old friend,
gave him a terrible shock; he had some fears of
assassination on account of it. It caused the death
of his only brother, Anthony, his " comfort," between
whom and himself existed the tenderest affection.
His mother had recently become violently insane.

The great object of his life, the reform of philosophy, seemed now even more remote from him than
ever. To use his own words, uttered a little while
before, he was indifferent whether God or Her Majesty called him.

" Here we see that agony and conflict which Professor Dowden so eloquently describes; here is the cry of anguish which
is echoed in Hamlet's strife with destiny, and in Lear's wild
wail of unutterable pain. If Professor Dowden had been able
to search in this direction for the original of the portrait which
he draws of the mind and art of Shakespeare, how would his
deepest speculations have been more than justified! What new
and profound and precious comments would he have made
could he have brought his glorious conjectures into this historic
environment! It is almost shocking, it is inexpressibly humiliating, to see his attempts to establish a *rapport* for them with

own bosom.' [Italics our own.] — *Ulrici's Shakespeare's Dramatic
Art*, p. 244.

The same critic finds, also, in the dissipations and frivolous excesses
which, according to tradition, marked Shakspere's youth, and which
finally drove him out of Stratford, matter for a sage reflection : —

" How often may we thus trace the guiding finger of God in the
errors of individuals, and the consequences to which they lead ! " —
Ibid., p. 74.

" Zeal without knowledge," is Mr. Lowell's comment on Ulrici's
book.

the vulgar, hollow mask of a life which is all that research can possibly find in the Stratford personality." — *Robert M. Theobald, Baconiana,* I. p. 63.

XI. The author of the plays was a great genius, not to be judged by ordinary standards, or under the common limitations of human nature.

Genius has no known antecedents; a man possessing it always takes the world by surprise. For this reason, the ancients were prone to regard genius, not as the natural resultant of qualities combined with infinite variations under the laws of heredity, but as something specially conferred upon favored individuals from a higher source.[1]

In modern times this view has become obsolete. What is merely wonderful (that is, unexplainable) has ceased to be miraculous. No one now pretends that Cæsar, or Plato, or any other highly endowed member of our race, was more than human. The old superstition still lingers, however, in a mild form around Shakspere. And no wonder; for what is displayed in his reputed writings and what we know of his life are so utterly at variance that, as Ralph Waldo Emerson declared, the twain cannot be united by a marriage ceremony. Nothing but a bolt from heaven could fuse them together.

" Nobody believes any longer that immediate inspiration is possible in modern times, and yet everybody seems to take it

---

[1] The number of progenitors that have contributed to make every man what he is, within the space of twenty generations only, or about six hundred years, exceeds a million. The individual variations in character and endowment are therefore almost infinite.

for granted of this one man, Shakespeare." — *Lowell's Among My Books*, p. 201.

But even this fanatical conception of "Shake-speare" is inadequate. It fails to account for the learning embedded in the plays, — learning so vast, so multifarious, and often so technically exact that twenty-four different occupations in life have in turn been assigned to the dramatist.

XII. Among Bacon's known works we find some fragments of verse which show him utterly wanting in the fine frenzy of the poet.

Bacon's acknowledged poetry, it is safe to say, would not have made him immortal. We know that he wrote a sonnet to the Queen, but, unless it be included in the "Shake-speare" collection, it is lost. Two years before he died, and while incapacitated by illness for good work, he paraphrased a few of the Psalms, which he afterward published, and which would seem to be at first sight only so many nails driven into the coffin of his poetic aspirations. It is manifestly unfair, however, to judge of his capabilities in this line by a sick-bed effort. He was necessarily hampered, too, by the restrictions that always attend the transplanting of an exotic in full bloom, lest the little tendrils of speech that give the flower its beauty and fragrance be broken. The president of a New England college once made a similar adventure with the Psalms; but when the book appeared, the author's friends bought up the entire edition, and suppressed it.

The following are two of the Psalms in Bacon's

version, — the two that represent, perhaps, the opposite extremes of merit among the seven: —

Psalm CIV.

Father and King of pow'rs, both high and low,
Whose sounding fame all creatures serve to blow,
My soul shall with the rest strike up thy praise,
And carol of thy works and wondrous ways.
But who can blaze thy beauties, Lord, aright?
They turn the brittle beams of mortal sight.
Upon thy head thou wear'st a glorious crown,
All set with virtues polish'd with renown;
Thence round about a silver veil doth fall
Of crystal light, mother of colors all.

The compass heav'n, smooth without grain or fold,
All set with spangs of glitt'ring stars untold,
And strip'd with golden beams of power unpent,
Is raised up for a removing tent.
Vaulted and archèd are his chamber beams
Upon the seas, the waters, and the streams.
The clouds as chariots swift do scour the sky,
The stormy winds upon their wings do fly;
His angels spirits are, that wait his will,
As flames of fire his anger they fulfil.

. . . .

Nor is it earth alone exalts thy name,
But seas and streams likewise do spread the same.
The rolling seas unto the lot doth fall
Of beasts innumerable, great and small;
There do the stately ships plough up the floods,
The greater navies look like walking woods.
The fishes there far voyages do make,
To divers shores their journey they do take.
There thou hast set the great Leviathan,
That makes the seas to seethe like boiling pan.

All these do ask of thee their meat to live,
Which in due season thou to them dost give.
Ope then thy hand, and then they have good fare:
Shut thou thy hand, and then they troubled are.

PSALM XC.

O Lord, thou art our home, to whom we fly,
   And so hast always been from age to age;
Before the hills did intercept the eye,
   Or that the frame was up of earthly stage;
One God thou wert, and art, and still shalt be;
The line of time, it doth not measure thee.

.   .   .   .

Teach us, O Lord, to number well our days,
   Thereby our hearts to wisdom to apply;
For that which guides man best in all his ways
   Is meditation of mortality.
This bubble light, this vapor of our breath,
Teach us to consecrate to hour of death.

Return unto us, Lord, and balance now,
   With days of joy, our days of misery;
Help us right soon, our knees to thee to bow,
   Depending wholly on thy clemency.
Then shall thy servants, both with heart and voice,
All the days of their life in thee rejoice.

Begin thy work, O Lord, in this our age,
   Show it unto thy servants that now live;
But to our children raise it many a stage,
   That all the world to thee may glory give.
Our handy-work, likewise, as fruitful tree,
Let it, O Lord, bless'd, not blasted, be.

"It is not safe to judge of his [Bacon's] poetical powers by
his paraphrase of the Psalms, which was written, just as Mil-

ton's paraphrase was written, in what is to-day the purest doggerel. But that these versions were so written purposely, in
order that the meanest intellects might commit them to memory
and sing them, no one at all familiar with the times can doubt
for a moment. If there is any degree in doggerel, Milton's
verses are the most ridiculous." — *Appleton Morgan.*

Milton was a Christian scholar, as well as a great
poet. No man ever lived better fitted than he was,
it would seem, to reproduce to our ears the devout
strains of Hebrew melody. For purposes of comparison we give, also, two of his Psalms out of the nineteen paraphrases which he attempted, as follows : —

PSALM VII.

Lord, my God, to Thee I fly,
  Save me and secure me under
Thy protection while I cry ;
  Lest as a lion (and no wonder)
  He haste to tear my soul asunder,
Tearing, and no rescue nigh.

.   .   .   .

God is a just judge and severe,
  And God is every day offended.
If the unjust will not forbear,
  His sword he whets, His bow hath bended
  Already, and for him intended
The tools of death, that waits him near.

(His arrows purposely made He
  For them that persecute.) Behold,
He travails big with vanity :
  Trouble he hath conceived of old
  As in a womb; and from that mould
Hath at length brought forth a lie.

He digged a pit, and delved it deep,
  And fell into the pit he made :
His mischief, that due course doth keep
  Turns on his head; and his ill trade
  Of violence will, undelayed,
Fall on his crown with ruin steep.

Then will I Jehovah's praise
According to his justice raise,
And sing the name and deity
Of Jehovah, the Most High."

PSALM VIII.

O Jehovah, our Lord, how wondrous great
  And glorious is Thy name thro' all the earth !
So as above the heavens Thy praise to set
  Out of the tender mouths of latest birth.

Out of the mouths of babes and sucklings Thou
  Hast founded strength, because of all thy foes :
To stint the enemy, and slack the avenger's brow,
  That bend his rage Thy providence to oppose.

.   .   .   .

Fowl of the heavens, and fish that thro' the wet
  Sea paths in shoals do slide, and know no dearth ;
O Jehovah, our Lord, how wondrous great
  And glorious is Thy name thro' all the earth.

We think our readers will agree with us that honors are at least easy between these distinguished
translators.

To find doggerel, however, we need not travel beyond the record in this literary suit. There are
astonishing specimens of it in " Shake-speare," even

in plays which are admitted by every one to be his
own from beginning to end. Richard Grant White
(who prided himself on the title which he had acquired as " Shakespeare's Scholar ") says of a passage
in ' King Lear ' : —

> " It is hardly more than a succession of almost trite moral
> reflections put in a sententious form, and written in verse as
> weak, as constrained, and as formal as that of a French
> tragedy."

We quote from Mr. White, also, in reference to another play of undoubtedly Shake-spearean origin : —

> " Although as a whole, ' A Midsummer Night's Dream ' is
> the most exquisite, the daintiest, and most fanciful creation
> that exists in poetry, and abounds in passages worthy even of
> Shakespeare in his full maturity, it also contains whole scenes
> which are hardly worthy of his 'prentice hand, and which yet
> seem to bear unmistakable marks of his unmistakable pen.   It
> is difficult to believe that such lines as —

> > ' Do not say so, Lysander ; say not so.
> > What though he love your Hermia ?   Lord, what though ? '

> were written by Shakespeare."

Think of the gems in this same wonderful drama,
— gems

> " That on the stretched forefinger of all time
> Sparkle forever,"

and then, by the side of them, of such a speech as this :

> " When at your hands did I deserve this scorn ?
> Is 't not enough, is 't not enough, young man,
> That I did never, no, nor never can,
> Deserve a sweet look from Demetrius' eye ? "

The truth is, Bacon's version of the Psalms is an essential part of our case; it explains what would otherwise have been inexplicable in "Shake-speare." The author of the plays, as Mr. White observes, was not always writing 'Hamlet.'[1]

> "It must be owned that, with all these great excellences, he [Shakespeare] has almost as great defects; and that, as he has certainly written better, so he has perhaps written worse, than any other." — *Pope.*

Fortunately, we have a specimen of Bacon's poetry for which we need not apologize. This is also a translation; but being in the precincts of profane literature, it justified a freer hand. We give it entire, as follows: —

> "The world 's a bubble, and the life of man
> Less than a span;
> In his conception wretched, from the womb
> So to the tomb;

[1] Wordsworth's 'Ode on Intimations of Immortality in Childhood' is, without doubt, the finest production of its kind in our language. Mr. Emerson pronounced it the "high-water mark" of the nineteenth century. Among other works of the same author, we find a poem of fifty pages, composed in 1798, and kept in manuscript for more than twenty years, subject to frequent revision, and intended, as the preface informs us, for a permanent place in the world's literature. When it finally appeared, Byron demanded to know whether such trash could evade contempt. Sir Walter Scott accused the author of "crawling on all fours." Indeed, we know of nothing in the whole range of English verse more dismally trivial than this poem, unless we may consider it redeemed by the amazing implication in one stanza that the planet Mars has a ruddy hue because the people who inhabit it are red-haired. In the Ode we have the sublimity of genius; its degradation in "Peter Bell." Petrarch has given us the finest hymn and the most wretched sonnet in the world.

Cursed from his cradle, and brought up to years
    With cares and fears ;
Who, then, to frail mortality shall trust
But limns the water, or but writes in dust.

" Yet whilst with sorrow here we live oppressed,
    What life is best ?
Courts are only superficial schools,
    To dandle fools.
The rural parts are turned into a den
    Of savage men :
And where 's the city from foul vice so free
But may be termed the worst of all the three ?

" Domestic cares afflict the husband's bed,
    Or pain his head.
Those that live single take it for a curse,
    Or do things worse.
Some would have children ; those that have them moan,
    Or wish them gone.
What is it, then, to have or have no wife,
But single thraldom, or a double strife ?

" Our own affections still at home to please
    Is a disease ;
To cross the seas to any foreign soil,
    Perils and toil.
Wars with their noise affright us ; when they cease,
    We 're worse in peace.
What then remains, but that we still should cry
Not to be born, or, being born, to die ? "

It is not known when the above was written. We
find it for the first time in a volume of Greek epi-
grams, published in 1629, three years after Bacon's
death, and ascribed to him on good authority. All
that is claimed for it is a high degree of skill in versi-
fication, — the opportunity not admitting a flight of

genius. The original is a dull, placid stream flowing through a meadow, — not a cataract from a mountain height.

" The merit of the original consists almost entirely in its compactness, there being no special felicity in the expression, or music in the metre. In the English, compactness is not aimed at, and a tone of plaintive melody is imparted, which is due chiefly to the metrical arrangement, and has something very pathetic in it to my ear." — *Bacon's Works* (Spedding), VII. 271.

We have seen that Bacon declared himself a "concealed poet" (p. 85); that he wrote a sonnet to Queen Elizabeth (p. 159); that he was probably author of another sonnet, which Florio commended as written by one who "loved better to be a poet than to be counted so" (p. 86); also, that John Aubrey, Milton's friend, pronounced Bacon "a good poet, but concealed" (p. 85). Edmund Howes, a contemporary, brings us another testimonial to the same general effect, for he reckoned Bacon among the poets then living, assigning him the eighth, and "Shake-speare" the thirteenth, place in the list. In a book published in 1645, and supposed to be by the eminent poet, George Withers, also a contemporary, an account is given of a great assize held on Mount Parnassus. In this assembly Apollo sits at the summit; but next to him, as chancellor of Parnassus, is placed Francis Bacon. Edmund Spenser appears as clerk.

But this is not all. Bacon himself once admitted, in the freedom of his private correspondence, that he was no stranger on these poetic heights. It was in

1595, at the very time when the "Shake-speare"
plays were coming out at the rate of two a year. It
was also immediately after Bacon had started his
famous scrap-book, in which so many turns of expression, appropriate only to dialogue, are noted,
and in which also we find that curious reference to
" law at Twickenham for the merry tales," — Twickenham being then his frequent place of abode.[1]

The Earl of Essex had been for several months
using his efforts to secure for Bacon an office under
the government, but with so many disappointments
that Bacon finally turned his own attention to something else, — perhaps to secure ready money, or
" quick revenue," as he called it, of which he was
then in pressing need, — for he wrote to the Earl as
follows : —

"I am neither much in appetite [for the office] nor much in
hope: for, as to the appetite, the waters of Parnassus are not
like the waters of the Spaw, that give a stomach, but rather they
quench appetites and desires."[2]

" Parnassus, a mountain in Central Greece, in mythology
sacred to the muses. The Delphian sanctuary of Apollo was
on its slope, and from between its twin summit peaks flows the
fountain of Castalia, the waters of which were imputed to impart the virtue of poetic inspiration." — *Century Dictionary.*

[1] The first entry was made in the Promus in December, 1594.
We have several letters written by Bacon in 1595, closing with the
words, "from my lodge at Twicknam."

[2] How far Essex' knowledge extended in this direction we do not
know; but we do know that, even if it covered the early dramas, it
would not have been considered by him of much importance; for,
with the exception of ' Hamlet ' in its first draft, and ' Romeo and
Juliet,' none of the great Tragedies had been written at the time of
his death. We must not measure the magnitude of the secret, as it
then was, by our present conceptions of it.

To get the full force of these facts, however, we must study Bacon's prose, which the critics, before the shadow of this controversy fell upon and chilled them, thus described : —

" In this band of scholars, dreamers, and inquirers appears the most comprehensive, sensitive, originative of the minds of the age, Francis Bacon ; a great and luminous intellect, one of the finest of this poetic progeny." — *Taine.*

" Like the poets, he peoples nature with instincts and desires ; attributes to bodies an actual voracity ; to the atmosphere, a thirst for light, sounds, odors, vapors, which it drinks in ; to metals, a sort of haste to be incorporated with acids." — *Ibid.*

" He thought in the manner of artists and poets, and spake in the manner of prophets and seers." — *Ibid.*

" His abilities were a clear confutation of two vulgar errors : first, that judgment, wit, fancy, and memory cannot conveniently be in conjunction in the same person ; whereas, our knight was a rich cabinet, filled with all four, besides a golden key to open it." — *Thomas Fuller's Worthies.*

" Abilities which commonly go single in other men are all conjoined in him." — *Dr. Rawley* (Bacon's chaplain).

" All his literary works are instinct with poetry in the wider sense of the term. Sometimes it is seen in a beautiful simile or a felicitous phrase ; sometimes in a touch of pathos. More often in the rhythmical cadence of a sentence which clings to the memory as only poetry can." — *A. F. Blaisdell.*

" In his style there is the same quality which is applauded in Shakespeare, — a combination of the intellectual and the imaginative, the closest reasoning in the boldest metaphor." — *Shaw.*

" The utmost splendor of imagery." — *Mackintosh.*

" Like unto Shakespeare, he takes good note of any deficiency of syllabic pulsations, and imparts the value of but one syllable to the dissyllables *heaven, many, even, goeth ;* and to *glittering* and *chariot* but the value of two, precisely as Shakespeare would." — *Prof. J. W. Tavener.*

" The style is quaint, original, abounding in allusions and

witticisms, and rich, even to gorgeousness, with piled-up analogies and metaphors." — *Encyc. Brit.*

" It is as an inspired seer, the prose-poet of modern science, that I reverence Lord Bacon." — *Sir Alexander Grant.*

" Few poets deal in finer imagery than is to be found in Bacon. . . . His prose is poetry." — *Lord Campbell.*

" Lord Bacon was a poet. His language has a sweet and majestic rhythm which satisfies the sense, no less than the almost superhuman wisdom of his philosophy satisfies the intellect. It is a strain which distends, and then bursts the circumference of the reader's mind, and pours itself forth with it into the universal element with which it has perpetual sympathy.

" Plato exhibits the rare union of close and subtle logic with the Pythian enthusiasm of poetry, melted by the splendor and harmony of his periods, which hurry the persuasion onward as in a breathless career. His language is that of an immortal spirit rather than of a man. Lord Bacon is, perhaps, the only writer who, in these particulars, can be compared with him." [1] — *Shelley.*

" Much of Bacon's life was passed in a visionary world, amidst things as strange as any that are described in the Arabian Tales." — *Macaulay.*

" The little volume of Bacon's 'Essays' exhibit, not only more strength of mind, more true philosophy, but more originality, more fancy, more imagination, than all the volumes of Plato." — *Walter Savage Landor.*

" We seldom fail to meet in his pages with some broad generalization, some color of fancy, some apt classical reference or startling epigram. No other man ever so illumined a mass of technical details with the light of genius." — *Nichol's Francis Bacon : His Life and Philosophy.*

---

[1] Our attention was called to this remarkable testimony of the poet Shelley by Mr. R. M. Theobald, who makes the following comment: "The truth is, that while the critics have their eye on the Baconian theory, they call Bacon prosy, unimaginative, and incapable of poetry. When they sincerely describe him, they one and all assign to him Shakespearean attributes ; so that, if you cull the eulogies passed on Bacon, you have a portrait of the author of Shakespeare."

" Bacon's anticipations [in physical science] are like those of the ' Fairy Queen ' about the stars, — flights of an imagination almost as unique in prose as Shakespeare's in verse." — *Nichol's Francis Bacon : His Life and Philosophy*, Part II. p. 193.

" It is his imagination which gives such splendor and attractiveness to his writings, clothing his thoughts in purple and gold, and making them move in majestic cadences." — *Whipple's Literature of the Age of Elizabeth*, p. 301.

" His superb rhetoric is the poetry of physical science. The humblest laborer in that field feels, in reading Bacon, that he himself is one of a band of heroes, wielding weapons mightier than those of Achilles or Agamemnon, engaged in a siege nobler than that of Troy." — *Ibid.*, p. 323.

" We have only to open ' The Advancement of Learning ' to see how the Attic bees clustered above the cradle of the new philosophy. Poetry pervaded the thoughts, it inspired the similes, it hymned in the majestic sentences of the wisest of mankind." — *E. Bulwer Lytton.*

" He seems to have written his essays with the pen of Shakespeare." — *Alexander Smith.*

" I infer from this sample that Bacon had all the natural faculties which a poet wants, — a fine ear for metre, a fine feeling for imaginative effect in words, and a vein of poetic passion." — *Spedding.*

It is admitted, then, that Bacon was at least a prose poet. No man ever caught more quickly or aptly the resemblances of things, or had a finer ear for the melody of speech. His metaphors trooped, as it were, to the sound of music. Professor Tavener compares his cadences to the swinging of a pendulum beating seconds. We know he was abnormally sensitive to the moods of nature, for he had fainting spells at every eclipse of the moon. We know he had a passion for the drama, shown by the part he took in devising stage performances before the Court, and in the revels at Gray's Inn. We know, also, he had an inexhaustible fund of humor, that poured from his tongue with the ripple of laughing waters, and needed only the constraints of a written dialogue to tumble and foam.

" The truth is that Bacon was not without the fine frenzy of the poet. . . . Had his genius taken the ordinary direction, I have little doubt that it would have carried him to a place among the great poets." — *Spedding's Life of Bacon.*

XIII. Bacon's want of natural sympathy, as shown in his treatment of Essex, fails to satisfy our ideal, derived from the dramas themselves, of their great author ; for the world has bestowed upon Shakespeare not only its reverence but its love.

It cannot be denied that the author of the plays possessed a heart of the most tender sensibilities. Like the tides of the ocean, his sympathies were " poured round all," penetrating every bay, creek, and river of human experience. The voyager o'er the mighty current of his thought always feels embarked on the bosom of the unbounded deep. It is not enough, therefore, that Bacon was a man of lofty aims; that he devoted his great powers with tireless assiduity to the interests of mankind; was he also of that rare type of character that, with greatness of intellect, glows and scintillates at every touch of feeling?

This brings us to a most important test, the personality of Lord Bacon himself. Time has scarcely dimmed his figure; we know him almost as intimately as though he were walking our streets. We see him gathering violets in his garden, stringing

pearls of thought in his essays, swaying the House
of Commons with his eloquence, holding the scales
of justice in the courts, marking the trend of social
progress in his histories, and breaking the chains
that had bound the human intellect from the days
of Aristotle. His mind and heart were in touch
with every interest of mankind. He was poet, orator,
naturalist, physician, historian, essayist, philosopher,
statesman, and judge. No man ever more completely
filled the ideal of the Roman poet : —

" Homo sum ; humani nihil a me alienum puto."

" The leading peculiarity of Bacon's literary style is its sym-
pathetic nature." — *Abbott's Life of Bacon.*

" Love of mankind with Bacon is not merely the noblest
feeling, but the highest reason ; a rich and mellow spirit of
humanity.
" Perhaps the finest sentence in his writings, certainly the one
which best indicates the essential feeling of his soul as he
regarded human misery and ignorance, occurs in his description
of one of the fathers of Solomon's House. ' His countenance,'
he says, ' was as the countenance of one who pities men.' " —
E. P. Whipple.

" The small, fine mind of Labruyère had not a more delicate
tact than the large intellect of Bacon. His understanding resembled the tent which the fairy Parabanon gave to Prince
Ahmed. Fold it, and it seemed a toy in the hand of a lady ;
spread it, and the armies of powerful sultans might repose
beneath its shade." — *Macaulay's Essay on Bacon.*

" A soft voice, a laughing lip, a melting heart, made him
hosts of friends. No child could resist the spell of his sweet
speech, of his tender smile, of his grace without study, his
frankness without guile." — *Hepworth Dixon's Personal History of Lord Bacon.* p. 8.

"All his pores lie open to external nature; birds and flowers delight his eye; his pulse beats quick at the sight of a fine horse, a ship in full sail, a soft sweep of country; everything holy, innocent, and gay acts on his spirits like wine on a strong man's blood. Joyous, helpful, swift to do good, slow to think evil, he leaves on every one who meets him a sense of friendliness, of peace and power. The serenity of his spirit keeps his intellect bright, his affections warm." — *Hepworth Dixon's Personal History of Lord Bacon*, p. 15.

He is accused of ingratitude toward his friend Essex, first, because he appeared against the accused at the trial; and, secondly, because by superior tactics he was the means of insuring conviction.

On the first point, it is sufficient to say that Bacon was present as an officer of the crown at the express command of the Queen, having repeatedly forewarned the Earl of the result of his evil courses, and duly notified him that, on any breach of the peace, he himself would support the government. The Earl richly merited his fate. His rebellion was one of the meanest, most causeless, and most contemptible that has stained the history of England.

"The rigor with which Bacon has been censured for acting on the fall of his patron Essex as advocate of the complainant, and afterwards laying before the public an account of the process justifying the Queen, appears unjust to any one who considers how Bacon exerted himself to bring the Earl to reason and the Queen to mercy, and at the same time, in virtue of his office, he was bound to perform whatever duty the Queen laid upon him." — *Erdman's History of Philosophy*, I. 669 [1890].

On the second, Bacon was prominent in the proceedings because his mental stature made him prominent. As well attempt to force an oak back into its acorn as to bring Francis Bacon on any occasion down to the level of ordinary men.[1]

In the matter of the bribes, he suffered for the sins of society. So far as he was personally culpable, it is manifest from his subsequent demeanor that chronic carelessness in money matters, and not any guile, was at the bottom of the difficulty. To be sure, he was lax in the administration of his household affairs; but so was William Pitt. Pitt could rule an empire, but not his own servants. Bacon conquered nearly every known realm of human knowledge, but he never invaded the dominions of his cook.[2] An imperial contempt for money dominated both. Venality is the very last sin in the whole catalogue of human frailties of which either of these two men could have been guilty, but it is the one with which Bacon has been most persistently, cruelly, mercilessly charged for more than two hundred and

---

[1] That he felt himself compromised in public estimation, we know very well, for in a letter to the Queen he says : —

"My life has been threatened and my name libelled."

We find the same lament in one of the "Shake-speare sonnets, as follows : —

"Then hate me if thou wilt; if ever, now,
Now while the world is bent my deeds to cross,
Join with the spite of fortune."   *Sonnet XC.*

In another sonnet, the author expresses fear of assassination, anticipating

"The coward conquest of a wretch's knife."   *LXX.*

[2] It was the waste of the servants' hall that impoverished them. In Pitt's case, the quantity of butcher's meat charged in the bills was nine hundred weight a week. The consumption of poultry, of fish, of tea, was in proportion. After his death, all parties in the House of Commons readily concurred in voting forty thousand pounds to satisfy the demands of his creditors.

fifty years. A Roman Emperor once indulged in the amiable wish that his people had but one head, that he might cut it off at a blow. He was a monster; but we confess we find some sad evidences of kinship with him in our own heart when we think of the calumniators of Francis Bacon, though the most brilliant essayist that has ever adorned the literary annals of England and the kindest of men be the chief offender. The fact that Bacon, with all his great abilities, known and acknowledged, could get no lucrative office under the government until he was forty-six years old, and that he was finally retired to private life by the machinations of men notoriously venal, may be taken as presumptive proof of the independence of his character, as well as of his rectitude and his honor.[1]

[1] Bacon's want of attention to his personal finances (a not uncommon failing in great men, due to a sort of instinct that the matter is beneath them) caused his mother the most lively concern. She even interfered at one time to protect him from his own servants. Spedding tells the following story in point : —

"In the year 1655, a bookseller's boy heard some gentlemen talking in his master's shop; one of them, a gray-headed man, was describing a scene which he had himself witnessed at Gorhambury. He had gone to see the lord chancellor on business, who received him in his study, and, having occasion to go out, left him there for a while alone. 'Whilst his lordship was gone, there comes,' he said, 'into the study one of his lordship's gentlemen, and opens my lord's chest of drawers wherein his money was, takes it out in handfuls, fills his pockets, and goes away without saying a word to me. He was no sooner gone but comes another gentleman, opens the same drawers, fills both his pockets with money, and goes away as the former did without speaking a word.' Bacon, being told, when he came back, what had passed in his absence, merely shook his head, and all he said was, 'Sir, I cannot help myself.' "

Montagu relates another incident to the same effect : —

One day, immediately after Bacon's removal from the chancellor-

" No one mistook the condemnation for a moral censure ; no one treated Lord St. Albans as a convicted judge. The House of Commons had refused to adopt the charge of bribery ; the House of Lords had rejected the attempt to brand him with a personal shame ; and society treated the event as one of those struggles for place which may hurt a man's fortunes without hurting his fame. The most noble and most generous men, the best scholars, the most pious clergymen, gathered round him in his adversity, more loving, more observant, more reverential, than they had ever been in his days of splendor.

" Such was also the reading of these transactions by the most eminent of foreign ministers and travellers. The French Marquis d'Effiat, the Spanish Conde de Gondomar, expressed for him in his fallen fortunes the most exalted veneration. That the judges on the bench, that the members of both Houses of Parliament, even those who, at Buckingham's bidding, had passed against him that abominable sentence, concurred with the most eminent of their contemporaries, native and alien, is apparent in the failure of every attempt made to disturb his judicial decisions. These efforts failed because there was no injustice to overthrow, and there was no injustice to overthrow because there had been no corruption on the bench." — *Dixon.*

" As regards the official impeachment of Bacon, if taken alone, it may establish no more against him than that, amid

ship, he happened to enter his servants' hall while the servants were at dinner. On their rising to receive him, he said : " Be seated ; your rise has been my fall."

" His principal fault seems to have been the excess of that virtue which covers a multitude of sins. This betrayed him to so great an indulgence toward his servants, who made a corrupt use of it, that it stripped him of all those riches and honors which a long series of merits had heaped upon him." — *Addison.*

" Bacon was generous, easy, good-natured, and naturally just ; but he had the misfortune to be beset by domestic harpies, who, in a manner, farmed out his office." — *Guthrie.*

One writer says that "three of his lordship's servants kept their coaches, and some kept race-horses."

the multitude of engrossing calls upon his mind, he did not extricate himself from the meshes of a practice full of danger and of mischief, but in which the dividing lines of absolute right and wrong had not then been sharply marked.   Hapless is he on whose head the world discharges the vials of its angry virtue ; and such is commonly the case with the last and detected usufructuary of a golden abuse which has outlived its time.   In such cases posterity may safely exercise its royal prerogative of mercy." — *W. E. Gladstone.*

History presents to us no more pathetic figure than that of the great Lord Bacon beseeching in vain that he might not be compelled to close his career, a career of unexampled usefulness to the world, in ignominy.   The authorities that condemned him remind us of a pack of wolves turning upon and rending a wounded comrade.

" I could never bring myself to condole with the great man after his fall, knowing as I did that no accident could do harm to his virtue, but rather make it manifest.   He seemed to me ever by his work one of the greatest men and most worthy of admiration." — *Ben Jonson.*

" A memorable example to all of virtue, kindness, peaceableness, and patience." — *Peter Boener (Bacon's Apothecary).*

" A friend unalterable to his friends." — *Sir Toby Matthew.*

" A man most sweet in his conversation and ways." — *Ibid.*

" It is not his greatness that I admire, but his virtue." — *Ibid.*

" May your good word grace it and defend it, which is able to add a charm to the greatest and least matters." — *Beaumont's Dedication of a Masque to Bacon,* 1612.

" I have been induced to think that, if ever there were a beam of knowledge derived from God upon any man in these modern times, it was upon him." — *Dr. Rawley.*

ST. MICHAEL'S CHURCH.

For my burial, I desire it may be in St. Michael's Church, near St. Albans : there was my mother buried. — FRANCIS BACON.

" He struck all men with an awful reverence." — *Francis Osborne.*

The above are testimonials of Bacon's friends, of members of his household, and of literary competitors.

" They bear witness to the stainlessness of his private life, his perfect temperance, self-possession, modest demeanor, and his innocent pleasantry." — *Nichol's Life of Bacon*, p. 202.

" Retiring, nervous, sensitive, unconventional, modest." — *Spedding's Life of Bacon.*

" Those who saw him nearest in his private life give him the best character." — *Ibid.*

" At the same time that we find him prostrating himself before the great mercy-seat and humbled under afflictions which lay heavy upon him, we see him supported by the sense of his dignity, his zeal, his devotion, and his love of mankind." — *Joseph Addison.*

" Beloved for the courteousness and humanity of his behavior." — *David Hume.*

" Bacon declared that his works were rather the fruit of his time than of his genius. — *Gervinus.*

" He attached little importance to himself. . . . No correct notion can be formed of Bacon's character till this suspicion of self-conceit is scattered to the winds." — *Abbott's Life of Bacon.*

" Weighted by the magnificence of his character." — *Ibid.*

" Of an unusually sweet temper and amiable disposition." — *Encyc. Brit., art. Bacon.*

" He was generous, open-hearted, affectionate, peculiarly sensitive to kindness, and equally forgetful of injuries." — *Fowler's Life of Bacon.*

" All who were great and good loved and honored him." — *Aubrey.*

"His acquaintance was eagerly sought by the eminent of every class, and by all whom an ingenuous love of excellence prompted to render homage to the greatest general philosopher, the first orator, and the finest writer of his age." — *Aikin's Court of James I.*, II. p. 201.

"He hungered, as for food, to rule and bless mankind." — *Hepworth Dixon.*

"One with whom the whole purpose of living was to do great things to enlighten and elevate his race, to enrich it with new powers, to lay up in store for all ages to come a source of blessings which should never fail." — *Church's Life of Bacon*, p. 1.

"His greatness, his splendid genius, his magnificent ideas, his enthusiasm for truth, his passion to be the benefactor of his kind, the charm that made him loved by good and worthy friends, amiable, courteous, patient, delightful as a companion, ready to take any trouble." — *Ibid.*

"It is not too much to say that in temper, in honesty, in labor, in humility, in reverence, he was the most perfect example that the world has yet seen of the student of nature." — *Ibid.*

"The name which he aspired to, and for which he was willing to renounce his own, was 'Benefactor of Mankind.'" — *Delia Bacon.*

"He stands almost alone in literature, a vast, dispassionate intellect, in which the sentiment of philanthropy has been refined and purified into the subtle essence of thought.
"It may be questioned whether Shakespeare himself could thoroughly have appreciated Bacon's intellectual character. He could have delineated Bacon in everything but in that peculiar philanthropy of the mind, that spiritual benignity, that belief in man and confidence in the future," which are Bacon's distinguishing characteristics. — *Whipple's Age of Elizabeth.*

"A deep sense of the misery of mankind is visible throughout his writings. . . . He has often been called a utilitarian, not because he loved truth less than others, but because he loved men more." — *Ellis's Preface to Bacon's Philosophical Works.*

"From the day of his death, his fame has been constantly and steadily progressive; and we have no doubt that his name will be named with reverence to the latest ages, and to the remotest ends of the civilized world." — *Macaulay.*

V.

COINCIDENCES.

LET us now mark certain coincidences in the composition of the plays with the well-known habits and studies of Francis Bacon.

a. A prominent characteristic of Bacon, in his literary work, was the frequency with which he invented new words. It is safe to say that no other writer, with possibly one exception, ever did so much to diversify and enrich our English tongue. We find many of these words actually taking shape before our eyes in the Promus, — perhaps a bright nucleus from the Latin in a nebulous envelope of prefixes and suffixes, preparing to shine forever with a radiance of its own in human speech.

"A dictionary of the English language might be compiled from Bacon's works alone." — *Dr. Johnson.*

In this business of word-building, however, Bacon had a strange double. It is estimated that Shakespeare gave three thousand new words, inclusive of old words with new meanings, to our language. And these additions were also, like Bacon's, derived chiefly from the Latin. They were such as only a scholar could impose upon the king's vernacular.

" Shakespeare's plays show forty per cent of romance or Latin words." — *Richard Grant White.*

" He did not scruple even to naturalize words for his own use from foreign springs, such as *exsufflicate* and *derascinate;* or to coin a word whenever the concurring reasons of sense and verse invited it, as in *fedary, intrinse, intrinsicate, insist-ure,* and various others." — *Hudson.*

" The vocabulary of Shakespeare became more than double that of any other writer in the English language. Craik esti-mates it at twenty-one thousand words, without counting in-flectional forms, while that of Milton was but seven thousand. . . . English speech, as well as literature, owes more to him than to any other man." — *Clark's Elements of the English Language,* p. 134.

" Shakespeare displayed a greater variety of expression than probably any other writer in any language." — *Müller's Science of Language,* 1st Series, p. 267.

Mr. Hallam calls attention to Shake-speare's fond-ness for words used in their primitive meanings. He sees a student's instinct in this attempt, contrary in many cases to popular usage, to keep our language true to its Latin roots. He gives the following examples: —

" Things base and vile, holding no *quantity* (value).
Rivers that have overborne their *continents* (the *continente ripa* of Horace).
Imagination all *compact.*
Something of great *constancy* (consistency).
Sweet Pyramus *translated* there.
The law of Athens which by no means we may *extenuate.*"

We append a few additional examples under this head: —

Expedient, a word derived from the Latin *expedire,* mean-ing to disentangle the foot, and thus to hasten. Shake-speare always uses it in this sense, as we do its cognate *expeditious*, never applying it to anything merely suitable or advantageous.

Extravagant, from *extra*, beyond, outside of; and *vagare*, to wander. Shake-speare applies the word to vagrancy, or straying beyond limits, only, as in 'Hamlet' : —

> "The extravagant and erring spirit hies
> To his confine." — I. 1.

Probation. This word ordinarily means a period of trial. In Shake-speare, however, it means proof, from *probare*, to prove.

> "The present object made probation."
> *Hamlet*, I. 1.

Discourse of reason, from *discurrere*, to run backward and forward between objects, as in *ratiocination*. A strict Latinism.

Contraction, from *contrahere* (p. p. *contractus*), to draw together; that is, to come to an agreement, as in marriage, not merely to lessen or condense.

> " O, such a deed
> As from the body of contraction plucks
> The very soul."
> *Ibid.*, III. 4.

A lust of the blood and a *permission of the will*. This is Shake-speare's definition of love. What is meant by " permission of the will " ?   Permission is from *permittere*, to send away completely, as when one, utterly banishing his will, gives full rein to a passion. This meaning of the word has never taken root in English.

Assume.

> " Assume a virtue if you have it not."
> *Ibid.*

Does Shake-speare instruct us to be hypocrites?   No, though all the commentators so agree. *Assume* is from *ad-sumere*, to take to. to acquire.

> Acquire a habit. if you have it not.

The context. especially in the folio. plainly points to the acquisition of virtue by studied formation of habits.

Modesty.

" An excellent play ; well digested in the scenes ; set down with as much modesty as cunning." — *Hamlet,* II. 2.

From *modestia,* meaning fitness of things, a whole in which all the parts have their proper places and proportions. Cicero uses the word in his ' De Officiis,' but feels compelled to explain it to the Romans themselves. He says it is equivalent to the Greek *εὐταξία.* In this sense it is so apt and so recondite that Dr. Furness, in his Variorum edition of ' Hamlet,' asks significantly, in italics, " Did not Sh. understand Latin ? "

These examples might be multiplied by the thousand. They are found as plentifully in the early plays as in the later ones.

b. Bacon had also a wonderful variety at his command in manner of writing. In this respect he was a literary chameleon. Abbott says of him : —

" His style varied almost as much as his handwriting; but it was influenced more by the subject-matter than by youth or old age. Few men have shown equal versatility in adapting their language to the slightest change of circumstance and purpose. His style depended upon whether he was addressing a king, or a great nobleman, or a philosopher, or a friend; whether he was composing a state paper, magnifying the prerogative, extolling truth, discussing studies, exhorting a judge, sending a New Year's present, or sounding a trumpet to prepare the way for the kingdom of man over nature."

It does not follow, of course, that because he had this "wonderful ductility," as Hallam calls it, therefore he wrote the plays. The converse of the proposition, however, is worth noting, viz., without it he would have been disqualified for the task.

We must venture one step farther. Did Bacon possess among his numerous varieties of style that which characterizes Shakespeare? On this point it may as well be conceded at once that the essays by which he is best known are, for purposes of this comparison, the least useful of his writings. They are *sui generis*, so closely packed with thought that they can be compared only to cannon-balls. Indeed, we should as soon think of comparing the chopped sea of the English Channel to the long, rolling swell of the Atlantic.

To face the difficulty squarely, and on terms most rigorous for Bacon, we give an example of each, as follows: —

FROM BACON.

" Prosperity is the blessing of the Old Testament ; adversity is the blessing of the New, which carrieth the greater benediction and the clearer revelation of God's favor. Yet, even in the Old Testament, if you listen to David's harp, you shall hear as many hearse-like airs as carols. And the pencil of the Holy Ghost hath labored more in describing the afflictions of Job than the felicities of Solomon. Prosperity is not without many fears and distastes, and adversity is not without many comforts and hopes. We see in needle-works and embroideries it is more pleasing to have a lively work upon a sad and solemn ground, than to have a dark and melancholy work upon a lightsome ground. Judge, therefore, of the pleasure of the heart by the pleasure of the eye. Certainly, virtue is like precious odors when they are incensed or crushed. For prosperity doth best discover vice. but adversity doth best discover virtue." — *Essay on Adversity.*

FROM SHAKESPEARE.

" Ay, but to die. and go we know not where ;
  To lie in cold obstruction, and to rot ;

This sensible warm motion to become
A kneaded clod; and the delighted spirit
To bathe in fiery floods, or to reside
In thrilling regions of thick-ribbed ice;
To be imprisoned in the viewless winds,
And blown with restless violence round about
The pendant world."
Measure for Measure, III. 1.

The passage quoted above from Bacon, written shortly before his death, is the one Macaulay selected to show that Bacon's writings, contrary to the ordinary course of things, grew more ornate and fanciful as he grew older. " With him," we are told, " the fruit came first, and remained till the last; the blossoms did not appear till late." Why is it that we cannot approach " Shake-speare," even on the side of Bacon, without encountering a miracle? Why do we always enter a land of enchantment, — the last refuge of dryads and fairies, where Nature's laws are suspended, where we have harvests without seed, fruits without buds or flowers, and a brilliant old age, preceded by a dull and passionless youth?

" Nature is always true to herself; her order was not reversed in the case of Bacon. The bud, the blossom, the fruit came in their proper and accustomed procedure. But what if, like a prudent husbandman, Bacon sent each to its appropriate market, — the flowers of his fancy to the wits and players, the fruits of his judgment to the sages and statesmen of his age ? " — *Smith's Bacon and Shakespeare*, p. 22.

In his ' History of Henry VII.,' Bacon adopted a style quite the reverse of that of the ' Essays.' It is here that he steps off the tripod. His sentences no longer keep step, as though on parade; they have a free-and-easy, almost frolicsome gait, unparalleled in the whole range of historical literature.

One cannot read a page of this work without meeting such specimens as these: —

" Empson would have cut another chop [of money] out of him if the king had not died in the instant."

" Perkin, for a perfume before him as he went, caused to be published a proclamation."

" One might know afar off where the owl was by the flight of birds."

" The King began to find where the shoe did wring him."

" It was an odious thing to the people of England to have a king brought in to them on the shoulders of Irish and Dutch."

" None could hold the book so well to prompt and instruct this stage-play as she could."

" She was to him as Juno was to Æneas, stirring both heaven and hell to do him mischief."

" Then did the King secretly sow Hydra's teeth."

" The marriage halted upon both feet."

" Their snowball did not gather as it went."

" The news came blazing and thundering over into England."

" From what coast should this blazing star appear? "

" With the first grain of incense that was sacrificed upon the altar of peace, Perkin was smoked away."

Bacon's letters give us still another style of composition, less severe than that of the Essays, and more elegant than that of the History. They contain jewels fit to sparkle with " Shake-speare's " —

" On the stretched forefinger of all time."

We have space for but one or two examples: —

" It may be you will do posterity good if, out of the carcass of dead and rotten greatness, as out of Samson's lion, there be honey gathered for future times."

How beautifully Bacon refers to the Hellenic myths as —

"Gentle whispers, which from more ancient traditions came at length into the flutes and trumpets of the Greeks."

It is characteristic of a very full mind that the flow of its thoughts is often disturbed by its own impetuosity. Ideas come from it with a rush. The well is bored so deep, and into a reservoir so vast, that the bursting current defies restraint. This was the case both with Bacon and with the author of the plays.

"Bacon's mind, with its fulness and eagerness of thought, was at all times apt to outrun his powers of grammatical expression." — *Spedding.*

"The tangled, elliptical, helter-skelter sentences into which the impetuous imagination of Shakespeare sometimes hurries him." — *Christopher North.*

Bacon's literary style had one peculiar feature, apparent under all its phrases, which we must not omit to mention, viz., a tendency to run into triple forms of expression. "There is no end to these forms in the writings of Bacon," says Professor Tavener. They beat upon the ear with a rhythm as unmistakable as that of the resounding sea. Indeed, we might have the courage to pronounce them, on the part of our author, an easily-besetting sin, *were they not equally conspicuous in* "*Shake-speare*," as the following examples will show : —

FROM BACON.

"Studies serve for delight, for ornament, and for ability."

"To spend too much time on studies is sloth : to use them too much for ornament is affectation ; to make judgment wholly by their rules is the humor of a scholar."

" Crafty men condemn studies, simple men admire them, and wise men use them."

" Read not to contradict and confute, nor to believe and take for granted, nor to find talk and discourse."

" Some books are to be tasted, others to be swallowed, and some few to be chewed and digested."

" Reading maketh a full man, conference a ready man, and writing an exact man."

" If a man write little, he had need have a great memory: if he confer little, he had need have a present wit; and if he read little, he had need have much cunning."

" A man cannot speak to his own son but as a father, to his wife but as a husband, and to his enemy but on terms."

" Give ear to precept, to laws, to religion."

" Judges ought to be more learned than witty, more reverent than plausible, and more advised than confident."

" Some ants carry corn, and some their young, and some go empty."

" They cloud the mind, they lose friends, they check with business."

" They dispose kings to tyranny, husbands to jealousy, wise men to irresolution."

" A man's nature is best perceived in privateness, for there is no affectation; in passion, for that putteth a man out of his precepts; and in a new case of experiment, for there custom leaveth him."

" Young men are fitter to invent than to judge, fitter for execution than for counsel, and fitter for new projects than for settled business."

" Nature is often hidden, sometimes overcome, seldom extinguished."

" It is heaven upon earth to have a man's mind move in Charity, rest in Providence, and turn upon the poles of Truth."

FROM "SHAKE-SPEARE."

"Some are born great, some achieve greatness, and some have greatness thrust upon them."

" It would be argument for a week, laughter for a month, and a good jest forever."

" One draught above heat makes him a fool, a second mads him, and a third drowns him."

" 'T is slander,
Whose edge is sharper than the sword, whose tongue
Outvenoms all the worms of Nile, whose breath
Rides on the posting winds."

" This peace is nothing but to rust iron, increase tailors, and breed ballad-makers."

" Vengeance is in my heart, death in my hand,
Blood and revenge are hammering in my head."

" Had I power, I should
Pour the sweet milk of concord into Hell,
Uproar the universal peace, confound
All unity on Earth."

" Alas, poor Romeo! he is already dead! stabbed with a white wench's black eye ; run through the ear with a love-song ; the very pin of his heart cleft with the blind bow-boy's butt-shaft."

" To be now a sensible man, by and by a fool, and presently a beast."

" Ay, but, lady,
That policy may either last so long,
Or feed upon such nice and waterish diet,
Or breed itself so out of circumstance,
That I, being absent and my place supplied,
My General will forget my love and service."

" 'T was mine, 't is his, and has been slave to thousands."

" This chair shall be my state, this dagger my sceptre, and this cushion my crown."

" She is a woman, therefore may be woo'd ;
She is a woman, therefore may be won ;
She is Lavinia, therefore must be loved."

" The birds chant melody on every bush ;
The snake lies rolled in the cheerful sun ;
The green leaves quiver with the cooling wind."

" Methinks she 's too low for a high praise, too brown for a fair praise, and too little for a great praise."

" She says she will die if he love her not, and she will die ere she make her love known, and she will die if he woo her."

" They say the lady is fair ; 't is a truth, I can bear them witness ; and virtuous ; 't is so, I cannot reprove it ; and wise, but for loving me."

" Fairest Cordelia, thou art most rich, being poor ;
Most choice, forsaken ; and most loved, despised."

" Like lean, sterile and bare land, manured, husbanded, and tilled."

" Her father loved me ; oft invited me ;
Still questioned me the story of my life,
From year to year — the battles, sieges, fortunes,
That I have passed."

" Sweet Hero ! she is wronged, she is slandered, she is undone."

" I have marked
A thousand blushing apparitions
To start into her face ; a thousand innocent shames,
In angel whiteness, bear away those blushes ;
And in her eye there hath appeared a fire,
To burn the errors that these Princes hold
Against her maiden truth."

" Who is here so base that would be a bondman ? If any, speak, for him have I offended. Who is here so rude that would not be a Roman ? If any, speak, for him have I offended. Who is here so vile that will not love his country ? If any, speak, for him have I offended."

The two authors balanced their sentences on the same scales.[1]

---

[1] For an admirable discussion on this subject, see Donnelly's Great Cryptogram, p. 481 *et seq.*

It is in minor peculiarities, however, that we find the strongest evidence of identity. A detective always looks at what is unaffected and unconscious in a man in order to unmask him. The shaping of a letter of the alphabet in handwriting, some little trick in gait or voice, an intonation that dates from childhood, these are clews compared with which elaborate tropes and figures of speech are of small account for our purpose. We want those sources of light which cannot be hid under a bushel. Dr. Theobald has found one in Bacon's use of the phrase " I cannot tell." It is an instance of *suppressio veri*, not, however, with intent to deceive, but to give the thought a greater spring. For example, referring to certain factious rulings in a lower court by Justice Coke, Bacon says, —

" Wherein your Lordships may have heard a great rattle, and a noise of *præmunire;* and " — here he adds, as a sort of contemptuous snapper to his lash — " I cannot tell what."

He simply means that the subject is beneath further notice.

Again, alluding to a possible war with Spain, he wonders that the people of England " should think of nothing but reckonings, and audits, and *meum*, and *tuum*, and I cannot tell what."

On another occasion he pours out his contempt upon the duelling code, on the ground that it rests upon absurd conceits; that is, as he says, " upon what's before-hand and what's behind-hand, and I cannot tell what."

So in a letter to the King, who was importuned to

grant further concessions in a matter in which the petitioners had already broken their agreements with him, Bacon recalls what had already been promised, — " lawful and settled trades, full manufactures, merchandise of all natures, poll money or brotherhood money, and I cannot tell what."

In all these cases, it will be observed, Bacon makes a pretence of ignorance for a purpose, — a rhetorical stratagem common enough of itself, but never before or since in English literature persistently associated with the words " I cannot tell." That is to say, never before or since with one exception, — in " Shake-speare." The author of the plays is constantly indulging in this same idiosyncrasy. For instance, in the 'Merchant of Venice' Shylock narrates the story of Jacob outwitting Laban in the breeding of sheep, and Antonio asks him, —

> " Was this inserted to make interest good,
> Or is your gold and silver ewes and rams? "

Shylock replies, —

> " I cannot tell; I make it breed as fast." — I. 3.

In Richard III. Queen Elizabeth demands to know why Gloster hates her and her family, and receives this answer: —

> " I cannot tell; the world is grown so bad
> That wrens may prey where eagles dare not perch.
> Since every Jack becomes a gentleman,
> There 's many a gentle person made a Jack."

That he could tell, and in fact did tell, her rejoinder implies: —

" Come, come, we know your meaning, brother Gloster ;
You envy my advancement, and my friends." — I. 3.

In 'Macbeth' a messenger brings to the King
news of a bloody battle in which Macbeth and
Banquo were victorious. He says of these war-
riors : —

" I must report they were
As cannons overcharg'd with double cracks ;
So they doubly redoubled strokes upon the foe ;
Except they meant to bathe in reeking wounds,
Or memorize another golgotha,
I cannot tell." — I. 2.

Not to multiply these examples further, as we
might easily do, we close with one which, though
negative in its character, is for that very reason the
stronger and more conclusive in our favor. Our
readers must thank Dr. Theobald, a singularly acute
and brilliant as well as fair-minded critic, for it.
We quote him as follows : —

" In 3 'Henry VI.' the Earl of Warwick gives a vivid description of the battle between the forces led by himself for the
King and those led by the Queen and Clifford on behalf of the
young prince. This passage appears in the original version,
' The Second Part of the Contention,' published in 1595, thus, —

' We at St. Albans met,
Our battle joined, and both sides fiercely fought.
But whether 't was the coldness of the King
(He looked full gently on his warlike Queen)
That robbed my soldiers of their heated spleen,
Or whether 't was report of her success,
Or more than common fear of Clifford's rigour,
Who thunders to his captains blood and death,
I cannot tell,' —

and then he proceeds to tell how shamefully they were defeated.

" Now in this case, *I cannot tell* is not used, as in the others which I have quoted, to express a mock perplexity; there is no counterfeit, no poetic lie here ; the doubt is real. The speaker really is unable, amongst all the possible causes of defeat, to select the true one, or to say how many causes were combined. Precisely the same passage occurs in 3 ' Henry VI.' [published in 1623], but now *I cannot tell* is changed into *I cannot judge,* evidently because, in the poet's mind, the words *I cannot tell* are applicable only to fantastic cases, not to cases of real and sincere suspense of judgment."

In further elucidation of this matter of style, the following examples are taken promiscuously from the two sets of works. We challenge our readers to draw the lines of cleavage between them, without assistance from the foot-notes : —

" It is a wonderful thing to see the semblable coherence of his men's spirits and his own : they, by observing him, do bear themselves like foolish justices ; he, by conversing with them, is turned into a justice-like serving man. . . . It is certain that either wise bearing or ignorant carriage is caught, as men take diseases, one of another ; therefore, let men take heed of their company." [1]

" Contrary is it with hypocrites and impostors, for they, in the church and before the people, set themselves on fire, and are carried, as it were, out of themselves, and becoming as men inspired with holy furies, they set heaven and earth together." [2]

" Suspicions among thoughts are like bats among birds, they ever fly by twilight." [3]

" Novelty is only in request: and it is as dangerous to be aged in any kind of course, as it is virtuous to be constant in any undertaking. There is scarce truth enough alive to make societies secure, but security enough to make fellowship accursed." [4]

[1] 2 Henry IV., V. 2.
[2] Bacon's Med. Sac.
[3] Essay on Suspicion.
[4] Measure for Measure.

" Extreme self-lovers will set a man's house afire to roast their own eggs.[1]

" I have thought that some of Nature's journeymen had made men, and not made them well ; they imitated humanity so abominably." [2]

" Faces are but a gallery of pictures, and talk but a tinkling cymbal, where there is no love." [3]

" False of heart, light of ear, bloody of hand ; hog in sloth, fox in stealth, wolf in greediness, dog in madness, lion in prey." [4]

" Weight in gold, iron in hardness, the whale in size, the dog in smell, the flame of gunpowder in rapid extension." [5]

" Men must learn that in this theatre of man's life it is reserved only for God and the angels to be lookers-on." [6]

" The King slept out the sobs of his subjects, until he was awakened with the thunderbolt of a parliament." [7]

" Or as a watch by night that course doth keep,
And goes and comes, unwares to them that sleep." [8]

" Or like the deadly bullet of a gun,
His meaning struck her, ere his words begun." [9]

" As smoke from Ætna that in fire consumes,
Or that which from dischargèd cannon fumes." [10]

" As if between them twain there was no strife,
But that life lived in death, and death in life." [10]

" As a tale told which sometimes men attend,
And sometimes not, our life steals to an end." [8]

" As silly, jeering idiots are with kings,
For sportive words and uttering foolish things." [10]

---

[1] Advancement of Learning.
[2] Hamlet.
[3] Essay on Friendship.
[4] King Lear.
[5] Novum Organum.
[6] Advancement of Learning.
[7] On Spanish Grievances.
[8] Translation of the Psalms.
[9] Venus and Adonis.
[10] Lucrece.

" For as the sun is daily new and old,
　So is my love still telling what is told." [1]

" And so in spite of death thou dost survive,
　In that thy likeness still is left alive." [2]

" So that with present griefs and future fears,
　Our eyes burst forth into a stream of tears." [3]

" Thus hast thou hanged our life on brittle pins,
　To let us know it will not bear our sins." [3]

" Like soldiers when their Captain once doth yield,
　They basely fly and dare not stay the field." [2]

" But like a stormy day, now wind, now rain,
　Sighs dry her cheeks, tears make them wet again." [2]

" Or as the grass which cannot term obtain,
　To see the summer come about again." [3]

" Or call it Winter, which, being full of care,
　Makes Summer's welcome thrice more wish'd, more rare." [1]

For the above metrical selections we are indebted to the Rev. L. C. Manchester, of Lowell, Massachusetts, who favors us with the following explanatory note : —

" As one interested in the discussion now going on, I send you some couplets from Bacon's verse and some from Shakespeare's, having a certain likeness to each other, but differing from the parallelisms already noted. Possibly similar likeness may appear between any other two writers in the same metre ; if not, I do not know what these prove, unless we are to think that Shakespeare wrote the ' Translation of the Psalms.' That veracious book, ' Shakespeare's True Life,' informs us that Shakespeare was often Bacon's guest at Twickenham, and was quite ' thick ' with him. Can it be that some day, when the two were together, lying perhaps in the shade of those cedars pictured in the book, the player gave the Translation to the philosopher ? The work is, for the most part, as much inferior to

---

[1] Sonnets.　　　　　　　　[2] Venus and Adonis.
[3] Translation of the Psalms.

Bacon's noblest poetical prose as it is to the grand verse of the
Shakespeare drama.

"The likeness of the stanzas in question is in the concluding
couplets, — Bacon's being in the metre of 'Venus and Adonis.'
It is not in sentiment or in word, but in the ending of the
stanzas with couplets of the same kind, either developing a
simile already introduced, or introducing a new one to complete the thought. ('Rhymes knit together and clinched by
a couplet.' — *T. Watts*, quoted by Tyler, in his edition of the
Sonnets.)"

Walter's 'True Life of Shakespeare,' referred to by
Mr. Manchester, reminds us of Lucian's 'Veracious
History;' but the author lacks the candor of the
Greek, who announced that *his* book contained "not
a single truth from beginning to end." It is a pity
that Mr. Walter did not redeem his otherwise admirable work with a similar confession. There would
have been, then, one truth in each.

After all, it must be remembered that the true
poetic spirit implies a state of being very different
from that in which the mind is ordinarily exercised.
The poet is a man "beside himself," — almost a
second personality. Instances are known where the
connection between them seemed for a time utterly
lost to consciousness. Goethe's fine instinct suspected depths of meaning, in the second part of
'Faust,' which he himself had not fathomed. A
certain orator is said to have sometimes wondered,
in the midst of his highest flights, what strange
power had taken possession of his mental faculties.
Thackeray often laughed aloud at some unexpected
joke cracked under his pen. Mrs. Stowe was be-
sought by her publishers to limit her great story to
one volume; she replied that the story was writing
itself, and could not be controlled. When Trollope

was asked why he had permitted Lily Dale to "marry that man," — "Confound it," was the reply, "she would do it!" It is manifestly impossible rightly to estimate a man under a condition like this from what we know of him under another and totally different condition. We are in the same predicament with Archimedes, who wanted to move the earth with his lever, but could find no place for the fulcrum. A garden viewed scientifically in the light of genera and species, with all its plants catalogued according to seasons of blooming, has little to remind us of one in which we notice only the perfumes and hues of the flowers; but the same person may be our guide in both. The seers of our race are those who look upon life with two angles of vision.

c. Bacon's versatility appeared also in his intercourse with persons of various trades and occupations in life. He had a distinct reputation among his contemporaries for ability to meet men on their own ground, and converse with them in the special dialects to which they were accustomed in their pursuits. He was especially a complete master of the language of the farm. His writings are full of homely provincialisms, such as the following: "Money is like muck, not good except it be spread;"[1] "If you leave

---

[1] Bacon further explained this function of money thus:—

"When it lies in a heap, it gives but a stench; when it is spread upon the ground, it is the cause of much fruit." — *Apothegm.*

So we find Cominius praising Coriolanus for looking

> "Upon things precious, as they were
> The common muck of the world."
> *Coriolanus,* II. 2.

"The annotators of 'Coriolanus' have not yet found out what Shakespeare meant by the 'common muck of the world.'" — *R. M. Theobald.*

your staddles too thick, you will never have clean underbrush;" and many of the flowers of rhetoric with which his works are bestrewed strike their roots down into hawking and hunting.

" I have heard him entertain a country lord in the proper terms relating to hawks and dogs; and at another time outcant a London chirurgeon." — *Francis Osborn.*

" In conversation he [Bacon] could assume the most different characters, and speak the language proper to each, with a facility that was perfectly natural, — a happy versatility of genius which all men wish to arrive at, but which one or two only in an age are seen to possess." — *Mallett's Life of Bacon.*

d. In another and (for our purpose) very important quality of mind the two authors were also conspicuously alike; they had each a wonderful faculty for detecting remote and subtle analogies. It is this that constitutes the essence of wit, and confers upon a writer the rare gift of enlivening, as we go along with him, even a worn and dusty highway with delightful vistas on either side.

" In wit, if by wit be meant the power of perceiving analogies between things which appear to have nothing in common, Bacon never had an equal, not even Cowley, not even the author of Hudibras. . . . Occasionally it obtained the mastery over all his other faculties, and led him into absurdities into which no dull man could have fallen." — *Macaulay's Essay on Bacon.*

" Shakespeare perceived a thousand distant and singular relations between the objects which met his view. He had the habit of that learned subtlety which sees and assimilates everything, and leaves no hint of resemblances unnoticed." — *Prof. Guizot.*

e. Again, Bacon was constantly making alterations in his writings, even after they had gone to press. Of the ten essays which he published in 1597, nearly all were more or less changed and enlarged for the edition of 1612. Those of 1612, including the ten before mentioned, were again enlarged for publication in 1625. It seems to have been almost impossible for an essay to get to the types a second time without passing through his reforming hand, — in one instance actually losing identity in the transition.

This was precisely the fate of the plays. Some of them underwent complete transformation between the quartos and the folio, becoming practically new compositions, and, what is very singular, working away from the requirements of the stage into forms more purely artistic and literary.

" Every change in the text of 'Hamlet' has impaired its fitness for the stage, and increased its value for the closet in exact and perfect proportion. . . . Scene by scene, line for line, stroke upon stroke, and touch after touch, he went over the old ground again, to make it worthy of himself and his future students." — *Swinburne.*

If there were two workshops, it is certain that one set of rules governed both.

f. Bacon's sense of humor, as has already been shown, was phenomenal, and yet it had one curb which it always obeyed.

In his ' Essay of Discourse ' he lays down the rule, among others, that religion should never be the butt of a jest. Accordingly, it is impossible to find, in all the wild, rollicking fun of the plays, even a flippancy at the expense of the Church.

g. In the local dialect of the University of Cambridge, students do not live, but " keep," in rooms.[1]

[1] Dickens's Dictionary of Oxford and Cambridge.

In 'Titus Andronicus,' one of the earliest of the plays, written, as White suggests, when the author's mind was fresh from academic pursuits, we find the following: —

"Knock at his study, where, they say, he keeps."

Bacon was educated at Cambridge.

h. The two authors had the same friends. Bacon and the Earl of Southampton were fellow-lodgers at Gray's Inn, and for many years devoted adherents of Essex. The "Shake-speare" poems, 'Venus and Adonis' and 'Lucrece,' were dedicated to Southampton. The Earls of Pembroke and Montgomery were shareholders with Bacon in Lord Somer's ill-fated expedition to America; to them was dedicated the first collected edition of the plays. They had also the same enemies. Lord Cobham was one of the leaders of the party opposed to Essex. Among his ancestors was the noble martyr, Sir John Oldcastle, whose name the dramatist, with his usual deference to the established order of things, at first adopted for the character of Falstaff. Even after he had made the change, he could not forbear the following sly hit at the family: —

"*Fal.* And is not my host of the tavern a most sweet wench ?
"*Prince Hen.* As the honey of Hybla, my old lord of the castle." — 1 *Henry IV.*, I. 2.

The head of the party to which Cobham belonged was Lord Burleigh. He was Bacon's uncle, but Bacon had private as well as public reasons for opposing him. Burleigh stood, like an angel with a drawn sword, directly in the path to that which Bacon coveted, — an office under the Queen. No entreaty, either of Bacon or of Bacon's mother, — except perhaps on one occasion, when he acted perfunctorily, — could move him. Even Anthony Bacon, who had spent thirteen years in France and Italy in voluntary service to the government without compensation, and who on his return home applied to Burleigh for some position that would enable him in a measure to recoup his depleted fortune, received only "fair words," — such words, according to his own account of them, as make "fools fair," but bitterly disappointing from one who had turned the applicant's "ten years' harvest into his own barn without a half-penny charge." It was this treatment that finally drove the two brothers into the ranks of the opposition, and at one time, to our amazement, involved them in attempts to displace Burleigh, and install Essex as chief counsellor of the crown.

The Lord Treasurer's conduct in this matter is easily accounted for without the usual imputation of unworthy motives: he did not appreciate his nephews. He saw in them, and particularly in Francis, qualities of mind which he deemed unsuited for official life. Himself a dull, plodding, unimaginative, thoroughly practical and conscientious statesman, he had no sympathy with any one who, as Essex said of Francis, was full of "poetic conceits." He contrived not to pay Spenser a small pension which the government had voted, evidently thinking, with Plato, that in a good commonwealth there is no place for a poet.

Bacon, as author of 'Hamlet,' took his revenge. He satirized his uncle as Polonius. What could represent the old minister's prolixity better than the following: —

> " *Pol.* My liege and madam, to expostulate
> What majesty should be, what duty is,
> Why day is day, night night, and time is time,
> Were nothing but to waste night, day and time.
> Therefore, since brevity is the soul of wit,
> And tediousness the limbs and outward flourishes,
> I will be brief.   Your noble son is mad.
> Mad call I it ; for, to define true madness,
> What is 't but to be nothing else but mad ?
>
> .   .   .   .
>
> And now remains
> That we find out the cause of this effect,
> Or rather say, the cause of this defect;
> For this effect defective comes by cause :
> Thus it remains, and the remainder thus.
> Perpend."   *Hamlet*, II. 2.

In early life Burleigh was offered the Secretary-ship by Queen Mary, with the proviso that he must change his religion.   His answer is historic: —

> " I have been taught and am bound to serve my God first, and next my Queen."

Polonius utters the same sentiment: —

> " I hold my duty as I hold my soul,
> Both to my God, one to my gracious king."

The ten famous precepts which Lord Burleigh gave to his son Robert, departing for Paris, are replete with worldly wisdom ; but they are eclipsed by the ten still more famous ones which Polonius deliv-

ered to *his* son Laertes, also on the eve of departure
for Paris : —

1.   " Give thy thoughts no tongue,

2. Nor any unproportion'd thought his act.

3. Be thou familiar, but by no means vulgar ;

4. The friends thou hast, and their adoption tried,
Grapple them to thy soul with hooks of steel,
But do not dull thy palm with entertainment
Of each new-hatch'd, unpledg'd comrade.

5.   Beware
Of entrance to a quarrel ; but, being in,
Bear 't that th' opposed may beware of thee.

6. Give every man thy ear, but few thy voice ;

7. Take each man's censure, but reserve thy judgment.

8. Costly thy habit as thy purse can buy,
But not expressed in fancy; rich, not gaudy ;
For the apparel oft proclaims the man ;
And they in France, of the best rank and station,
Are most select and generous, chief in that.

9. Neither a borrower nor a lender be ;
For loan oft loses both itself and friend,
And borrowing dulls the edge of husbandry.

10. This above all, — to thine own self be true ;
And it must follow, as the night the day,
Thou canst not then be false to any man."

              Hamlet, I. 3.

One of the most prominent features of Burleigh's
administration was his reliance upon the help of spies
and informers. For twenty years he kept a small
army of these emissaries under his pay, hesitating at
no espionage or treachery to gain the secrets of his

enemies. "They were a vile band," says a recent writer in the Dictionary of National Biography, "the employment of which could not but bring some measure of dishonor upon their employer. Hence the shame and indelible reproach which attach themselves to Cecil's conduct of affairs, and which not all the difficulties of his position or the unexampled provocations which he endured can altogether excuse." He even forced Bishop Parker to take the confessions of a prisoner whom torture could not affect, in the disguise of a Catholic priest.

It is to this conspicuous trait in Burleigh's character that we owe the following exquisite scene : —

"*Enter* POLONIUS *and* REYNALDO.

Pol.　Give him this money, and these notes, Reynaldo.

Rey.　I will, my lord.

Pol.　You shall do marvellous wisely, good Reynaldo,
Before you visit him, to make inquiry
Of his behaviour.

Rey.　My lord, I did intend it.

Pol.　Marry, well said ; very well said.　Look you, sir,
Inquire me first what Dansksters are in Paris :
And how, and who ; what means, and where they keep ;
What company, at what expense ; and finding,
By this encompassment and drift of question,
That they do know my son, come you more nearer
Than your particular demands will touch it.
Take you, as 't were, some distant knowledge of him ;
As thus, — 'I know his father, and his friends,
And, in part, him : ' — do you mark this, Reynaldo ?

Rey.　Ay, very well, my lord.

Pol.　'And, in part, him ; but,' you may say, 'not well ;
But, if 't be he I mean, he 's very wild,
Addicted so and so ; ' and there put on him
What forgeries you please ; marry, none so rank

As may dishonor him ; take heed of that ;
But, sir, such wanton, wild, and usual slips
As are companions noted and most known
To youth and liberty.

Rey.   As gaming, my lord.

Pol. Ay, or drinking, fencing, swearing, quarrelling,
Drabbing ; — you may go so far.

Rey. My lord, that would dishonor him.

Pol. 'Faith, no ; as you may season it in the charge.
You must not put another scandal on him,
That he is open to incontinency ;
That's not my meaning ; but breathe his faults so
    quaintly,
That they may seem the taints of liberty ;
The flash and out-break of a fierce mind ;
A savageness in unreclaimed blood,
Of general assault.

Rey.   But, good my lord, —

Pol. Wherefore should you do this ?

Rey.   Ay, my lord,
I would know that.

Pol.   Marry, sir, here's my drift ;
And, I believe, it is a fetch of warrant.
You, laying these slight sullies on my son,
As 't were a thing a little soil'd i' th' working,
Mark you,
Your party in converse, him you would sound,
Having ever seen in the prenominate crimes
The youth you breathe of guilty, be assur'd,
He closes with you in this consequence :
' Good sir,' or so ; or ' friend,' or ' gentleman,' —
According to the phrase, or the addition,
Of man and country.

Rey.   Very good, my lord.

Pol. And then, sir, does he this, — he does —
What was I about to say ?   [By the Mass] I was
About to say something ; where did I leave ?

Rey. At ' closes in the consequence,'
As ' friend or so,' and ' gentleman.'

Pol. At 'closes in the consequence,' — ay, marry,
He closes with you thus ; — ' I know the gentleman ;
I saw him yesterday, or t' other day.
Or there, or then ; with such or such ; and, as you say,
There he was gaming ; there o'ertook in 's rouse ;
There falling out at tennis ; or perchance,
' I saw him enter such a house of sale ' —
Videlicet, a brothel, — or so forth. —
See you now ;
Your bait of falsehood takes this carp of truth,
And thus do we of wisdom and of reach,
With windlaces, and with assays of bias,
By indirections find directions out.
So by my former lecture and advice,
Shall you my son. You have me, have you not?
Rey. My lord, I have.
Pol.   God b' wi' you ; fare you well.
Rey. Good my lord.
Pol. Observe his inclination in yourself.
Rey. I shall, my lord.
Pol. And let him ply his music.
Rey.   Well, my lord.   [*Exit.*"

An intelligent writer in ' Notes and Queries ' (January 31, 1863) declares that " Polonius is not so much a satire as a portrait of Lord Burleigh." He adds innocently, " Shakespeare may have had some prejudices against this celebrated minister." Considering the relations that existed between Francis Bacon and his cousin Robert Cecil, and the well-known character of the latter, we doubt whether anything more comical than the foregoing scene in ' Hamlet ' can be found in the whole range of English literature.

Bacon's most implacable enemy, however, was Sir Edward Coke. The two were constant rivals for the favor of the court and for the highest honors of the profession to which they belonged. They were rivals, too, for the hand of Lady Hatton, the beautiful widow, who finally waived the eight objections which her friends urged against Coke (his seven children and himself), and gave him the preference. At one time the contention became so personal and bitter that Bacon appealed to the government for help.

In 'Twelfth Night,' we find the following portraiture of Coke, drawn by no friendly hand : —

"*Sir Toby.* Taunt him with the license of ink; if thou thou'st him thrice,[1] it shall not be amiss; and as many lies as will lie in thy sheet of paper, although the sheet were big enough for the Bed of Ware in England, set 'em down." — III. 2.

"Coke was exhibited on the stage in 'Twelfth Night' for his ill usage of Raleigh." — *Disraeli's Curiosities of Literature*, II. 531.

i. The philosopher and the dramatist were at one, also, in the ease and frequency, not to say unscrupulousness, with which they appropriated to their own use the writings of others. Bacon's audacity in this respect is unequalled in all the world's literature, unless we except " Shake-speare." Both authors lit their torches, as Rawley says of Bacon, "at every man's candles."

j. Bacon's home was at St. Albans, on the river Ver, especially interesting as the site of the ancient

---

[1] A reference to Coke's brutal speech at the trial of Sir Walter Raleigh, in which occur these words : " Thou viper ! for I thou thee, thou traitor ! " Theobald (1733) cites the passage as a proof of " Shake-speare's " detestation of Coke.

city of Verulamium. Among the local traditions of
the place, verified by old coins found in the soil, is
one respecting a king named Cymbeline, who reigned
there in the early part of the Christian era, and who
had intimate relations with Rome. The story of
Cymbeline furnished some of the incidents, even to
minute particulars, of the Shakespearean play that
bears his name.

k. Bacon was very fond of puns. He not only
handed down to posterity numerous specimens found
in his reading, but he immortalized some of his own
in the Apothegms. The Spanish Ambassador, a Jew,
happening to leave England Easter morning, paid
his parting respects to Bacon, wishing him a good
Easter. Bacon replied, wishing his friend a good
pass-over. The plays also abound in this species of
wit. A remarkable instance may be quoted from the
' Merry Wives of Windsor,' thus : —

" *Evans. Accusativo, hing, hang, hog.*
" *Quick.* Hang hog is Latin for Bacon, I warrant you." —
IV. I.

This refers to a pun perpetrated by Sir Nicholas
Bacon, father of Francis. One day a culprit, named
Hog, appealed to Judge Bacon's mercy on the ground
that they were of the same family. " Aye," replied
the Judge, " but you and I cannot be kindred except
you be hanged ; for hog is not bacon until it be well
hanged."

The appearance of this family pun in the plays is
significant.[1]

[1] " Bacon was fond, also, of speaking of his great contemporaries,
of quoting their wit and recording their sayings. In his apothegms

l. Bacon's prose works overflow with citations from classical literature. They are filled to saturation with ancient lore. This is true also of the plays. They make us breathe the very air of Greece and Rome. The following is only a partial list of the classical authors, the influence of whose writings has been traced in them: Homer, Plato, Aristotle, Sophocles, Euripides, Æschylus, Lucian, Galen, Ovid, Lucretius, Tacitus, Horace, Virgil, Plutarch, Seneca, Catullus, Livy, and Plautus, all of whom were known to Bacon. A curious instance is the following: —

> " Thy promises are like Adonis' gardens,
> That one day bloomed and fruitful were the next."
>
> 1 *Henry VI.*, I. 6.

This reference puzzled all the commentators for nearly three hundred years, — Richard Grant White declaring that " no mention of any such gardens in the classic writings of Greece or Rome is known to scholars." It has recently been found, however, in Plato's ' Phœdrus,' — a work that had not been translated into English in Shakespeare's time.

" It is the ease and naturalness with which the classical allusions are introduced to which it is the most important that we we find nearly all that is known of Raleigh's power of repartee. How came such a gatherer of wit, humors, and characters to ignore the greatest man living ? Had he a reason for this omission ? It were idle to assume that Bacon failed to see the greatness of Lear and Macbeth."— *The (London) Athenæum*, Sept. 13, 1856.

" Although Bacon quotes nearly every great writer in his works, he never quoted Shakespeare. Is it for the same reason that the author of the ' Waverley Novels ' used, as quotations for the headings of his chapters, passages from every poet but Scott ? " — *George Stronach, in Bacon Journal,* 1886.

should attend. They are not purple patches sewed on to a piece of plain homespun ; they are inwoven in the web.

" He [Farmer] leaves us at full liberty, for anything he has advanced, to regard Shakespeare as having had a mind richly furnished with the mythology and history of the times of antiquity, an intimate and inwrought acquaintance, such as perhaps few profound scholars possess." — *Hunter*.

" What kind of culture Shakespeare had is uncertain ; how much he had is disputed; that he had as much as he wanted, and of whatever kind he wanted, must be clear to whoever considers the question. Dr. Farmer has proved, in his entertaining essay,[1] that he got everything at second-hand from translations, and that where his translator blundered he loyally blundered too. But Goethe, the man of widest acquirement in modern times, did precisely the same thing." — *Lowell's Among My Books*, p. 188.

m. Bacon spent several years in study and travel on the Continent; it is said that he was meditating a tour in the East when the sudden death of his father called him home. Internal evidences make it almost absolutely certain that the author of the plays acquired his exact knowledge of Italian scenes and customs from actual residence in Italy.

" The most striking difficulty lies, perhaps, in the descriptions of foreign scenes, particularly of Italian scenes, — descriptions so numerous and so marvellously accurate that it is almost impossible to believe that they were written by a man who lived in London and Stratford, who never left this island, and who saw the world only from a stroller's booth." — *The (London) Athenæum*, Sept. 13, 1886.

" It cannot be denied that Shakespeare, in the ' Merchant of Venice,' has carefully observed and wonderfully hit the local

---

[1] In three papers, marked by his well-known learning and literary power, Dr. Maginn pierced the pedantic and inflated essay of Farmer into hopeless collapse." — *Prof. Baynes, Frazer's Magazine*, 1879.

coloring. There lies over this drama an inimitable and decidedly Italian atmosphere. Everything in it is so faithful, so fresh, and so true to nature, that in this respect the play cannot possibly be excelled.

" Portia sends her servant to Padua to fetch certain ' notes and garments,' and then meet her at the ' common ferry' trading to Venice. If Shakespeare had taken the ride himself before describing it, as Sir Walter Scott took that from Loch Vennachar to Stirling, described in the · Lady of the Lake,' the statements could not agree better.

" The ferry takes us across the ' Laguna Morta,' and up the great canal to the city, where we in spirit land at the Rialto. Shakespeare displays no less accurate knowledge of this locality than of the villas along the Brenta, as he does not confound the Isola di Rialto with the Ponte di Rialto. He knows that the ' exchange where merchants most do congregate' is upon the former." — *Elze's Essays on Shakespeare*, p. 278.

> " ' This night, methinks, is but the daylight sick ;
>   It looks a little paler; 't is a day
>   Such as the day is when the sun is hid.'
>   *Merchant of Venice*, V. 1.

" The light of the moon and stars [in Italy] is almost as yellow as the sunlight in England. . . . Two hours after sunset, on the night of the full moon, we have seen so far over the lagunes that the night seemed only a paler day, — 'a little paler.' " — *Charles Knight.*

A correspondent of the 'Baltimore Sun' writing under date of August 16, 1895, at Rome, says: —

" It seems natural that the Italians should give attention to the Shakespearean drama. Much of it has been taken from Italian sources. I am inclined to think that no less than two-thirds of the plays of Shakespeare are derived, in a more or less direct form, from Italian sources, — either renaissance Italian or ancient Roman. But not only will the student of Shakespeare discover this prominence in the works of the great poet, but the close searcher into the byways of Italian literature will discover that not only are the plots taken from Italy, but in several cases the very words are translations, more or less faithful, from Italian authors of mediocre fame.

" There is no doubt that the English poet knew Italy well, and with an observant, intimate knowledge of not only the outward aspects of the places and people, but also an intuitive knowledge which enabled him to penetrate, as it were, into their hearts and minds, and show them forth on the stage verily 'in their habit as they lived.' It is George Augustus Sala, himself the descendant of a Roman family of ancient lineage, who pointedly refers to this quality of Shakespeare's knowledge of Italy. In his 'Life and Adventures,' published a few months ago, Mr. Sala writes: 'Wandering from Milan to Mantua, and from Padua to Verona and Vicenza, there grew up in me day after day a stronger and stronger impression — an impression which has become an unalterable conviction — that Shakespeare knew every rood of ground and every building in the cities in which he had laid the scenes of the " Merchant of Venice," " The Two Gentlemen of Verona," of " Romeo and Juliet," and of " The Taming of the Shrew." Few tourists who have visited Northern Italy have escaped being pestered by ciceroni, who have offered to show them the tomb of Juliet at Verona, the shop of the apothecary at Mantua, and the Palazzo del Moro (the residence of Othello) on the Grand Canal at Venice. But it was the constant study of ostensibly petty details in Shakespeare's Italian plays that led me to the full and fast belief that he was familiar, from actual experience and observation, with the Northern Italy of his time.'

" To one who resides constantly in Italy, and is gifted with observation, the truth of this is most convincing and evident. A short time ago I visited the cities which are the chief scenes of his more prominent Italian plays, — Venice, Verona, Padua, Mantua. It was simply surprising to note how marvellously the view of the place, carefully studied, threw light on the play for which it furnished the scene. Shakespeare was evidently of the opinion of Proteus. in 'The Two Gentlemen of Verona,' 'that home-keeping youths have ever homely wits,' and undoubtedly he did extend his travel beyond the space which lies between London and Stratford-upon-Avon. I have not to account for the time in which this continental tour was accomplished, — that is the task of the biographer; but the intimate knowledge of Italian towns, manners, and customs cannot intelligently and satisfactorily be accounted for otherwise."

Professor Elze gives us, also, some curious information regarding " Shake-speare's " knowledge of Italian art, — knowledge that could have been derived, it would seem, only from personal inspection on the spot. For instance, in the ' Winter's Tale,' " Shakespeare " tells us that the statue of Hermione was the work of Giulio Romano; he dwells upon the merits of it, and of Romano's artistic qualities as a sculptor, with discriminating and enthusiastic praise.

" There is, perhaps, no description of statuary extant so admirable for its truth and beauty." — *Green's Shakespeare and the Emblem Writers*, p. 108.

But who ever heard, until recently, that Romano was a sculptor? Certainly not the Shakespearean critics, for they have almost universally assumed that this great master in the art of painting, Raphael's favorite pupil and successor, simply colored in this case the work of another artist. Such coloring was then, indeed, quite in vogue. Shakspere's bust at Stratford was treated in this manner, and continued so — with red lips, brown eyes, and auburn hair — until Mr. Malone, himself a learned critic, employed a common house-painter to cover it with a coat of white paint. Other critics, such as the editor of the ' Saturday Review ' and Mr. Andrew Lang, characterize this reference to Romano as one of "Shakespeare's" blunders.[1]

It happens, however, that Vasari, who published in 1550 a work on Italian art, and who was a contemporary and personal acquaintance of Romano, states distinctly that Romano was not only a painter, but an architect and sculptor also. The statement appears in a Latin epitaph given in the book. Vasari revised and enlarged his work for a second edition in 1568, but, curiously enough, omitted the epitaph. The first edition (which was, of course, in Italian) was never translated into a foreign tongue. It was the second edition only that became known, through translations, outside of Italy. "We now stand," says Professor Elze, "before this dilemma": Either the author of the plays had read, when he wrote the 'Winter's Tale,' a copy of Vasari in the first edition (one that had long been supplanted by another, and that has not been translated to this day), and found what nobody else found for nearly three hundred years afterwards, or he had been in Mantua and seen Romano's works.

It is hardly necessary to add that every effort to find the slightest hint of foreign travel in the life of Shakspere, though made with great persistence, has thus far signally failed.

n. Bacon's paramount aspiration was to possess and impart wisdom. He was indefatigable in his search for it, analyzing motives, and turning the light

---

[1] "The egregious blunder of calling him a sculptor." — *Saturday Review.*

For Mr. Lang's assumption to the same effect, see 'Harper's Monthly,' April, 1894, art. 'Winter's Tale.'

of his genius upon the most hidden springs of conduct. Nothing was too remote or recondite for his use. It was inevitable, then, that his mind should fall easily and naturally into those channels of thought which the "wit of one and the wisdom of many" have worn deep in human experience. The Promus fairly sparkles with proverbs. Nearly every known language appears to have been ransacked for them. From the Promus they were poured copiously into the plays. Mrs. Pott finds nearly two thousand instances in which they beautify and enrich these wonderful works.

" In Bacon's works we find a multitude of moral sayings and maxims of experience from which the most striking mottoes might be drawn for every play of Shakespeare, — aye, for every one of his principal characters, . . . testifying to a remarkable harmony in their mutual comprehension of human nature." — *Gervinus.*

" As a student of human nature Bacon is hardly yet appreciated ; his beneficent spirit and rich imagination lend sweetness and beauty to the homeliest practical wisdom.

" As well as he thought he understood [physical] nature, he understood human nature far better.

" Not the abstract qualities and powers of the human mind, but the combination of these into concrete character, interested Bacon. He regarded the machinery in motion ; the human being as he thinks, feels, and moves ; men in their relations with men."[1] — *E. P. Whipple.*

" The study of mankind occupied the largest part of his time." — *Prof. Minto's Manual of English Prose Composition,* p. 243.

" The original ten essays contain almost nothing but maxims of prudence." — *Ibid.*

" The main study of his life was how to 'work' men." — *Ibid.,* p. 254.

" He was more eminently the philosopher of human than of general nature." — *Hallam.*

---

[1] How exactly this characterization fits " Shake-speare " also !

QUEEN ELIZABETH.

o. Bacon's whole life was passed in the atmosphere of the Court. At the age of ten he was patted on the head by Queen Elizabeth, and called her "young lord keeper." When sixteen he went to Paris in the suite of the British ambassador, and lived three years in that gay capital and its vicinity, studying not only the arts of diplomacy, but all the penetralia of Court life. On his return he was freely admitted to the presence of royalty, was the friend of princes, and, filling the highest offices in the gift of the king, was elevated to the peerage. It is not surprising, therefore, that the plays, almost without exception, have their movement in the highest circles of society. The common people are kept in the background, and are referred to in terms, often bordering on contempt, that show the author to have been a man of rank. It is certain that he was familiar with Court etiquette, even to the nicest details.

"Shakespeare despised the million, and Bacon feared, with Phocion, the applause of the multitude." — *Gervinus.*

"He [Shakespeare] was a constitutional aristocrat." — *Appleton Morgan.*

"Men of birth and quality will leave the practice [of duelling] when it comes so low as barbers, surgeons, butchers, and such base mechanical persons." — *Bacon.*

"The ignorant and rude multitude." — *Ibid.*

"The rude multitude; the base vulgar." — *Shake-speare.*

p. Bacon was continually hiding his personality under disguises. One of the first acts of his public career was to invent a cipher for letter-writing. He even invented a cipher within a cipher, so that if the first should by any chance be disclosed, the other, imbedded in it, would escape detection. At one time he carried on a fictitious correspondence, intended for the eye of the queen, between his brother Anthony and the Earl of Essex, composing the letters on both sides, and referring to himself in the third person. He published one of his philosophical works under a pseudonym, and another as though it were the wisdom of the ancients stored in fables.

In Sonnet LXXVI. we find the following : —

> " Why write I still all one, ever the same,
>   And keep invention in a noted weed,
>   That every word doth almost tell my name,
>   Showing their birth and whence they did proceed ? "

Here is a plain statement that the author of this sonnet was writing under a disguise.

The same remarkable admission appears in Bacon's prayer : —

" The state and bread of the poor and oppressed have been precious in mine eyes; I have hated all cruelty and hardness of heart; I have, though in a despised weed, sought the good of all men."

The word *weed* signifies garment; particularly, as both Bacon and " Shake-speare " use it, one that disguises the wearer.[1] It will be noted that this confession

---

[1] " *Luc.*   But in what habit will you go along ?
      Jul.   Not like a woman. . . .
              Gentle Lucetta, fit me with such weeds
              As may beseem some well-reputed page."
                          Two Gentlemen of Verona, II. 7.

" This fellow . . . clad himself like a hermit, and in that weed wandered about the country, until he was discovered and taken." — *Bacon's History of Henry VII.*

reveals at once Bacon's views of the drama (already quoted) as a means of promoting public virtue, those of the people around him (who despised it), and his *incognito.*

q. Early in life, Bacon determined to make all knowledge his province. He became fired with this ambition at college, when he discovered that the authority of Aristotle, then supreme over the minds of men, was based on erroneous postulates. Accordingly he resolved, single-handed, to demolish the whole structure of philosophy as it then existed, and at least to indicate the methods by which it should be rebuilt. To accomplish this, he knew he must compass all the knowledge of his time, as the great Stagirite had done before him. How well and faithfully he fulfilled his task, let the gratitude and veneration of mankind make answer. Among the names of the five most illustrious men of all the world, Bacon's has a place, and that place at or near the head.

Of the various arts and sciences into which he pushed his investigations, we may specify the following : —

Philosophy. — Bacon has been called the father of inductive philosophy, because he, more than any other, taught the natural method of searching for truth. Before his time, men had conceived certain principles to be true, and from them had reasoned down to facts. The consequence was that facts became more or less warped to fit theories, and the discovery of new facts out of harmony with the theories a matter of regret and even of condemnation. Under this system, obviously, the world could make but slow progress.

Bacon started at the other end. The cast of his mind was distinctively synthetical. His choice of the inductive method for his investigations, a process from the particular to the general and from the general to the universal, shows the direction of his intellectual fibre. In this he simply obeyed a law of his being, as a carpenter drives his plane with the grain of the wood.[1] He had no knowledge of mathematics, a science almost purely analytic.[2] He discarded the syllogism, because it opens with a broad assumption and reasons downward. On the other hand, he had an ability, as we have already stated, to detect analogies and to combine, never surpassed, perhaps never equalled, among the children of men. In a word, his mind was phenomenally comprehensive, able to project a vast temple of science in which every department should have its appropriate space, but not to excavate to solid rock on which to lay the foundations and erect the structure. Even at this distance of time we are amazed at the mass of materials gathered together by this intellectual giant from all quarters, and lying about in great promiscuous heaps on the ground where he toiled.

Bacon's eminence as a philosopher is one of the interesting paradoxes of our time. On one point

---

[1] " With a synthetic power rarely equalled, Bacon was an indifferent analyst ; his care was not to part and prove, but to announce and harmonize." — *Nichol's Francis Bacon*, Part II. p. 194.

[2] He "was not only entirely unacquainted with geometry and algebra, but evidently insensible even of their value or their use." — *Craik's English Literature and Language*, II. 143.

only are all agreed, viz., that he is a resplendent orb in the light of which, across an interval of three centuries, every man still casts a shadow. His brightness prevents a clear definition of his disk. No two critics agree as to the nature or cause of the profound impression he has made on mankind. Their comments remind us of the inscription on a monument in Athens, " To the unknown God."[1]

Bacon himself was full of contradictions. He often violated his own precepts. He declared he was only " ringing a bell" for others, and yet he took no notice of those who, as it were, obeyed his summons. He sneered at Copernicus, and at the theory of the solar system with which that illustrious name is linked forever. He betrayed no sympathy with Galileo. He turned a deaf ear to Harvey, the discoverer of the circulation of the blood; to Gilbert, who first proclaimed the earth a magnet; to Napier, the inventor of logarithms; and to Kepler, whose formula of planetary laws imparts dignity to human nature itself. All these, with the exception of Copernicus, were his contemporaries, illustrating his own favorite methods and adding glory before his face to his own glorious age. Any estimate of Bacon into which these facts do not fit is utterly worthless.

Various notable attempts have been made to explain this anomaly. According to Baron Liebig, Bacon was an impostor; this is the Explanation Brutal. According to Spedding, he had a wonder-

---

[1] " There is something about him not fully understood or discerned, which, in spite of all curtailment of his claims in regard to one special kind of eminence or another, still leaves the sense of his eminence as strong as ever." — *Craik's English Literature and Language*, I. 613.

ful talent for detecting resemblances, but none at all for distinguishing differences; this is the Explanation Nonsensical. Dr. Draper in his 'Science and Religion' comes nearer the truth; he holds that Bacon's entire system of philosophy is "fanciful."

The only rational and consistent view is this: Bacon was, first, a poet; secondly, a philosopher. Over and above his other faculties towered the creative, — that which gave eloquence to his tongue, splendor to his style, and an exhaustless illumination to his whole being. If he sometimes failed to discern a truth close at hand in the practical affairs of life, he was like the angels before the Throne, hiding their eyes under their wings.

"A similar combination of different mental powers was at work in them; as Shakespeare was often philosophical in his profoundness, Bacon was not seldom surprised into the imagination of the poet." — *Gervinus.*

"If we look carefully into the matter, it is not on the prescribed method of Bacon that his fame was built. It was the power of divination in the man which made him great and influential. . . . He was very near discovering the law of the correlation of forces." [1] — *Ingleby's Essays,* p. 182.

"His services lay not so much in what he did himself, as in the grand impulse he gave to others." — *Prof. Minto's English Prose Composition,* p. 239.

"No man would go to Bacon's works to learn any particular science or art, any more than he would go to a twelve-inch globe in order to find his way from Kennington turnpike to

[1] History is full of instances of this same poetic divination. Ten years before Darwin's 'Origin of Species' appeared, Emerson wrote : —

> "And striving to be man, the worm
> Mounts through all the spires of form."

Clapham Common. The art which Bacon taught was the art of inventing arts." — *Macaulay's Essay on Bacon.*

" The glance with which he surveyed the intellectual universe resembled that which the archangel from the golden threshold of heaven darted down into the new creation." — *Ibid.*

" Il se saisit tellement de l'imagination, qu'il force la raison à s'incliner, et il les éblouit autant qu'il les éclaire." — *M. Remusat: Bacon, sa vie, son temps, sa philosophie, et son influence.* Paris: 1857.

" Truly it may be said both of Bacon and of Shakespeare, that equally they never argue; they decree." — *O'Connor's Hamlet's Note-Book,* p. 60.

" He was a seer, a poet, rather than a natural philosopher." — *R. M. Theobald.*

" Some of Bacon's suggested experiments on light might well be supposed to have been borrowed from Newton ; and the results at which he arrived in the investigation of heat, he sets forth in language not greatly differing from that which in modern times describes heat as a mode of motion." — *Baron Liebig, Macmillan's Mag.,* 1863.

" Bacon was the prophet of things that Newton revealed." — *Horace Walpole.*

" The change is great when in fifty years we pass from the poetical science of Bacon to the mathematical and precise science of Newton." — *Church's Life of Bacon.* p. 181.

" The *Novum Organum* is a string of aphorisms, a collection, as it were, of scientific decrees, as of an oracle who foresees the future and reveals the truth. . . . It is intuition, not reasoning." — *Taine's History of English Literature,* I. 154.

History. — Historical literature had a special charm for Bacon. His history of the reign of Henry VII. is an English classic ; his portraiture of Julius Cæsar, an epitome of one of the world's most interesting and important epochs.

Shakespeare's mind ran in the same channels. Nearly half the plays are historical, and they deal with those periods to which Bacon gave particular attention, the English Henries and the career of Rome.

" ' Where have you learned the history of England?' it was asked of the greatest statesman of the last century. Lord Chatham replied, ' In the plays of Shakespeare.' " — *Dean Stanley.*

" The marvellous accuracy, the real, substantial learning of the three Roman plays of Shakespeare, present the most complete evidence to our minds that they were the result of a profound study of the whole range of Roman history." — *Knight.*

" Where, even in Plutarch's pages, are the aristocratic republican tone and the tough muscularity of mind, which characterized the Romans, so embodied as in Shakespeare's Roman plays? Where, even in Homer's song, the subtle wisdom of the crafty Ulysses, the sullen selfishness and conscious martial might of broad Achilles, the blundering courage of thick-headed Ajax, or the mingled gallantry and foppery of Paris, so vividly portrayed as in 'Troilus and Cressida'?" — *Richard Grant White.*

" Delicate and subtle distinctions are made between the manners of different epochs of Roman history. For instance, the language, turn of thought, and local coloring in ' Coriolanus,' ' Antony,' and ' Julius Cæsar ' are exquisitely and profoundly Roman ; yet the reader is conscious that the Romans in ' Coriolanus ' are as different from the Romans of the other two plays as was the Roman people at the two different epochs in question. . . . We have here the very essence and soul of classicism, and we have, too, what the ancients have not given us, the household and private physiognomy of their times." — *Shaw's English Literature*, p. 121.

Law. — Bacon began the study of law at nineteen, several years before the appearance of the first of the Shakespeare plays. His mastery of the subject was prompt and thorough. At fifty he was the leading jurist of the age.

The use of legal terms in the plays, always in their exact significance, and sometimes showing profound insight into the principles on which they rest, has long excited the wonder of the world. On this point we have already given the opinion of Chief Justice Campbell; we will add the testimony of Richard Grant White, a witness also on the other side, and now speaking as it were under cross-examination, as follows : —

"No dramatist of the time, not even Beaumont, who was a younger son of a judge of the Common Pleas, and who, after studying in the inns of court, abandoned law for the drama, used legal phrases with Shakespeare's readiness and exactness. And the significance of this fact is heightened by another, that it is only to the language of the law that he exhibits this inclination. The phrases peculiar to other occupations serve him on rare occasions, generally when something in the scene suggests them; but legal phrases flow from his pen as part of his vocabulary and parcel of his thought. . . . And besides, Shakespeare uses his law just as freely in his early plays, written in his first London years, as in those produced at a later period. Just as exactly, too; for the correctness and propriety with which these terms are introduced have compelled the admiration of a chief justice and a lord chancellor."

The conclusion is well-nigh irresistible that a trained lawyer was the author of the plays.[1] The

---

[1] "The notion that he was an attorney's clerk is blown to pieces." — *Richard Grant White.*

"The worst of it is, for the theory of his having been an attorney's clerk, that it will not account for his insight into law; his knowledge is not office sweepings, but ripe fruits, mature, as though he had spent his life in their growth." — *Gerald Massey.*

"It is demonstrated that he [Shakespeare] was no attorney's clerk, as Lord Campbell believed, but a ripe, learned, and profound lawyer, so saturated with precedents that at once in his highest and

only possible escape from it is through Portia's unprecedented rulings in the trial scene in 'The Merchant of Venice;' as though a beautiful damsel, sitting as judge on the bench, and in love with one of the parties interested in the suit, were expected to follow legal precedents!

It is not necessary, however, to poise this argument on a jest. Thanks to Mr. John T. Doyle, a complete explanation of these seemingly anomalous proceedings is easily given. That is to say, the trial was in exact accordance with the rules of procedure that formerly obtained in the courts of Spain, and, it may fairly be presumed, also in those of Venice.

In 1852–53 Mr. Doyle resided in Nicaragua, once a Spanish colony, and still under the sway of Spanish customs, and there, as agent of a trading company, became involved in considerable litigation. The account which he gives of the course pursued in one of his causes, and substantially in them all, is extremely interesting, particularly in view of the light thrown by it on the case *Shylock* vs. *Antonio.*

First, the judge ascertained the facts in the usual way, by questioning the parties to the suit, and ex-

sweetest flights he colors everything with legal dyes." — *Appleton Morgan.*

"Genius would not here guide without technical lore. . . . Are the devotees of Shakespeare resolved to make him a miracle?" — *Prof. Francis W. Newman.*

A writer in 'Baconiana' (London, November, 1893) shows with admirable clearness and force that out of two hundred and fifty points of law treated in the plays, two hundred and one of them are stated with more or less fulness in Bacon's legal tracts, published by Spedding, and easily accessible to any student.

amining the witnesses; then, taking the case under
advisement, he continued it to another day. In due
time the parties were again called together and a
written statement of the matters in controversy was
submitted to them by the judge, who, with their con-
currence, immediately appointed a certain person, of
high reputation for capacity and legal attainments, to
act as referee. This person, who happened to live in
a distant city, submitted his opinion in writing, as the
final decision of the court. Subsequently a *gratification* in his behalf was demanded of the successful
suitor. Mr. Doyle's comments on the case are so
clever that we present them entire: —

" With this experience, I read the case of Shylock over
again, and understood it better. It was plain that the sort of
procedure Shakespeare had in view, and attributed to the Venetian court, was exactly that of my recent experience. The trial
scene in the ' Merchant of Venice ' opens on the day appointed
for final judgment: the facts had been ascertained at a previous
session, and Bellario had been selected. as the jurist, to deter-
mine the law applicable to them. The case had been submitted
to him in writing, and the court was awaiting his decision. The
defendant, when the case is called, answers, as is done daily in
our own courts. ' Ready, so please your Grace.' ' Shylock, the
plaintiff, is not present. In an English, or any common-law
court, his absence would have resulted in a nonsuit, but not so
here; he is sent for, just as my adversary was, and comes.
After an ineffectual attempt to move him to mercy, the Duke
intimates an adjournment, unless Bellario comes. And it is
then announced that a messenger from him is in attendance;
his letter is read, and Portia is introduced. Bellario's letter
excuses his non-attendance on a plea of illness, and proposes
her, under the name of Balthasar. as a substitute. ' I acquainted
him [he writes] with the cause in controversy between the Jew
and Antonio, the merchant: we turned o'er many books to-

gether; he is furnished with my opinion, which, bettered with his own learning, the greatness whereof I cannot enough commend, comes with him at my importunity to fill up your Grace's request in my stead. . . . I leave him to your acceptance, whose trial shall better publish his commendation.' The Duke, of course, had the right, so far as concerned himself, to accept the substitution of Balthasar for Bellario; but Shylock, I take it, would have had his right to challenge the substitute, and perhaps it is to avoid this, by disarming his suspicions, that all Portia's utterances in the case, until she has secured his express consent to her acting, are favorable to him. Thus, —

> ' Of a strange nature is the suit you follow,
> Yet in such rule that the Venetian law
> Cannot impugn you as you do proceed ; '

and again, after her splendid plea for mercy, —

> ' I have spoken thus much,
> To mitigate the justice of thy plea,
> Which, if thou follow, this strict Court of Venice
> Must needs give sentence 'gainst the merchant here.'

" Shylock would have been mad to object to a judge whose intimations were so clearly in his favor. He first pronounces her ' A Daniel come to judgment ! yea, a Daniel ! ' This does not, however, amount to an express acceptance of her as a substitute : it is but an expression of high respect, consistent with a refusal to consent to the proposed substitution. She carries the deception still farther, pronounces the bond forfeit, and that —

> ' Lawfully, by this the Jew may claim
> A pound of flesh, to be by him cut off
> Nearest the merchant's heart,'

and again pleads for mercy.

" The poor Jew, completely entrapped, then 'charges her by the law to proceed to judgment.' Antonio does the same, and, both parties having thus in open court accepted her as such, she is fairly installed as the *judex substitutus* for Bellario, and almost immediately afterwards suggests the quibble over the drop of blood and the exact pound of flesh on which Antonio escapes.

"To complete the parallel to my Nicaraguan experience, above recounted, we find, after the trial is over, and the poor, discomfited Jew has retired from the court, the Duke says to the defendant, whose life has been saved by Portia's subtlety, —

> 'Antonio, *gratify* this gentleman,
> For, in my mind, you are much bound to him.'

That is, give him a 'gratification,' or *honorarium;* and Bassanio offers her the three thousand ducats which were the condition of the bond." [1]

Mr. Doyle also finds, in a Mexican case, a precedent for the action of the Venetian court in fining Shylock. He then adds: —

" It seems to me that Shakespeare was acquainted (however he acquired the knowledge) with the modes of procedure in tribunals administering the law of Spain, as well as with those of his own country; if like practice did not obtain in Venice, or if he knew nothing of Venetian law, there was no great improbability in assuming it to resemble that of Spain, considering that both were inherited from a common source, and that the Spanish monarchs had so long exercised dominion in Italy."

Bacon's residence in France and in Southern Europe for several years sufficiently accounts for the special knowledge shown by " Shake-speare " in the conduct of this case.

Medicine. — Upon the theory and practice of medicine, Bacon lavished at times all his powers. The study seems to have had a special fascination for him. He was puddering in physic, he says, all his life. He even kept an apothecary among his per-

---

[1] *Shakespeariana,* 10, 57.

sonal retainers, seldom retiring to bed without a
dose.

Physicians tell us that the writer of the plays was
a medical expert. Dr. Bucknill has written a book
of three hundred pages, and Dr. Chesney one of two
hundred, to prove this. We know that the names of
Galen and Paracelsus roll from the tongues of the
dramatis personæ like household words. Bacon's
mother was afflicted in the latter part of her life with
insanity. The portrayal of that dreaded disease in
'Hamlet' and 'King Lear' is to this day a psychological marvel.[1]

"We confess, almost with shame, that, although nearly two
centuries and a half have passed since Shakespeare wrote 'King
Lear,' we have very little to add to his method of treating the
insane, as there pointed out." — *Dr. Brigham.*

"Diseases of the nervous system seem to have been a
favorite study, especially insanity." — *B. Rush Field's Medical
Thoughts of Shakespeare*, p. 13, 2d ed.

"That abnormal states of mind were the favorite study of
Shakespeare would be evident from the mere numbers of char-

[1] It has been conjectured that Shakespeare derived his knowledge
of medical science from his son-in-law, Mr. Hall, who was a physician.
This is negatived by two considerations, viz.: 1. Hall married Susanna
Shakespeare in 1607, twenty years after the plays began to appear,
and long after those were written in which this specialty is most displayed. 2. His professional attainments were of too low a character
to sustain such an inference. Fortunately, we have his memorandum
book, in which he noted down his most important cases, and the
methods of treatment he applied to them. Conspicuous among his
remedies are powdered human skull and human fat, tonics of earth
worms and snails, solution of goose excrements, frog-spawn water,
and swallows' nests, — straw, sticks, dung, and all.

This was in the days when country practitioners advised people,
on the ground of health, to wash their faces but once a week, and to
dry them only on scarlet cloth.

acters to which he has attributed them. On no other subject has he written so much: on no other has he written with such mighty power." — *Bucknill's Psychology of Shakespeare,* p. vii.

Natural History. — No department of science was more thoroughly explored by Bacon than natural history. If he had anticipated a general deluge of ignorance, he could not have gathered into an ark a more complete menagerie than the one we find in his 'Sylva Sylvarum' and other works. Nearly every living species, the name and habits of which had been given in books, is represented there.

In one other author alone, not professedly technical, do we find equally copious references to animals and plants. That author is " Shake-speare." The books that have been written to show his knowledge on this subject are very numerous. We have one by Harting, on the Ornithology of " Shakespeare; " another by Phipson, on his Animal Lore; three by Ellacombe, Beisly, and Grindon, on his Plant Lore; and an elaborate treatise by Patterson, on the insects mentioned in the plays.

The resemblance between the two goes further; it exists not only in the multiplicity of these references, but in the character of them also.

Bacon was born in London; he passed the most of his days in the city, or in its immediate suburbs. We have no reason to believe that he was especially fond of country life, or that he studied nature personally in the fields and woods. His love of garden plants, however, as already shown, was deep and tender; he wanted some of them in bloom about him all the year round. He likened their perfume to the war-bling of birds. He once accepted an invitation to make a social visit, with the remark that he would be delighted to pluck violets in his friend's garden. In the science of horticulture, therefore, no one could be more thoroughly at home than Francis Bacon, or possess a knowledge much more minute and accurate.

On the other hand, for what he wrote on the great world of nature beyond the precincts of his garden, on trees and shrubs, on birds and fish and undomesticated animals generally, he was obliged to go to the shelves of his library. He went to Aristotle's 'Problems,' to Pliny's 'Natural History,' to Sandys' 'Travels,' to Scaliger's 'De Subtilitate,' to Porta's 'Magic,' and to several others. He viewed each of these works as a collection, and accordingly he called his own, in which they were all to some degree incorporated, 'Sylva Sylvarum, or Collection of Collections.' Rawley tells us that he himself foraged through all this literature for the facts which Bacon recorded.

The dependence on books was so absolute that, though no mention is made by Bacon of Sandys or of Sandys' travels, we know almost exactly what countries the latter visited, and even the order in which he visited them, from what is contained in the 'Sylva Sylvarum.'

Under these circumstances one result was inevitable. Allowing for the full exercise of Bacon's scientific intuition, we must still expect to find, as Baron Liebig has found, numerous errors in the text. The stream never rises higher than the source, and the source in this case was fact and fiction inextricably mixed.

It is startling to find the same line of demarcation between the knowledge of horticulture and the knowledge of the great world of physical nature outside of horticulture, and the same indifference to charges of plagiarism, in " Shake-speare " precisely as in Bacon. What " Shake-speare " has written about garden-plants is accurate to the minutest details. He is here evidently on his own ground, giving the results of his own observations, and spreading over them the glow of his personal feelings.

In the domain of animated nature at large, however, we encounter a different state of things. Over every kind of wild animal, including birds and insects mentioned in the plays, with one curious exception, our literary Jupiter nods ; but he nods so gracefully as to deceive even the very elect of the critics. Thanks to an intelligent writer in the 'Quarterly,' we now know to what books he went for his facts, and how and why he blundered.

" He borrows from Gower and Chaucer and Spenser ; from Drayton and Du Bartas and Lyly and William Browne ; from Pliny, Ovid, Virgil, and the Bible ; borrows, in fact, every-where he can, but with a symmetry that makes his natural his-tory harmonious as a whole, and a judgment that keeps it always moderate and possible." — *Quarterly Review*, April, 1894.

Take the description, for instance, of the ideal horse in ' Venus and Adonis ; ' it is borrowed, almost word for word, from Du Bartas. Here are all of " Shake-speare's " phrases as they occur in that fa-

mous description, and, in brackets, those of the
original, as given in the 'Quarterly': —

"Round hoofed [round hoof]: short jointed [short pasterns];
broad breasts [broad breast]; full eye [full eye]; small head
[head but of middle size]; nostrils wide [nostril wide]; high
crest [crested neck, bowed]: straight legs [hart-like legs]; and
passing strong [strong]; thin mane [thin mane]; thick tail [full
tail]; broad buttock [fair, fat buttocks]; tender hide [smooth
hide]."

Now take an illustration among the birds. The
lark seems to have been a favorite with the author
of the plays. The allusions are as follows: —

" The 'morning lark' (so in Lyly); the 'mounting lark'
(William Browne): the 'merry lark' (Spenser) ; 'herald of the
morning' (Chaucer): 'shrill lark' (Spenser); 'summer's bird'
(Spenser): the 'busy day, waked by the lark' ('the busy lark,
waker of the day,' Chester);

> 'Hark ! hark! the lark at heaven's gate sings,
>   And Phœbus 'gins arise,'
> (' At Heaven's gate she claps her wings,
>   The morn not waking till she sings.' — *Lyly*)."

The writer in the 'Quarterly' accepts the tradi-
tional Shakspere, but he cannot avoid expressing a
certain disappointment (in which he has our entire
sympathy) as follows: —

" Shakespeare was curiously unobservant of animated Nature.
. . . He seems to have seen very little. . . . Stratford-on-Avon
was, in his day, enmeshed in streams, yet he has not a single
kingfisher. Not on all his streams or pools is there an otter, a
water-rat, a fish rising, a dragon-fly, a moor-hen, or a heron.
. . To the living objects about him he seems to have been
obstinately purblind and half-deaf. His boyhood was passed
among the woods, and yet in all the woods in his plays there is
neither woodpecker nor wood-pigeon: we never hear or see a
squirrel in the trees, nor a night-jar hawking over the bracken."

The plain answer to this is, of course, that the author of the plays never lived in Stratford; he was not a countryman; he never roamed through the woods, or fished in the streams. On the contrary, he passed his boyhood in a city, where language was free from *patois ;* his youth, in a university, from which he poured the classics into his earliest plays; and his manhood, in courts of law and royalty, with the manners, customs, and learning of which he was so thoroughly familiar.

We are now prepared to understand why " Shakespeare" made so many errors in his descriptions of animals, — he looked at them, contrary to Dryden's dictum, through the " spectacles of books." For example : —

> " We 'll follow where thou lead'st,
> Like stinging bees in hottest summer's day,
> Led by their master to the flower'd fields."
>> *Titus Andronicus,* V. 1.

" The passage is of course ridiculous, but it is taken from Du Bartas." — *Quarterly.*

Again : —

> "Our thighs packed with wax, our mouths with honey,
> We bring it to the hive."
>> 2 *Henry IV.,* IV. 4.

" Bees do not carry wax on their thighs but in their tails; and honey, not in their mouths, but in their stomachs. However, the line is borrowed from Lyly's ' Euphues.' " — *Quarterly.*

Again, —

" The old bees die, the young possess their hive."

"Of anything else in the world this might be true, but said of the bee it is a monumental error, the most compendious mis-statement possible. There are no generations of bees; they are all the offspring of the same mother; and they possess the hive by mutual arrangement, and not by hereditary succession ; for when it gets too full, the superfluous tenth goes off with a queen bee to the colonies." — *Quarterly.*

The most elaborate description of a bee-hive and its inmates in " Shake-speare " is given in ' Henry V.,' as follows : —

> " For so work the honey-bees,
> Creatures that by a rule in nature teach
> The act of order to a peopled kingdom ;
> They have a king and officers of sorts :
> Where some, like magistrates correct at home,
> Others, like merchants, venture trade abroad,
> Others, like soldiers, armed in their stings,
> Make boot upon the summer's velvet buds ;
> Which pillage they with merry march bring home
> To the tent-royal of their emperor ;
> Who, busied in his majesty, surveys
> The singing masons building roofs of gold,
> The civil citizens kneading up the honey,
> The poor mechanic porters crowding in
> Their heavy burdens at his narrow gate,
> The sad-eyed justice, with his surly hum,
> Delivering o'er to the executors pale
> The lazy yawning drone." — I. 2.

On this the writer in the ' Quarterly ' com-ments : —

" As poetry, it is a most beautiful passage ; as a description of a hive, it is utter nonsense, with an error of fact in every line, and instinct throughout with a total misconception of the great bee-parable. Obviously, therefore, there could have been no personal observation. How, then, did the poet arrive at the beautiful image? From the 'Euphues' of Lyly."

On the same authority it appears that what "Shake-speare" says of the cuckoo comprises "two proverbs, two misstatements, and the completest possible misconception of the cuckoo idea in nature;" and of the weasel, "two proverbs and two misstatements." "Shake-speare" seems to have been very fond of the dove, and to have some accurate knowledge of it; but it is the domesticated dove which he describes, such as had its habitat at Gorhambury and Twickenham Park, and not its congener in the woods.

To all this, however, we find one significant exception, — the author of the plays describes with accuracy and, what is more remarkable still, with perfect sympathy, the animals of the chase.

"With the boar, the hare, and the deer the facts are reversed. Whether Shakespeare ever saw a boar-hunt is a matter for conjecture, but he gives a superb description of the animal and its chase in 'Venus and Adonis.' . . . It is very noteworthy as an illustration of the poet's treatment of a real animal in which he felt an actual personal interest. Take again in the same poem the exquisite description of a hunted hare, and note the force and beauty which the lines derive from his accuracy and sympathy. He had observed what he there described, and the result is such a poem as to make other poets despair.

"Or what can be said that is too appreciative of Shakespeare's deer? He was here perfectly at home, and thoroughly familiar from personal observation with the haunts and habits of the animal he was describing. The result is a detailed and most beautifully accurate history of the deer, whether stag, hart, or hind, buck, or doe. Above all, it is marked, as in the case of the hare, with a most touching sympathy for the hunted beast." — *Quarterly.*

Bacon was thoroughly familiar with hunting and hawking, as, indeed, was every one at that time in his station of life; and if we may judge from his temperament and the state of his health, sympathy with the hunted animal must have been a predominant feeling with him. This is the kind of exception that proves a rule.

Religion. — The Bacon family was Catholic under Mary, and Protestant under Elizabeth; as a consequence, Francis had no strong predilections in favor of either sect. In religion as in philosophy, he abhorred sects, and sought only what was universal. The sincerity of his faith in an overruling Providence we have no reason to doubt, though his own statement that "a little philosophy inclineth man's mind to atheism, but depth in philosophy bringeth men's minds about to religion," may have been, intentionally or unintentionally, autobiographical, indicating some laxity of opinions on this subject in the early part of his life. The anxieties and constant admonitions of his mother, culminating in the dethronement of her reason, as well as the subsequent battles of religious controversialists over his *status*, would seem to justify this inference.[1]

---

[1] According to Evelyn and Aubrey, Bacon was the true founder of the Royal Society. He inspired it with his own cosmopolitan spirit against the religious passions of the age so effectually that when, a hundred years afterwards, the Society for the Promotion of Christian Knowledge wished simply to meet in its rooms, the request was refused. . . . Bacon's name has been found in a list of rejected candi-

"He was in power at the time of the Synod of Dort, and must for months have been deafened with talk about election, reprobation, and final perseverance. Yet we do not remember a line in his works from which it can be inferred that he was either a Calvinist or an Arminian." — *Macaulay.*

"From his exhaustive enumeration of the branches of human knowledge Bacon excluded theology, and theology alone." — *Greene's Short History of England*, p. 596.

Shakespeare's religion was also an anomaly. Several books have been written on it, but they might well have been compressed into the dimensions of Horrebow's famous chapter on reptiles in Iceland. Some infer, from his toleration amid the fierce resentments of his time, that he was a Catholic; others, from the defiance hurled at the Pope in 'King John,' and from the panegyric on Cranmer in 'Henry VIII.,' that he was a Protestant; while others still, finding no consolations from belief in a future life in the plays, proclaim him an infidel. Indeed, pious commentators always approach this subject walking backward and holding a mantle before them. They know instinctively that the great poet was also a great philosopher, building solidly on human reason, and from the summit of his magnificent structures allowing not even a vine to shoot upward.

"In his great tragedies he traces the workings of noble or lovely human characters on to the point, and no further, where they disappear in the darkness of death : and ends with a look *back*, never on toward anything beyond." — *F. B. West: Browning as a Preacher.*

dates for admission to membership in the Academy of Florence, an institution founded for the cultivation of the physical sciences. M. de Rémusat assigns the rejection to theological grounds.

"No church can claim him." — *Richard Grant White.*

"Both have an equal hatred of sects and parties : Bacon, of sophists and dogmatic philosophers ; Shakespeare, of Puritans and zealots. . . . Just as Bacon banished religion from science, so did Shakespeare from art. . . . In both, this has been equally misconstrued, Le Maistre proving Bacon's lack of Christianity, as Birch has done that of Shakespeare." — *Gervinus.*

Poetry. — Bacon defined poetry as " feigned history ; " that is to say, history not according to actual occurrences which seldom satisfy the moral sense, but of a higher order, so written as to exhibit in one picture the natural and in the end inevitable results of a given line of conduct. The office of the true poet is thus to bring to virtue its reward, and to vice its punishment within certain time limits, and on the grandest scale to which his genius can attain. It is to grind at once what the mills of God grind slowly. This was Bacon's favorite idea, illustrated also in his definition of Art compared with Nature. Art, he said, is superior to Nature, but superior to it only while obedient to its rules. Architecture may be " frozen music," but it must be in harmony with what Bacon calls the " nature of things," to make melody in our souls.

It is impossible to conceive of compositions more faithful to this dramatic ideal than the plays of " Shake-speare." The very anachronisms in them emphasize the distinction between poetry and history ; and the plays always meet the ends of justice, for they are always true to the fundamental principles of our nature.

" Nature is made better by no mean,
But Nature makes that mean ; so, over that art,
Which, you say, adds to Nature, is an art
That Nature makes.   You see, sweet maid, we marry
A gentler scion to the wildest stock ;
And make conceive a bark of baser kind
By bud of nobler race.   This is an art
Which does mend nature."

Winter's Tale, IV. 3.

" His contemporary, Bacon, gave to poetry this great vocation; as the world of the senses is of lower value than the
human soul, so poetry must grant to men what history denies;
it must satisfy the mind . . . with a more perfect order and a
juster relation of things than are to be found there.   Shakespeare appears to have held the same views." — *Gervinus' Com.*,
II. 549.

The plays are " the most consummate style of the art that
mends nature." — *Holmes' Authorship of Shakespeare*, p. 200.

" In one short but beautiful paragraph concerning poetry,
Bacon has exhausted everything that philosophy and good
sense have yet had to offer on what has been since called the
Beau Ideal." — *Dugald Stewart.*

Music. — Both authors took great delight in music.
Bacon devoted a long chapter of his ' Natural History' to the consideration of sounds and the laws of
melody.   In the plays we find nothing sweeter than
the strains that " creep in our ears " as we read
them.

" Lord Bacon has given a great variety of experiments,
touching music, that show him to have been not barely a philosopher, an inquirer into the phenomena of sound, but a master
of the science of harmony, and very intimately acquainted with
the precepts of musical composition." — *Sir John Hawkins.*

" Shakespeare seems to have been proficient in the art." —
Richard Grant White.

" He [Shakespeare] seems also to have possessed, in an un-usual degree, the power of judging and understanding the theory of music, — that upon which the performance and execution of music depends. In the 'Two Gentlemen of Verona' (I. 1), where the heroine of the play is conversing with her maid, there is a passage which enters so fully into the manner of how a song should be sung, that it seems to have been inserted in-tentionally to exhibit the young poet's knowledge in this branch of art. And Burney draws attention to the fact that the critic who, in the scene referred to, is teaching Lucetta Julia's song, makes use of no expressions but such as were employed by the English, as *termini technici* in the profession of music." — *Ulrici.*

One of the points upon which Bacon expended much thought was the harmonic relations of the tones composing the modern diatonic scale. The interval of the perfect fourth, which comprises two major seconds and a minor second, he carefully analyzed, reaching a conclusion which has been frequently cited in treatises on the subject. Concerning this interval he writes, that "after every three whole notes [tones] nature requireth for all harmonical use one half note [tone] to be interposed." Thus, for instance, from C to F, which comprises a perfect fourth, we have three whole tones, C, D, and E, fol-lowed by a semitone, F. The augmentation of this interval, by sharpening the F, so as to give an inter-val of three full tones, was not permissible in Bacon's day, and he sought to base the prohibition on a nat-ural law.

Again Bacon writes: "For discords, the second and seventh are of all others the most odious in har-mony to the sense ; whereof the one is next above the unison, the other next under the diapason, which may shew that harmony requireth a competent distance of notes." Here is evidence of his perfect familiarity with a technical question; is it possible that Shakespeare also possessed the same abstruse knowledge? We quote from 'King Lear': —

"Oh, these eclipses portend these divisions! — fa, sol, la, mi." — I. 2.

"In Shakespeare's time, and until a comparatively recent date, the syllables for solmization, instead of do, re, mi, fa, sol, la, si, were fa, sol, la, fa, sol, la, mi;" so that 'fa, sol, la, mi' covered the interval of an augmented fourth, "ending upon the seventh or leading note of the scale, which, unless followed by the tonic, or used for some very special effect, is a most distracting figure based upon the most poignant of discords." — *Richard Grant White.*

"Shakespeare shows by the context that he was well acquainted with the property of these syllables in solmization, which imply a series of sounds so unnatural that ancient musicians prohibited their use. The monkish writers on music say, *mi contra fa est diabolus.* The interval, *fa* mi, including a tritonus or sharp 4th, consisting of three tones without the intervention of a semitone (expressed in the modern scale by the letters F G A B), would form a musical phrase extremely disagreeable to the ear. Edmund, speaking of eclipses as portents and prodigies, compares the dislocation of events, the times being out of joint, to the unnatural and offensive sounds, *fa, sol, la, mi.*" — *Dr. Burney.*

Oratory. — Bacon was a natural orator. Ben Jonson says of him : —

"There happened in my time one noble speaker who was full of gravity in his speaking. . . . His hearers could not cough, or look aside from him without loss. He commanded where he spoke, and had his judges angry and pleased at his will. No man had their affections more in his power. The fear of every man who heard him was lest he should make an end."

Another contemporary pronounced him "the elo-
quentest man that was born in this island."
Turning to the plays, we find there the most wonderful speech that ever passed, or was supposed to
pass, human lips. In power of sarcasm, in pathos,
in sublimity of utterance, and, above all, in rhetorical
subtlety, Mark Antony's oration over the body of
Cæsar has no equal in forensic literature.

"Every line of this speech deserves an eulogium; . . . neither Demosthenes, nor Cicero, nor their glorious rival, the immortal Chatham, ever made a better." — *Sherlock.*

"The first of dramatists, he might easily have been the first
of orators." — *Archbishop Whately.*

Printing. — Bacon's knowledge of the printer's art
extended to the minutest details. His first book was
published when he was twenty-four, but under so
heavy a title, 'The Greatest Birth of Time,' that it
sank at once into the sea of oblivion. The mysteries
of the craft, however, finally became very familiar to
him. In the 'Novum Organum' he announced his
intention of writing a treatise on the subject, going
so far as to include ink, pens, paper, parchment, and
seals in his prospectus for it.

The encyclopedic "Shake-speare" was also at
home in the composing and press rooms. "He
could not have been more so," says Dr. Appleton
Morgan, "if he had passed his days as a journeyman
printer."

"A small type, called *nonpareil*, was introduced in English
printing-houses from Holland about the year 1560, and became
admired and preferred beyond the others in common use. It
seems to have become a favorite with Shakespeare, who calls
many of his lady characters ' nonpareils.' " — *Morgan.*

"What printer is there who has put to press the second edition of a book, working page for page in a smaller type and shorter measure, but will recognize the typographer's reminiscences in the following description of Leontes' babe by Pauline: —

> 'Behold, my lords,
> Although the print be little, the whole matter
> And copy of the father: . . .
> The very mould and frame of hand, nail, finger.'
> *Winter's Tale*, II. 3.

Is it conceivable that a sentence of four lines, containing five distinct typographical words, three of which are especially technical, could have proceeded from the brain of one not intimately acquainted with typography?" — *Blades' Shakespeare and Typography*, p. 42.

Astrology. — In common with most of his contemporaries, Bacon had a lingering belief in astrology. So had the author of the plays. The planets are "good," "favorable," "lucky," or "ill-boding," "angry," and "malignant," according to their position at the moment of one's birth.

Navigation. — Among the subjects investigated by Bacon, that which surprises us most to find is, perhaps, the art of navigation. He went into it so thoroughly, however, that in his 'History of the Winds' he gives us the details of the rigging of a ship, as well as the mode of sailing her.

We are still more astonished — or should be if we were not prepared for it — to find that "Shakespeare" had the same unusual knowledge. He not only "knows the ropes," but he knows exactly what to do on shipboard in a storm. Even the dialect of the forecastle is familiar to him.

" Of all negative facts in regard to his [Shakespeare's] life,
none perhaps is surer than that he never was at sea." —
Richard Grant White.

" Shakespeare's seamanship during the tempest in the first
scene [of the Tempest] is beyond criticism. No order of the
Boatswain is superfluous; no order is omitted that skill can
suggest to save the craft. Turn to Dryden, where, amidst a
wild and incoherent mass of nautical nonsense, orders are issued
which, if obeyed, would drive the ship straight to destruction."
Furness' Variorum, IX.

Heraldry. — In the ' De Augmentis,' Bacon defines
an emblem as a " sensible image," — one that " strikes
the memory more forcibly, and is more readily impressed upon it than an object of the intellect." He
includes the emblematic art in the list of those subjects that seemed to him to require careful investigation. That he was especially fond of studies of this
nature is evident throughout his works. Fables with
esoteric meanings, symbolical pictures, cipher writings, anything occult or cabalistic, strongly appealed
to his imagination. The frontispiece of the ' Novum
Organum' is a ship under full canvas, passing between
the pillars of Hercules in search of a new world of
science. A picture of the winged Pegasus adorns
another of his books. His Essays bear the title, ' In-
teriora Rerum,' or the Interior of Things. Indeed, a
cloud of mystery envelops nearly all his first editions,
to the despair of the uninitiated, from that day to this.
He named his whole system of philosophy, 'The Restoration,' because he thought there had once been an
' Age of Reason,' the records of which are now lost,
and that nothing is needed for its recovery but a
combined effort on the part of mankind to repossess
Nature's secrets. In his view, Plato and Aristotle

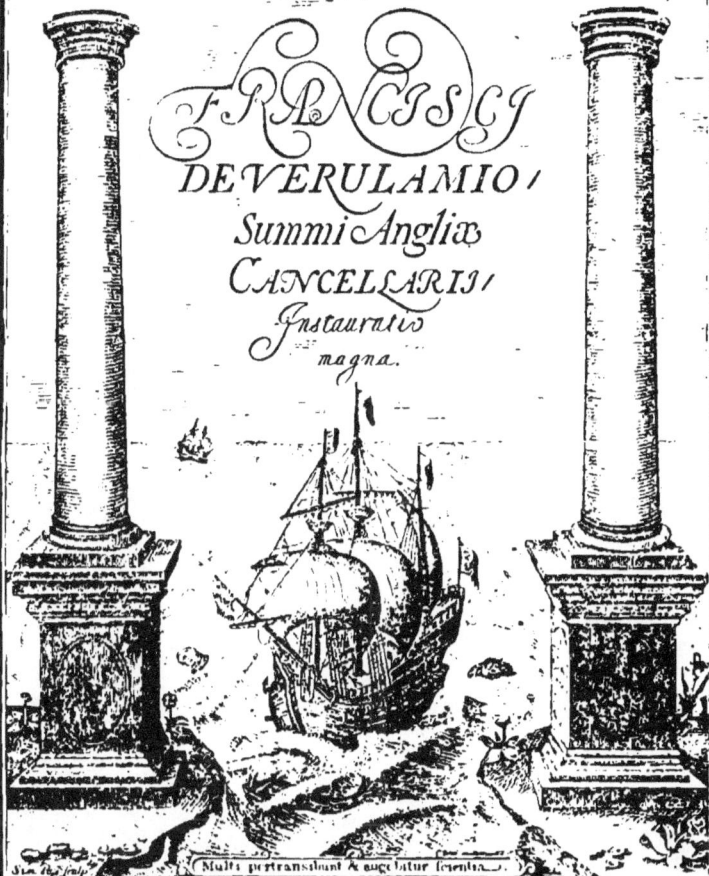

FRANCISCI

DE VERULAMIO,
Summi Angliæ
CANCELLARII,
Instauratio
magna.

Multi pertransibunt & augebitur scientia.

Anno

LONDINI
Apud Joannem Billium
Typographum
Regium.

1620.

are among the lighter objects that have floated down to us on the stream of Time, — the heavier and more valuable having sunk before they reached us.

Of "Shake-speare's" familiarity with the works of the emblematists we have abundant proofs. That he had read, in 1593, Whitney's 'Choice of Emblems,' an English publication of 1586, the following parallelism may indicate : —

FROM DEDICATION OF 'CHOICE OF EMBLEMS' TO EARL OF LEICESTER.	FROM DEDICATION OF 'VENUS AND ADONIS' TO EARL OF SOUTHAMPTON.
"Being abashed that my hability can not afford them such as are fit to be offered up to so honorable a survey; yet, if it shall like your honor to allow of any of them, I shall think my pen set to the book in happy hour; and it shall encourage me to assay some matter of more moment, as soon as leisure will furnish my desire in that behalf."	"I leave it to your honorable survey, and your Honour to your heart's content; only if your Honour seem but pleased, I account myself highly praised, and vow to take advantage of all idle hours till I have honoured you with some graver labour."

In the triumph scene of 'Pericles' six knights successively cross the stage. The author thus describes their armorial bearings : —

> "*Sim.* Who is the first that doth prefer himself?
> *Thai.* A knight of Sparta, my renowned father ;
> And the device he bears upon his shield
> Is a black Ethiope reaching at the sun ;
> The word, ' Lux tua vita mihi.' "

This motto, says Green, in his ' Shakespeare and the Emblem Writers ' (to whom we are indebted for much curious and valuable information on this subject), is almost identical with that of the Blount fam-

ily, several members of which are introduced to us
in the plays. The origin of the device itself — "a
black Ethiope reaching at the sun" — is unknown.

> *Sim.* Who is the second that presents himself ?
> *Thai.* A prince of Macedon, my royal father;
>   And the device he bears upon the shield
>   Is an arm'd knight that's conquer'd by a lady;
>   The motto thus, in Spanish, ' Piu por dulzura que por
>   fuerza. ' "

Moderata vis impotenti violentia potior.

Freitag, 1579.

The motto means, "More by gentleness than by
force," and, though here given in Spanish, has been
found only in a French work, "of extreme rarity"
(as Green says), Corrozet's 'Hecatomgraphie,' Paris,
1540. There it reads, "plus par doulceur que par

force," and is illustrated in the original work with a wood-cut, representing the well-known fabled contest between the Wind and the Sun over a traveller's cloak.

We know that this fable subsequently became very popular on the Continent, for we find it again in Freitag's Latin work, ' Mythologia Ethica.'

Freitag's work in Latin came from the press in Antwerp in 1579, the year that terminated Bacon's sojourn in France.

> " *Sim.* And what 's the third ?
> *Thai.* The third of Antioch
> And his device, a wreath of chivalry ;
> The word, ' Me pompæ provexit apex.' "

Me pompæ prouexit apex.

Paradin, 1562.

The laurel-wreath, which this knight wore emblazoned on his shield, and the words, meaning, " The crown of triumph has impelled me on," are given, precisely as Shakespeare has represented them, in

Paradin's 'Devises Héroïques,' published in French in Antwerp in 1562. The accompanying cut (p. 257) is taken from that work.

> "*Sim.* What is the fourth?
> *Thai.* A burning torch that 's turned upside down;
> The word, 'Quod me alit, me extinguit.' "

For this, the author of 'Pericles' went to Symeoni's French work, 'Tetrastichi Morali' (1561), or to Whitney's translation of it, in both of which the device is represented as follows: —

SIGNOR DI S.
VALIER.

Symeoni, 1561 *(diminished copy).*

Symeoni's explanation of the device is in these words : —

"In the battle of the Swiss, routed near Milan by King Francis, M. de Saint-Valier bore a standard whereon was painted a lighted torch with the head downward, on which flowed so much wax as would extinguish it, with this motto, 'Qui me alit, me extinguit.' It is the nature of the wax, which is the cause of the torch burning when held upright, that with the head downward it should be extinguished. Thus he wished to signify that, as the beauty of the lady whom he loved nourished all his thoughts, so she put him in peril of his life."

> "*Thai.* The fifth, a hand environed with clouds,
> Holding out gold that's by the touchstone tried,
> The motto thus, 'Sic spectanda fides.'"

Crispin de Passe, about 1595.

We find this device, with the motto, " So is fidelity to be proved," in Paradin, who thus explains it : —

"If in order to prove fine gold or other metals, we bring them to the touch, without trusting to their glitter or their sound, so to recognize good people and persons of virtue it is needful to observe the splendor of their deeds, not words."

Several of the kings of France adopted this device for their escutcheons.

> "*Sim.*   And what 's
> The sixth and last, the which the knight himself
> With such a graceful courtesy deliver'd?
> *Thai.* He seems to be a stranger: but his present is
> A withered branch, that 's only green at top;
> The motto, ' In hac spe vivo.' "

Paradin, 1562.

Concerning this, Mr. Douce in his ' Illustrations of Shakespeare ' comments as follows : —

"The sixth device, from its peculiar reference to the situa-tion of Pericles, may perhaps have been altered from one in Paradin, used by Diana of Poictiers. It is a green branch

springing from a tomb, with the motto, ' Sola vivit in illo,' —
Alone on that she lives."

Mr. Green, however, thinks that " Shake-speare "
invented for himself the sixth knight's device and its
motto, " In hac spe vivo." He adds : —

" The step from applying so suitably the emblems of other
writers to the construction of new ones would not be great ; and
from what he has actually done in the invention of emblems
in the ' Merchant of Venice,' he would experience very little
trouble in contriving any emblem he needed for the completion
of his dramatic plans. The Casket Scene [in the ' Merchant of
Venice '] and the Triumph Scene [in ' Pericles '], then, justify
our conclusion that the correspondencies between Shake-speare
and the Emblem writers which preceded him are very direct
and complete. It is to be accepted as a fact, that he was acquainted with their works, and profited so much from them as
to be able, whenever the occasion demanded, to invent, and
most fittingly illustrate, devices of his own." — p. 185.

It is evident that the author of ' Pericles ' had made
a thorough study of heraldry. If he wrote the play
previously to 1586, as he probably did (Dryden says
it was his first), he acquired his knowledge of the
subject from Latin, French, and Italian sources. In
either event, we must recognize his easy familiarity
with the literature of courts.

Witchcraft. — Bacon believed in witchcraft, but at
the same time deprecated the ease with which judges
and juries accepted the confessions — " recent confessions," as he called them — of the poor deluded
creatures on trial for their lives. He treated the
subject in the ' Advancement of Learning ' (1605),
and in the ' Sylva Sylvarum.' Among the most
conspicuous instances of the kind to which he al-

ludes were those investigated by Dr. Harsnet, and made public by him in a book entitled 'Declaration of Egregious Popish Impostures' in 1603.

That the author of 'King Lear' (1606) went to this same book for information on witchcraft is perfectly well known. The same extraordinary devils are introduced to us in both of these works under the following names: —

FROM HARSNET'S 'DECLARATION.'	FROM 'KING LEAR.'
Fliberdigibet	Flibbertigibbet
Hoberdidance	Hobbididance
Haberdicut	Obidicut
Flateretto	Flateretto
Smolkin	Smolkin
Modu	Modo
Maho	Mahu

Passages in the text of 'King Lear' can also be traced to Harsnet, particularly Edgar's references to knives and halters (articles that played an important part in the proceedings at Denham), and the character of the seven devils mentioned, each of which represented a deadly sin in human nature. The likeness extends in one case even to the curling of the hair. Indeed, Mr. Spalding, in his 'Elizabethan Demonology,' is enabled from this source to correct a line in the drama, ordinarily rendered,

" Pur! the cat is gray" (III. 6),

by showing that Purre was one of the fiends that figured at the trial, and was compared to a cat, as others were compared to hogs, wolves, dogs, and lions.

" Hog in sloth, fox in stealth, wolf in greediness, dog in madness, lion in prey." — III. 4.

" A comparison of the passages in ' King Lear,' spoken by Edgar when feigning madness, with those given by Harsnet, will show that Shakespeare has accurately given the contemporary belief on the subject. Mr. Spalding also considers that nearly all the allusions in ' King Lear' refer to a youth known as Richard Mainey, — a minute account of whose supposed possession has been given by Harsnet." — *Dyer's Folk-Lore in Shakespeare*, p. 56.

Freemasonry. — The corner-stone of the Memorial Edifice at Stratford-upon-Avon was laid in 1877 with full masonic ceremonial, under the assumption, based exclusively on the plays, that the dramatist was a member of the order. It bears the following inscription : —

THIS STONE WAS LAID ON

April 23rd, 1877,

BY

THE RIGHT HONOURABLE AND RIGHT WORSHIPFUL

LORD LEIGH,

P. G. M., Warwickshire.

Many scholars, who have brought great learning to bear upon the point, both in England and in Germany, Mr. Wigston especially, are assured that the founder of Freemasonry was Francis Bacon. The fraternity may, indeed, be said to rest on the ' New Atlantis' as its foundation. The pillars of ' Solomon's House,' as Bacon called his wonderful imaginary structure, are FAITH and LOVE.

VI.

DISILLUSION, A GAIN.

HERE, then, is our "Shake-speare." A man born into the highest culture of his time, the consummate flower of a long line of distinguished ancestry; of transcendent abilities, dominated by a genius for hard work; of aims in life at once the boldest and the most inspiring which the heart of man ever conceived; in originality and power of thought, in learning, in eloquence, in wit, and in marvellous insight into character, the acknowledged peer of the greatest of the human race. "Surely," says Holmes, "we may exclaim with Coleridge, not without amazement still, ' Merciful, wonder-making Heaven! what a man was this Shakespeare! Myriad-minded, indeed, he was!'"

Ours is an age of disillusion. Heroes whose names have kindled the flame of devotion to duty in the hearts of millions are fading into myths. The majestic form of William Tell is found to be but a lengthened shadow thrown across the page of history. Even the faithful dog Gelert, over whose fate so many children have shed tears, has become as purely symbolic as the one that followed Yudhish-thira to the holy mount, and was thence, for his virtues, translated into heaven. Why should the world longer worship at the shrine of a man of whose life it knows, almost literally, in a mass of disgusting fiction, but one significant fact, viz., that in his will, disposing of a large property, he left to the wife of his youth and the mother of his children nothing but his " second-best bed " !

The conclusion of the whole matter may be stated thus : —

The Sonnets will lose none of their sweetness, and the Plays none of their magnificence, by a change in the ascription of authorship. The world, however, will gain much. It will learn that effects are always commensurate with their causes, and that industry is the path to greatness.

VII.

BIOGRAPHY OF SHAKSPERE.

SHAKSPERE IN FACT.	SURMISES, LEGENDS, AND MYTHS STATED AS FACTS BY THE BIOGRAPHERS.

1564, April 26. Baptized at Stratford-on-Avon.

"Saxon by his father and Norman by his mother; . . . one lobe of his brain seems to have been Normanly refined, and the other Saxonly sagacious."[1]—*James Russell Lowell.*

[1] It is fortunate, in one sense, for Shakspere that so little is known of his life; the critics can create him to suit themselves. On this point one of the latter takes us into his confidence, for he says (Wise's 'Shakespeare, his Birthplace and its Neighborhood'), "it is best for us to draw our own ideal." Mr. Lowell furnishes us with the first specimen of this kind of carpentry.

Shakspere's lineage baffles research. Of his grandparents one only is known, Robert Arden, not of the gentry, as often said, but a husbandman. Richard Shakspere, of Snitterfield, also a husbandman, is supposed to have been his paternal grandfather, simply because two young men, John and Henry Shakspere, were living at the same place at the same time and "of the age which Richard's sons might be." This John Shakspere is likewise merely supposed to have been the reputed poet's father. In the mathematical formulæ of Shakespeareans, however, two suppositions combined equal a certainty; whereas it is evident that the strength of a conclusion depending upon repeated hypotheses is in inverse ratio to the number on

1571-78. " Received the technical or scholastic part
of his education in the
Grammar School of his
native town." [1] — *Prof.
Baynes, Encyc. Brit.*

" " " Remained at school
for at least six years." [2]
— *Ibid.*

" " " At school Shake-
speare acquired some
knowledge of Latin and
of Greek." [3] — *Richard
Grant White.*

" " " Taken by his father
to see [dramatic] per-
formances at Strat-
ford." [4]—*Prof. Baynes.*

" " " At Shottery the
poet met his future

which it rests. The maiden names of the two grandmothers are irrecoverably lost.

"Shakspere was not on his mother's side of Norman blood, as
some have concluded." — *Richard Grant White.*

[1] No record. First mentioned by Rowe in 1709 on the authority
of Thomas Betterton, the actor, who visited Stratford in the latter
part of the seventeenth century, or more than one hundred years
after Shakspere had attained school age.

How much information Betterton gathered up may be inferred
from the character of Rowe's Biography, which was largely based
upon it, and in which, as Malone says, there are eleven statements of
fact, two of them true, one doubtful, and eight false.

[2] No record. Stated on the authority of Betterton.

[3] An inference only, derived from the plays. No evidence exists
that he attended any school whatever. All the traditions respecting
his early life, his domestic surroundings and the indications derived from his handwriting afford presumptive proof that he was
uneducated.

[4] Wholly imaginary.

1582, Nov. 28. Licensed to
marry Anne Hatha-
way.

bride, in all the charm
of her sunny girlhood ;
and they may be said
to have grown up to-
g e t h e r ."[1] — *Prof.
Baynes.*

1582, Dec. " M a r r i e d."[2] —
Richard Grant White.

1583, May 26. His daughter
Susanna baptized.

1584, Feb. 2. Hamnet and Judith, twins, baptized.

1585.   " The   substantial
facts in the story [of the
deer-stealing] are that
Shakspere in his youth
was fond of woodland
sports, and that in one
of his hunting adven-
tures he came into col-

---

[1] Wholly imaginary and absurd. She was nearly eight years his
senior, and "might have dandled him in his infancy," as White says,
"upon her knee."

"The marriage-bond of November, 1582, includes the only evidences respecting Anne Hathaway during her maidenhood that have
yet been discovered." — *Halliwell-Phillipps' Outlines*, Vol. II. p. 183.

"There is unhappily no tradition indicating the birthplace of
Shakspere's Anne upon which the least reliance can be placed." —
Ibid., p. 189.

In the entry on the Episcopal register for a marriage license, November 27, 1582, the bride is called Anne Whateley of Temple Graf-
ton ; in the bond given the next day to expedite the banns, the name
appears as Anne Hathwey of Stratford. The first mention of the
cottage at Shottery, now shown to visitors as her maiden residence,
was made by Samuel Ireland (father of the celebrated forger), in a
book entitled "Picturesque Views on the Warwickshire Avon," in
1795, or nearly two and a half centuries after Anne Hathwey's birth.

[2] No record. A pure invention as to date.

lision with Sir Thomas Lucy's keepers."[1]— *Prof. Baynes.*

1585-87. "With 'Venus and Adonis' written, [2] if nothing else, Shakespeare went to London."— *Richard Grant White.*

1592. In London. His name parodied as *Shake-scene* in Greene's 'Groatsworth of Wit.'

1592. "He had already tested his faculty for acting by occasional essays on the provincial stage."[3]— *Prof. Baynes.*

---

[1] Reported as a tradition by Betterton, Capell, and Oldys, about a century after the alleged event. Based probably on the first scene of 'The Merry Wives of Windsor,' and therefore fictitious.

[2] Unsupported by testimony of any kind and incredible. Will it be believed that, in inserting the qualifying clause, "if nothing else," White actually had in mind the tragedy of 'Hamlet'?

[3] A good illustration of the manner in which Shakspere's life has been written. In a prior part of the same article, Professor Baynes says : "It is not improbable that in connection with some of the companies [on their tours into the country], Shakespeare may have tried his hand both as poet and actor before leaving Stratford. . . . He may have been pressed by the actors to appear in some secondary part on the stage." It is not often that conjecture and fact are brought so closely together. Usually, it has taken two authors, one succeeding the other, to get a fact by this process into Shakspere's life.

Mr. Lowell found a similar artifice in Masson's 'Life of Milton': "What he puts by way of a query on page 402 has become downright certainty nine pages farther on." — *Among My Books*, p. 267.

A curious instance of this easily besetting sin in Shakespearean commentators is found in the Rev. William Harness' 'Life of Shakspere.' In 1768 Capell advanced the absurd hypothesis that Shak-

1592.   " Chettle apologizes
to and commends Shak-
spere, saying ' he was as
sorry as if the original
fault had been his own,
to have offended a man
so courteous, so gifted,
and one who, by his
worth and his ability,
had risen in the esteem
of many of his superi-
ors in rank and sta-
tion.' . . . Thus Shak-
spere, within six or
seven years of his de-
parture from Stratford,
a fugitive adventurer,
had won admiration
from the public, re-
spect from his superi-
ors, etc."[1]— *Richard
Grant White.*

1593.   " The Earl of Southampton . . . had a spe-
cial fondness for the
drama; and, being a
constant attendant up-

spere was afflicted with lameness, basing it on the following lines in
the ' Sonnets ' : —

" So I, made lame by fortune's dearest spite." — No. XXXVII.
" Speak of my lameness, and I straight will halt." — No. LXXXIX.

Fifty-seven years afterward, Mr. Harness, without mentioning
Capell, proclaimed the lameness as a fact, whereupon the announce-
ment at once went the rounds of the newspaper press that three of
England's greatest poets, Scott, Byron, and Shakspere, were cripples !

[1] A mistake.   Chettle neither made an apology to Shakspere nor
commended him.   The entire fabric, venerable with age, rests on a
misapprehension.   See pp. 150–153.

on the theatre, he saw much of Shakespeare and his plays."[1] — *Richard Grant White.*

1593. To the Earl of Southampton Shakespeare dedicated "his 'Venus and Adonis,' although he had not asked permission to do so, as the dedication shows; and in those days and long after, without some knowledge of his man, and some opportunity of judging how he would receive the compliment, a player would not have ventured to take such a liberty with the name of a nobleman."[2] — *Ibid.*

1596, Aug. 11. His son, Hamnet, buried at Stratford.

1597.   Bought New Place in Stratford.

1598. Oct. 25. Returned on the rolls of Stratford as the holder (during a famine) of ten quarters of corn.

"   Sold 1 load of stone to Town of Stratford for 10*d.*

---

[1] As to Shakspere, wholly imaginary. Not the slightest evidence exists that Shakspere, the actor, was patronized by the Earl of Southampton.

[2] A just commentary, discrediting Shakspere as the author of the poem. Southampton and Bacon were intimate friends.

1598, Feb. 4.   Richard Quiney
addresses a letter to
Shakspere, asking a
loan of £30 on secur-
ity. [1]

1599.	Applied for a grant of coat-armor to his father." [2]	1599.	"The patent of arms granted to his father." [3] — *Prof. Baynes.*

1600.   Sues John Clayton
for £7, and obtains
verdict.

1602.   Buys two parcels of
land and a cottage in
Stratford.

1603.   Appointed one of
His Majesty's servants
for theatrical perform-
ances.

1604.   Sues Philip Rogers
at Stratford for £1
15*s*. 10*d*. for malt delivered, including 2*s*.
loaned.

1605.   Purchases a moiety   " King James, it is
of the tithes of Strat-   well known, honored

[1] The only letter to him extant. None from him to any one ever
heard of.

[2] " There can hardly be any doubt that the pedigree which he
constructed for himself in order to obtain a coat-of-arms from the
Herald's College, and so enter the ranks of 'gentlemen,' was 'wholesale lying,' and that Shakspere knew it was." — *Thomas Davidson.*

" It was for this social consideration that he toiled and schemed."
— *Richard Grant White.*

[3] The application appears to have been rejected.   No record of a
grant on the books of the Herald's College has ever been published.

" It seems that the grant was not ratified." — *Henry Morley, English Writers,* Vol. X. p. 498.   (1893.)

ford, Old Stratford, Bishopton, and Welcombe for £440.

1607, June 5. His daughter Susanna marries Dr. John Hall, at Stratford.

1608. Sues John Addenbroke of Stratford, obtaining judgment for £6, together with £1 4s. costs. Addenbroke not being found, sues his bondsman Hornby.

" Present, as sponsor, at baptism of son of Henry Walker, in Stratford.

1610. Purchases 20 acres of pasture land in Stratford.

Shakespeare so far as to write to him with his own hand."[1] — *Schlegel.*

1608. He was in the habit of visiting at several titled houses, amongst others those of the Earl of Bedford and Sir John Harrington."[2] — *Prof. Baynes.*

" " The only known volume that certainly belonged to Shakspere and contains his autograph is Florio's version of Montaigne's Essays in the British Museum." [3] — *Ibid.*

[1] First mentioned nearly one hundred and fifty years after Shakspeare's death, by Oldys, who said he received the story from Sheffield, Duke of Buckingham, who in turn claimed that he received it from the notorious Sir William Davenant. Suitable only for the most robust credulity.

"There is no proof that any personal patronage was extended to Shakspere by either Elizabeth or James." — *Ward's English Dramatic Literature,* Vol. II. p. 279.

[2] A sheer fabrication. "Of Shakspere's social life during his long residence in London we have not even a tradition." — *Richard Grant White.* About 1603, Sir Walter Raleigh founded the Mermaid Club, which, Mr. White says, "owes its wide celebrity and perpetual fame chiefly to Shakespeare," although (he adds naïvely) "there is no evidence that Shakspere was one of its members."

[3] The alleged autograph being beyond all reasonable doubt a forgery, it is safe to say that Shakspere never possessed the book.

1612.   Brings suit to protect his interest in the
tithes of corn, grain,
hay, wool, lambs, etc.,
of Stratford.

1610–13.   " He returned to
S t r a t f o r d a disap-
pointed   m a n ." [1] —
Richard Grant White.

1613, March 10.   Purchases a
house in London for
£140.

"   March 11. Mortgages the
same for £60.

"   June. Mrs. Hall brings
suit against John Lane
for slander.[2]

1614, Oct. 28.   Guaranteed by
William Replingham
against loss by enclos-
ure of commons at
Stratford.

---

[1] A total error.   Shakspere returned to Stratford in middle life,
possessed of that which had evidently been the sole object of his ambition, a large fortune.   We have no hint from any source whatever
that the society of his illiterate neighbors, in a "dirty village"
(White), was not perfectly congenial to him.

[2] " In June, 1613, there was a tiresome bit of gossip in circulation
at Stratford-on-Avon, respecting Mrs. Hall, Shakespeare's elder
daughter, and Ralph Smith and John Palmer.   Matters came to such
a pass that Dr. Hall deemed it advisable to take proceedings in the
Ecclesiastical Court against one of the persons who had slandered
his wife.   The case was heard at Worcester, July 15, 1613, and appears to have been conducted somewhat mysteriously, the deposition
of Robert Whatcot, the poet's intimate friend, being the only evidence recorded, and throwing no substantial light on the merits of the
dispute." — *Halliwell-Phillipps' Outlines,* p. 168.

Lane made no defence, and was excommunicated.

[3] Shakspere at first opposed the enclosures as contrary to his per-

1614, Nov. 16. Comes to London.

1614, Nov. 17. Explains to Thomas Greene how far the enclosure at Welcombe will extend.[1]

1616, Feb. 11. His daughter Judith marries Thomas Quiney without a license.[2]

" Bridegroom and bride arraigned before the Ecclesiastical Court at Worcester for violation of law.

1616, March 25. Makes his will.[3]

sonal interests, but afterwards, on being privately guaranteed against loss by the promoter of the scheme, withdrew his opposition. The remonstrance of the town, addressed to him on behalf of the poorer classes, seems to have had no effect.

"It is certain that the poet was in favor of the enclosures." — *Halliwell-Phillipps' Outlines*, p. 168.

"That Shakspere was accessory to an attempt to enclose the common lands of Stratford and so oppress the poor, is beyond a doubt." — *Thomas Davidson, N. Y. World*, 1887.

[1] One of the two conversations only in which Shakspere is reported to have taken part. The other is given by Manningham.

[2] "Judith's marriage with Mr. Quiney was a mysterious and hurried one. There appears to have been some reason for accelerating the event." — *Halliwell-Phillipps' Outlines*, p. 182.

Mr. Quiney was a liquor-dealer; he was fined by the town for profanity and for making a public nuisance of his tippling-shop.

[3] "Shakspere's will was one of great particularity, making little legacies to nephews and nieces, and leaving swords and rings to friends and acquaintances; and yet his wife's name is omitted from the document in its original form, and only appears by an afterthought, in an interlineation, as if his attention had been called to the

1616, April. "T w o o f t h e
most cherished of his
companions and fellow-
poets, Drayton and Ben
Jonson, had paid a visit
to Stratford and been
entertained by Shak-
spere only a few days
before his death." [1] —
Prof. Baynes.

1616, April 23.   His death.

1635, Nov. 25.   D r . H a l l' s
death. [2]

1642.   Mrs. Hall sells her
husband's note-book
under peculiar circum-
stances. [3]

omission, and for decency's sake he would not have the mother of his
children unnoticed altogether. The lack of any other bequest than
the furniture of her chamber is of small moment in comparison with
the slight shown by that interlineation. A second-best bed might be
passed over; but what can be done with second-best thoughts?" —
Richard Grant White.

"She was left by her husband without house or furniture (except
the second-best bed), or a kind word, or any other token of love." —
Chief Justice Campbell's Legal Acquirements of Shakespeare, p 106.

" He had forgot her." — *Malone.*

" In his will he only sparingly and meanly bequeathed to her his
second-best bed." — *Gervinus.*

[1] A tradition not heard of till fifty years after Shakspere's death.

[2] Dr. Hall was expelled from the corporation of Stratford in
1633.

[3] Dr. Cooke, who published this note-book in 1659, states in the
preface how he came into possession of it. It appears that at the
beginning of the civil war, probably in 1642, he was acting as surgeon
to a Roundhead troop stationed at Stratford Bridge; and, having
been invited to visit New Place, was shown by Mrs. Hall some books
and manuscripts that had belonged to her deceased husband. He
was also informed that she had in the house some other books, once

1649, July 11. Mrs. Hall's
    death.

1662, Feb. 9. Mrs. Quiney's
    death.

1669-70. Death of Elizabeth,
    the only grandchild
    and last lineal de-
    scendant of William
    Shakspere of Strat-
    ford-on-Avon.

In 1780 George Steevens wrote the following oft-quoted summary : —

" All that is known with any degree of certainty concerning Shakspere is — that he was born at Stratford-upon-Avon — married and had children there — went to London, where he commenced actor and wrote poems and plays — returned to Stratford, made his will, died, and was buried."

We venture to bring this summary to date, as follows : —

All that is known with any degree of certainty concerning Shakspere is, that he was born at Stratford-upon-Avon ; married, and had children there ; went to London, where he became an actor, and was reputed to be the author of poems and plays ; acquired wealth ; applied for a title, which was refused ;

the property of a physician who had pledged them to Dr. Hall for money advanced. Then ensued the following conversation: " I told her that if I liked them I would give her the money again. Mrs. Hall then brought them forth, amongst which there was this, with another of the author's, both intended for the press. I, being acquainted with Mr. Hall's hand, told her that one or two of them were her husband's and showed them to her. She denied, I affirmed, till I perceived she began to be offended, and at last I returned her the money."

invested money in real estate, and in the tithes of his
native town; instituted many lawsuits; returned to
Stratford; sold malt; entertained a preacher at his
house, and drew on the town for one quart of claret
wine and one quart of sack (20*d.*) for the occasion;
favored a conspiracy to enclose the commons there;
made his will, died, and was buried.

"There is not recorded of him [Shakspere] one noble or
lovable action." — *Thomas Davidson.*

"An obscure and profane life." — *Ralph Waldo Emerson.*

"A record unadorned by a single excellence or virtue." —
William O'Connor in Hamlet's Note-Book.

"I am not sure that we should not venerate Shakespeare as
much if the biographers had left him undisturbed in his obscurity. To be told that he played a trick on his brother player in
a licentious amour, or that he died of a drunken frolic . . .
does not exactly inform us of the man who wrote 'Lear.'" —
Hallam.

"Whether Bacon wrote the wonderful plays or not, I am
quite sure the man Shakspere neither did nor could." — *John
G. Whittier.*

"I am a firm believer in the Baconian theory." — *Benj. F.
Butler.*

"I would not be surprised to find myself ranged with Mrs.
Pott and Judge Holmes on the side of the philosopher against
the play-actor." — *Oliver Wendell Holmes.*

"Any man who believes that William Shakspere of Stratford wrote 'Hamlet' or 'Lear' is a fool." — *John Bright.*

"Ask your own hearts, ask your common sense, to conceive the possibility of the author of the plays being . . . the
anomalous, the wild, the irregular genius of our daily criticism."
— *Coleridge.*

In a word, to look persistently to this source for
the literary masterpieces of all time is to illustrate
that subtle and practically unlimited power of the

human will to ignore, in the face of consequences
deemed objectionable, the most elementary laws of
evidence. It is necessary, perhaps, that the car of
progress be equipped, like our railway trains, with a
dozen brakemen to one stoker; but the time will
come, we do not hesitate to predict, when this un-
reasoning and perverse, not to say intemperate, con-
servatism in the public mind on the subject of the
authorship of "Shake-speare" will be universally
regretted as a reflection upon the scholarship of our
age.

VIII.

SUMMARY.

ONE word more. A common farm-laborer in England uses, it is said, five hundred words; the average educated business man, three thousand; a writer like Thackeray, five thousand; the great poet, scholar, and publicist, John Milton, "who carried the idiomatic powers of the English tongue," says Macaulay, "to their highest perfection, and to whose style every ancient and every modern language contributed something of grace, of energy, and of music," used seven thousand. How many words did the author of "Shake-speare" use? According to Professor Craik, a recognized authority in this branch of science, twenty-one thousand, — inflectional forms not counted.

Who was it, living in England in the latter part of the sixteenth and the early part of the seventeenth centuries, that compassed so enormous a range of diction? Was it William Shakspere, the actor, born and bred in what Halliwell-Phillipps called a "bookless neighborhood," where the number of books outside of the school and the church could not have exceeded, as Richard Grant White tells us, a half-dozen in the whole town, — where, in a population of about twelve hundred, not more than fifty, or at most one

hundred, persons could read or write, whose own
father and mother could not read or write, and both
of whose daughters went to their graves late in life
without having read, it is supposed, a line of their
father's works, if he ever wrote any, — one of them
even selling the manuscript copy of a book, written
by her deceased husband for publication, because
she could not identify the handwriting, though repeatedly urged to do so? Was this the man, uneducated, as his contemporaries called him, an impostor,
as every one who knew him in the character of a
dramatist called him, — was this the man whose vocabulary, enriched with the spoils of five languages
besides his own, was greater, three times greater, it
would seem, than that of any other mortal who ever
lived? Must we permit the nineteenth century to go
out and join the vast congregation of the ages stained
with a superstition so palpable, so humiliating to us,
so unspeakably absurd as this?

Let us rather turn to the man who at the age of
twelve entered Cambridge University; who at fifteen
exhausted that fount of learning, and left it without
taking his degree; who then devoted three years to
the further study of literature, art, science, government, and the modern languages, on the Continent;
who on his return home notified his uncle, the Prime
Minister of England, that he had made all knowledge,
ALL KNOWLEDGE, his province; who was kept from
active service in political life till he was nearly fifty
years old, and was then found to be in the possession
of phenomenal habits of study which his acknowledged works do not account for, — the first of his
philosophical series not appearing till he had been

twenty-nine years out of college; whose mind was comprehensive rather than analytical, unable to grasp the commonest physical science in which mathematics plays a prominent part, but conspicuously rich in that which makes the plays immortal, — practical wisdom, knowledge of human nature, and of the secret springs of human conduct; whose manner of writing was wonderfully varied and ductile; who has justly been styled the Prose-Poet of Modern Science; who privately styled himself a " concealed poet; " who in the most solemn manner before his death claimed to have sought the good of all men in some work or works which were " despised," which he had therefore written, as he said, " in a weed," or under a pseudonym, and which Sir Toby Matthew undoubtedly referred to when he pronounced the author the *most prodigious wit of all the world, though known by the name of another ;* and, finally, whose intellectual eminence is to this day one of the unsolved enigmas of mankind.

INDEX.

www.ingramcontent.com/pod-product-compliance
Lightning Source LLC
Chambersburg PA
CBHW021215270326
41929CB00010B/1135